Scaling up Education Reform:
Addressing the Politics of Disparity

R. Bishop, D. O'Sullivan, and M. Berryman

NZCER PRESS

Wellington 2010

NZCER PRESS

New Zealand Council for Educational Research
PO Box 3237
Wellington 6140
New Zealand

ISBN 978-1-877398-54-4

Designed by Cluster Creative

Printed by Printlink, Wellington

Cover by Donn Ratana

The mangōpare (hammerhead shark) symbolises strength
and sustenance. When caught, it was an essential source
of many resources that enabled people to flourish. As well
as food and oil, the bones were used to make tools such
as sawing implements, needles and fish hooks. Thus,
within the mangōpare was the means of making the
hooks required for the next catch.
Sustainable educational reform must also have the
means of sustaining itself from the very outset. Therefore,
the mangōpare image is used on the cover of this book to
symbolise sustainable educational reform that can
strengthen and sustain education for all students.

Distributed by NZCER Distribution Services
PO Box 3237
Wellington 6140
New Zealand
www.nzcer.org.nz

Contents

Acknowledgements

He mihi maioha ki a koutou te whānau o Te Kotahitanga.

We wish to thank all the students, teachers, leaders, principals, boards of trustees and communities of the schools currently in Te Kotahitanga. Also the New Zealand Ministry of Education for funding the Te Kotahitanga project. Without their ongoing commitment, we would not be where we are today.

We also wish to acknowledge the funding provided by Ngā Pae o Te Māramatanga, (the Māori Centre of Research Excellence) for the initial iteration of this book.

To our kaumātua whakaruruhau, who have provided us with cultural support from the outset of Te Kotahitanga: Nā koutou te kākano i ruia.

To our research and professional development colleagues from the Te Kotahitanga project who have contributed over the years, kei runga noa atu.

We have also been the recipients of much support from our colleagues both within the University of Waikato, the Ministry of Education and others in New Zealand and overseas. Kia ora koutou mo o koutou tautoko.

Nā manaakitanga katoa.

We dedicate this book to our families for it is their ongoing support that allows us to continue on the journey of discovery that is Te Kotahitanga and all that is associated with this project.

Introduction

We are dealing, it would seem, not so much with culturally deprived children as with culturally deprived schools. And the task to be accomplished is not to revise, and amend, and repair deficient children, but to alter and transform the atmosphere and operations of the schools to which we commit these children. Only by changing the nature of the educational experience can we change the product. To continue to define the difficulty as inherent in the raw material, the children, is plainly to blame the victim and to acquiesce in the continuation of educational inequality. (Ryan, 1976, pp. 61–62)

This book is about scaling up, about extending and sustaining educational reform. It is our contention that scaling up educational reform has the potential to have a major impact on the disparities that exist in our society. In most cases these disparities are historical, ongoing and seemingly immutable. However, we are not claiming that educational reform on its own can cure historical disparities. We are saying that educational reform can play a major part in a comprehensive approach to addressing social, economic and political disparities. However, like all human activities, attempts to address disparities and realise the potential of groups currently minoritised[1] run into power differentials in society; hence the subtitle *Addressing the Politics of Disparity* to acknowledge that much of what we talk about in this book is highly contested.

Current approaches to scaling up educational reform have not worked for minoritised students. Most attempts are short term, poorly funded at the outset and often abandoned before any real changes can be seen, to be replaced by some "bold new initiative". In contrast, we are talking about the need for educational reforms that have built into them, from the very outset, those elements that will see them sustained in the original sites and spread to others. It is our contention that these elements will allow educational reforms to be scaled up with the confidence that the reform will not only be able to be sustained in existing and new sites, but that, above all, they will work to reduce disparities and realise the potential of those students currently not well served by education. Put simply, educational reforms that can be sustained and extended can have an impact on educational and social disparities through increasing the educational opportunities for students previously denied these options.

The major social challenge facing New Zealand today is the continuing social, economic and political disparities within our nation, primarily between the descendants of the European colonisers (Pākehā) and the indigenous Māori people. Having said that, we acknowledge that there are many other minoritised groups in our society, such as involuntary migrant ethnic groups, those of all races with special needs and the children of other marginalised groups. However, we as Māori are the indigenous population of Aotearoa New Zealand, and we have rights under international agreements. We also have the Treaty of Waitangi as a national foundation, guaranteeing us the full benefits of living within the nation of New Zealand, which was established in 1840. That these benefits have yet to be realised is the focus of this book.

However, we have found that in addressing the disparities that affect Māori we can also help others. We will present evidence later in this book to show that focusing reform on Māori also benefits other minoritised peoples, whereas focusing reform on all peoples tends to benefit those who have been benefiting all along—not those who really need it.

Although some progress has been seen in recent times, Māori continue to have higher levels of unemployment, are more likely to be employed in low-paying employment, have much higher levels of incarceration, illness and poverty than do the rest of the population and are generally underrepresented in the positive social and economic indicators of

---

1   "Minoritised" is a term used in Shields, Bishop, and Mazawi (2005) to refer to a people who have been ascribed characteristics of a minority. To be minoritised one does not need to be in the numerical minority, only to be treated as if one's position and perspective are of less worth; to be silenced or marginalised. Hence, for example, in schools on the Navajo reservation with over 95 percent of the population being Navajo, or in Bedouin schools, we find characteristics of the students similar to those we may find among Māori in mainstream schools in which they are actually in the numerical minority.

society. These are all outcomes of a process of colonisation that removed Māori control and power over their resource base, language and culture, and which, given a different set of relationships, could have seen Māori people being full participants in the emerging economy and society of the new nation, instead of being overrepresented in the negative indices (Bishop & Glynn, 1999; Walker, 1990). As Colin James (2008) wrote recently in a *New Zealand Herald* column under the title "Nation's Duty to Protect Vulnerable":

> Iwi and hapu were protected in theory by the Treaty of Waitangi. Maori were made equal 'subjects' (citizens). In fact, they were largely dispossessed of their assets, their culture and their self-respect. It wasn't genocide but it crushed morale. Hapu and whanau were less able to ensure their members' welfare. In part the gang violence can be traced to that dispossession and demoralisation. In short, Governments here for 140 years failed the 'responsibility to protect' test for a large and distinguishable minority of our citizens. Only with the initiation of the Treaty of Waitangi process of truth and reconciliation and compensation a generation ago have governments recognised this past failure and attended to it … Rebuilding assets and morale is a multi-generation task … [and indicates] the paramount necessity [for the state] to invest well in our children … reversing the demoralisation of iwi is a demanding project, this responsibility to protect.

The necessity to invest well in our children was also the subject of a recent report to Parliament, entitled the *Inquiry into Making the Schooling System Work for Every Child*, by the Education and Science Committee of the House of Representatives (2008). In its report the committee points to the part education should play in addressing disparities in terms of the impact on Māori as a people, and as people expected to contribute to the nation. The committee pointed out that because Māori represent 28 percent of newborn New Zealanders, the increasing proportion of Māori in the population means that unless "the gap between the performance of Māori students and others is not addressed, the negative consequences for New Zealand will grow exponentially" (p. 10). Professor Mason Durie is quoted as saying that "until the disparity in Māori achievement is corrected, Māori will continue to feature disproportionately in indicators of poor outcomes, *and will be a wasted resource for New Zealand*" (p. 10, emphasis added). The report then identifies how this situation not only affects those who fail at school later in life, in terms of their earning and employment potential, their health and wellbeing and the strong "connection between non-engagement with school and youth offending" (p. 11), but also has effects on the wider society:

> As employment becomes less labour-intensive, and more dependent on the use of technology, fewer jobs will be available for those who lack functional literacy and numeracy. The larger the group, the more difficult will it be for New Zealand to create and sustain a high-performing, internationally competitive economy. (p. 11)

The Education Counts website[2] also identifies a substantial body of evidence that demonstrates that students who are not well served by the education system are heavily disadvantaged in later life. For example, those with higher levels of education are more likely to participate in the labour market, face lower risks of unemployment, have greater access to further training and receive higher earnings on average. Conversely, people with no formal school qualifications have unemployment rates far exceeding those with qualifications, and have the lowest median incomes:

> In 2006, the unemployment rate for those with a bachelor's degree or higher was 2.1 percent; for those with another tertiary qualification 2.9 percent; with only a school qualification 4.1 percent; and with no qualification 5.2 percent … The median weekly income for those with bachelors' and higher degrees was $785; for those with other tertiary qualifications it was $575; for those with school qualifications it was $335; and for those with no qualifications $310. (Education and Science Committee, 2008, pp. 10–11)

The Education Counts website also contends that young people leaving school without any qualifications may have difficulty performing in the workforce and may face difficulties in terms of lifelong learning or returning to formal study in later years. It suggests that a considerable number of research studies show a strong connection between early school leavers and unemployment and/or lower incomes, which are in turn generally related to poverty and dependence on income support.

In his submission to the Education and Science Committee (cited above), Judge Andrew Becroft, the Principal Youth Court Judge, estimated that up to 80 percent of offenders in the Youth Court are not attending school, either because they are not enrolled or because they are suspended or excluded. He continued by suggesting that between 25 and 30 percent of youth offending takes place between 9 am and 3 pm. Judge Becroft proposed that "[e]ngaging all young people of compulsory school age in education would reduce the crime rate among this group significantly" (p. 11).

In terms of offending, the report noted that young Māori offend at twice the rate of young Pasifika people and at four times the rate of young Pākehā, and in the experience of Judge Becroft failure at school contributes to the establishment of a vicious circle that leads to recidivist offending. The Ministry of Social Development also presented evidence that gaining stable employment helps young offenders to desist from offending, particularly if their jobs offer learning opportunities. However, "[s]tudents who fail at school clearly have less chance of obtaining such employment" (pp. 10–11).

Despite the choice provided by Māori-medium education in New Zealand,[3] the vast majority of Māori students attend public/mainstream schools and are taught by non-Māori teachers who have problems relating to and addressing the educational needs of

---

2 http://www.educationcounts.govt.nz/, retrieved 2007.
3 Adrienne Alton-Lee (2008) provides us with evidence that students in Māori-medium classrooms are achieving at higher rates than their contemporaries in mainstream schools.

Māori students (Bishop & Berryman, 2006). In addition, decades of educational reforms and policies such as integration, multiculturalism and biculturalism have failed to support teachers adequately to address systemic shortcomings. These reforms have made very little difference for the large proportion of Māori students who have attended mainstream schools since these educational disparities were first statistically identified over 40 years ago (Hunn, 1960).

It is unfortunate that despite these attempts at reform, and encouraging indications that disparities began to reduce in 2005 (Hood, 2008), disparities still remain. The overall academic achievement levels of Māori students are low; more leave school without any qualifications than do their non-Māori counterparts; their retention rate to age 17 is far less than that for non-Māori; their rate of suspension from school is three to five times higher, depending on gender; they are overrepresented in special education programmes for behavioural issues; they enrol in preschool programmes in lower proportions than other groups; they tend to be overrepresented in low-stream education classes; they receive less academic feedback than do children of the majority culture; they are more likely than other students to be found in vocational curriculum streams; they leave school earlier, with fewer formal qualifications; and they enrol in tertiary education in lower proportions (Hood, 2008; Ministry of Education, 2005b).

Addressing these educational disparities is a difficult, yet necessary task for educators at all levels within our system. Most countries that have diverse ethnic student populations will attest to this fact, for this is where educational disparities really show themselves: among the marginalised and minoritised peoples within mainstream educational settings.

In 2001 we, Russell Bishop and Mere Berryman, began an educational reform project called Te Kotahitanga,[4] which aims at improving the educational achievement of indigenous Māori students in mainstream secondary schools. Over the past eight years the project has spread to 33 secondary schools in New Zealand, where we are now seeing some remarkable changes in Māori student engagement with learning and achievement. The project is funded by the New Zealand Ministry of Education and is based on a theoretical approach to research and development termed "kaupapa Māori".[5] The project developed from a unique perspective, in that it draws on the ways of knowing

4   Te Kotahitanga literally means unity of purpose, but it has increasingly come to embody its figurative meaning of unity through self-determination. Many Māori meeting houses and marae are named Te Kotahitanga in acknowledgement of the movement of the same name that developed in New Zealand in the late 19th century, and which had self-determination for Māori as one of its key policies.

5   Kaupapa Māori is a discourse of proactive theory and practice that emerged from within the wider revitalisation of Māori communities that developed in New Zealand following the rapid Māori urbanisation in the 1950s and 1960s. This movement grew further in the 1970s, and by the late 1980s had developed as a political consciousness among Māori people, which promoted the revitalisation of Māori cultural aspirations, preferences and practices as a philosophical and productive educational stance and resistance to the hegemony of the dominant discourse.

of the people most affected by educational disparities, and the project has built on Māori aspirations, preferences and practices for educational reform (Bishop, Berryman, Cavanagh, & Teddy, 2007; Bishop, Berryman, Tiakiwai, & Richardson, 2003).

Having said that, this book is not about the project as such. Instead, it seeks to address an even more complex question than how to design and implement effective educational reform. It seeks to understand how to develop an educational reform programme that is both extendable and sustainable; that is, a model that addresses both the quantitative and qualitative aspects of education reform. In other words, a model of scaling up educational reform that not only addresses the need to expand enclaves of successful reform to more schools and classrooms, but also addresses the qualitative complexity that lies beneath reform efforts in ways that sustain "change in a multi-level system characterized by multiple and shifting priorities" (Coburn, 2003, p. 3). In this way, we understand that educational reform will play a part in impacting on social disparities by impacting on educational disparities.

This book considers the conditions that are necessary for extending and sustaining educational reform by considering what McLaughlin and Mitra (2001) term "theory or principle-based educational reforms". Fullan (2007) terms these "large-scale reforms". Such reforms focus on improving student outcomes by creating a professional learning context in which teachers acquire an in-depth understanding of the underlying theoretical principles of the reform so that they can use their learning flexibly in their classrooms when new situations and challenges arise. Such reforms are initiated and designed outside of schools and focus on the need to reform educational practice at a number of levels—the classroom, the school and the education system as a whole—in order to improve student outcomes.

Scaling up theory- or principle-based reforms requires that all of those currently involved deepen their understanding of their practices in response to changing circumstances within existing reform sites, as well as broadening the reach of the reform to these teachers' other classrooms, to other teachers' classrooms within the initial and new schools and to policy makers at the national level. As Glennan, Bodilly, Galegher, and Kerr (2004) observe, from their detailed meta-analysis of attempts to scale up a number of large-scale, theory-based educational reforms in the United States, scaling up an educational reform is no longer thought of in terms of a one-way replication model that simply seeks to increase the number of sites involved in the reform. Rather, scaling up is seen as a "non-sequential process of interaction, feedback, and adaptation among groups of actors—teachers, providers, schools, and district and state administrators" (p. 27). In other words, reform participants are not acted upon but are active participants in an *iterative* process. Successful scale up of educational reform requires of active participants that they not only change core instructional practices from those currently dominant in the schools, but also provide infrastructural and organisational support at a variety of levels—within the schools and beyond, and within the system itself. This may extend to changing "policies governing standards, assessments and accountability; the supporting infrastructure, including incentives for teachers and other actors; funding and resource allocations patterns; and networking arrangements" (ibid.).

Issues of extending and sustaining educational reforms are not mutually exclusive: they are two sides of the same coin. Extending education reform means broadening the reform to other sites, be they classrooms, schools or regions. By sustainability we follow the understandings of Coburn (2003), Elmore (1996), McLaughlin and Mitra (2001), and Timperley, Wilson, Barrar, and Fung (2007), who stress that sustainability means more than simply maintaining the practices of the reform over time, or even continuing the level of implementation achieved when the reform design team leaves the school. Rather, by sustainability we mean *the provision of a means whereby the reform is able to be deepened and extended by teachers, school leaders and policy makers in response to a changing student curriculum, and context, over time and circumstance.*

Following Coburn (2003), Elmore (1996) and McLaughlin and Mitra (2001), we emphasise that issues of extension and sustainability are addressed by the same means, and that these means need to exist from the very inception of the reform and be built into the design and implementation of the reform from its very outset. In other words, "issues of invention, implementation, sustainability, and scale occur simultaneously when going deeper and broader with theory-based change" (McLaughlin & Mitra, 2001, p. 301).

Sarason (1996) warns that, despite the initial success of a reform, reforms tend to founder once external support and funding are withdrawn, personnel and policies shift and competition for internal resources grows. Theory-based reforms are designed to counter this tendency in that, while they are generally large scale, they have a motivating theoretical base which establishes core principles or norms of practice that define the change in terms of the theoretical foundations of classroom practice. This flexibility allows the reform to be appropriate to and owned by practitioners in a wide range of settings and circumstances. Indeed, what is crucial is that the local participants be able to adapt and modify their actual activities in line with the reform's principles to make the reform relevant to their own setting. As Coburn (2003) notes, to deepen and extend the reform, schools, teachers and students need to be able to take *ownership* of the reform in order to maintain the focus in the face of competing interests and agendas.

Along with Freire (1970) and Fullan (1993), we acknowledge that too many educational reform initiatives have been top down, drawing on expert theories of change while ignoring the necessary involvement and ownership by those on the ground. Although theory-based reforms are usually externally generated, they are given practical form in school settings, often requiring "significant teacher learning and contextualization if they are to change teaching and learning in significant, sustained ways" (McLaughlin &

Mitra, 2001, p. 302). In short, theory-based reforms are externally generated, contain core principles and allow for "co-invention and flexible implementation in practice" (ibid.).

Such an approach is vital, for, as Elmore (1996) notes, "innovations that require large changes in the core of educational practice seldom penetrate more than a small fraction of US schools and classrooms and seldom last for very long when they do" (p. 1). By the core of education, Elmore means:

> how teachers understand the nature of knowledge and the student's role in learning, and how these ideas about knowledge and learning are manifested in teaching and classwork. The 'core' also includes structural arrangements of schools, such as the physical layout of classrooms, student grouping practices, teacher responsibilities for groups of students, and relations among teachers in their work with students, as well as processes for assessing student learning and communicating it to students, teachers, parents, administrators, and other interested parties. (p. 1)

This book is about educational reform at three levels: the classroom; the school; and the system. As Datnow and Stringfield (2000), Fullan (2007) and Glennan et al. (2004) all stress, it is the interdependence of the actors at all the levels of the education system that is crucial for sustaining and expanding educational reform. Such an approach is necessary, for although we understand clearly that teachers in classrooms are the engine room of educational reform, as Elmore (2004) suggests, the key to change is teacher action supported by responsive structural reform. Or, as Glennan et al. (2004) observe, "new teaching methods are doomed to fade if not supported by school- and district-wide policies and infrastructure" (p. 29).

It is worth noting that in Bolman and Deal's (2006) model, infrastructure ranges from and includes school management structures, organisation and reporting systems, such as staffing role allocations and capability-building procedures, decision-making processes, through to the symbolic representation of what is important to the school. Our earlier work (Bishop et al., 2003, 2007) has investigated what effective teacher action looks like in depth, and we will draw on that work here. However, now it is also timely to consider just what "responsive structural reform" looks like in practice and how to implement this at the school and system-wide levels. Based on our experiences of working within a large educational reform project with 33 secondary schools, their teachers, leaders and communities (some for over five years), and with reference to the literature in this field, we have developed in this book a model for sustaining and extending theory-based educational reforms.

CHAPTER ONE

Towards a Model for Sustaining and Extending Theory-based Educational Reforms

> Let's be explicit. The only goal worth talking about is transforming
> the current school system so that large-scale, sustainable,
> continuous reform becomes built in. (Fullan, 2003, p. 29)

Introduction

This chapter details the history of the Te Kotahitanga project and the impact this project is having on the students, teachers and schools currently in the project. We then address the conditions necessary to develop an educational reform project so that it is sustainable and extendable.

Te Kotahitanga Phase I

In 2001 and 2002 the first phase of the Te Kotahitanga research project was undertaken by the Māori Education Research Team at the School of Education, University of Waikato, in partnership with the Poutama Pounamu Education Research and Development Centre, based at Tauranga.

We began the project by talking to Years 9 and 10 Māori students (and other participants in their education) in a range of schools. These schools covered a range of criteria, including single sex to co-educational, high to low decile,[1] urban to rural, large

---

1   This term refers to the categorisation of schools according to the average socioeconomic status of the parents of the students attending the schools.

to small, and high to low proportions of Māori students. The aim of our conversations was for us to gain a better understanding of Māori students' experiences in the classroom (and of those others involved in their education). We then sought to develop a means of passing this understanding on to their teachers in a way that might lead to improved pedagogy, which would ultimately result in reducing educational disparities through improving Māori student achievement. In doing so, we sought to identify those underlying teacher and school behaviours and attitudes that make a difference to Māori achievement. Overall, the research was concerned with finding out how schooling could reduce educational disparities through raising the educational achievement of Māori children.

The project commenced with a short scoping exercise in which we found the value of the student voice (Bishop et al., 2001a). This exercise guided the subsequent longer term project, which commenced with the gathering of a number of narratives of classroom experience by the process of collaborative storying (Bishop, 1996) from a range of engaged and nonengaged Māori children in five unmodified public/mainstream schools. It was from these stories that the rest of the project developed.

In their narratives the children clearly identified that the main influence on their educational achievement was the quality of the in-class relationships and interactions they had with their teachers. They also shared how, by changing the ways they related and interacted with Māori students in their classrooms, teachers could create a context for learning in which Māori students' educational achievement could improve. It was clear from these stories that if Māori students are to achieve at higher levels, teachers must theorise differently about these students and about their own ability to help Māori students to reach higher levels of achievement. In short, "they must alter their beliefs and conceptions of practice, their 'theories of action'" (Smylie, 1995, p. 93).

On the basis of these suggestions from Years 9 and 10 Māori students, together with other information from relevant literature and the experiences of the students' caregivers, principals and teachers, the research team developed an Effective Teaching Profile (see Box 1.1). This profile formed the basis of the Te Kotahitanga professional development innovation. When this innovation was implemented with a group of 11 teachers in four schools in 2001, it resulted in improved learning, behaviour and attendance outcomes in the classrooms of those teachers who had been able to participate fully in the professional development intervention (Bishop et al., 2003).

Fundamental to the Effective Teaching Profile is teachers' understanding of the need to explicitly reject deficit theorising as a way of explaining Māori students' educational achievement levels, and take an *agentic* position in their theorising about their practice. That is, practitioners need to express their professional commitment and responsibility to bring about change in Māori students' educational achievement by accepting professional responsibility for the learning of all their students.

Box 1.1 The Te Kotahitanga Effective Teaching Profile

Effective teachers of Māori students create a culturally appropriate and responsive context for learning in their classroom. In doing so they:
- positively and vehemently reject deficit theorising as a means of explaining Māori students' educational achievement levels (and professional development projects need to ensure that this happens)
- know and understand how to bring about change in Māori students' educational achievement and are professionally committed to doing so (and professional development projects need to ensure that this happens).

They do this in the following observable ways:
1. Manaakitanga: They care for the students as culturally located human beings above all else.
   Mana refers to authority and akiaki to the task of urging someone to act. Manaakitanga refers to the task of building and nurturing a supportive environment.
2. Mana motuhake: They care for the performance of their students.
   In modern times mana has taken on various meanings, such as legitimation and author-ity, and can also relate to an individual's or a group's ability to participate at the local and global level. Mana motuhake involves the development of personal or group identity and independence.
3. Whakapiringatanga: They are able to create a secure, well managed learning environment by incorporating routine pedagogical knowledge with pedagogical imagination.
   Whakapiringatanga is a process wherein specific individual roles and responsibilities are required to achieve individual and group outcomes.
4. Wānanga: They are able to engage in effective teaching interactions with Māori students as Māori.
   As well as being known as a Māori centre of learning, a wānanga as a learning forum involves a rich and dynamic sharing of knowledge. With this exchange of views, ideas are given life and spirit through dialogue, debate, and careful consideration in order to reshape and accommodate new knowledge.
5. Ako: They can use a range of strategies that promote effective teaching interactions and relationships with their learners.
   Ako means to learn, as well as to teach. It refers both to the acquisition of knowledge and to the processing and imparting of knowledge. More importantly, ako is a teaching–learning practice that involves teachers and students learning in an interactive dialogic relationship.
6. Kotahitanga: They promote, monitor, and reflect on outcomes that in turn lead to improvements in educational achievement for Māori students.
   Kotahitanga is a collaborative response towards a commonly held vision, goal, or other such purpose or outcome.

Source: Bishop et al., 2003

These two central concepts are manifested in the teachers' classrooms when teachers demonstrate on a daily basis that they:
- care for the students as culturally located individuals
- have high expectations for students' learning
- are able to manage their classrooms so as to promote learning
- are able to engage in a range of discursive learning interactions with students, or facilitate students to engage with others in these ways
- know a range of strategies that can facilitate learning interactions
- collaboratively promote, monitor and reflect on students' learning outcomes in order to modify their instructional practices in ways that will lead to improvements in Māori student achievement
- share this knowledge with their students.

The implementation of the Effective Teaching Profile allows educators to create learning contexts that will improve the learning engagement and achievement of Māori students by developing learning–teaching relationships where the following notions are paramount:
- *power is shared*: Learners can initiate interactions, and a learner's right to self-determination over learning styles and sense-making processes are regarded as fundamental to power-sharing relationships, and collaborative critical reflection is part of an ongoing critique of power relationships.
- *culture counts*: Classrooms are places where learners can bring "who they are" to the learning interactions in complete safety, and where their knowledge is *acceptable* and *legitimate*.
- *learning is interactive and dialogic*: Learners are able to be co-inquirers (i.e., raisers of questions and evaluators of questions and answers); learning is active and problem based, integrated and holistic; learning positioning is reciprocal (ako); knowledge is co-created; and classrooms are places where young people's sense-making processes and knowledge are validated and developed in collaboration with others.
- *connectedness is fundamental to relations*: Teachers are committed to and inextricably connected to their students and the community; and school and home/parental aspirations are complementary.
- *there is a common vision*: There is an agenda for excellence for Māori in education.

In short, implementing the Effective Teaching Profile provides an opportunity for educators to develop an education in which power is shared between self-determining individuals within nondominating relations of interdependence; where culture counts; where learning is interactive, dialogic and spiral; and where participants are connected and committed to one another through the establishment of a common vision of what constitutes excellence in educational outcomes. In this way, following Cummins (1995), Gay (2000), Sidorkin (2002) and Villegas and Lucas (2002), we propose that the above context for learning can best be described as a *culturally responsive pedagogy of relations.*

What we learnt from Phase I

In the first phase of Te Kotahitanga we noted that the small number of teachers who worked with Te Kotahitanga were isolated and vulnerable within the change process. During this phase the research/professional development team had worked with only a select number of teachers in a range of schools to ascertain if the programme would work with individual teachers in a variety of classrooms. The programme did work well for most of the teachers, in particular those who were able to be supported in the project to an optimal level and where improvements in Māori student achievement were systematically monitored in a way that informed ongoing teaching practice. This optimal level, however, was only achievable when there was consistent and reliable in-class support available to teachers to provide objective and ongoing feedback on their practice. This latter finding demonstrated the importance of schools developing systems to provide ongoing support to teachers in their classrooms.

Furthermore, because the first phase involved only a very small number of teachers in each school, the teachers tended to become somewhat isolated enclaves within their respective schools. In addition to the improvements in students' achievement, anecdotal evidence indicated that children in the optimally supported target teachers' classrooms had improved their behaviour, reduced their absenteeism and were intending to continue their education beyond the junior school. However, in their other classes taught by nontarget teachers, the behaviour of these same students had in some cases worsened, selective absenteeism ("wagging" selected classes) had increased and the general level of frustration of all concerned had risen.

Consequently, it was recommended that the focus of the professional development intervention in future should be the whole staff rather than just a few teachers. It was felt that this would infuse the changes taking place in the teachers' classrooms throughout the whole school and create a "cultural change" in the school so that all teachers would be supportive of and knowledgeable about the new approaches, and school structures and systems could be developed to support the reform initiative. In addition, in a more cohesive, strategic way it would allow their students to experience consistency across as many of their subject classrooms as possible.

In one of the four schools in Phase 1 we had been able to arrange for the same class to be taught by three Te Kotahitanga teachers. Of all the classes we observed in the four schools, the students in this class appeared to make the greatest progress from their starting baseline over a range of indicators. This indicated that the whole-school approach (and our working with as many teachers as possible for each group of students) was a better way to proceed than working with teachers in isolated classrooms.

Following on from the successful implementation of the professional development model in the first phase of the project, refinements were made to the model and it was trialled in a second phase.

Te Kotahitanga Phase 2

Initially, in its first phase the project was conducted by a small team of researchers/professional developers external to the school, with the express intention of seeing if changing classroom relationships and interactions could bring about changes in Māori student outcomes (Bishop et al., 2003). However, as the numbers of schools and teachers involved in the second phase grew, the in-school component of the project was conducted by teams of in-school facilitators, who were provided with professional development and supported by the external developers of the project. These facilitators were staff released from their usual teaching duties to undertake training and to implement the project in their schools. Resource Teachers: Learning and Behaviour (RTLBs) and Schools' Advisory Services staff were also included as part of the implementation teams in schools and were trained to implement the reform activities and conduct the follow-up sessions.

The professional development approach used was very similar to that developed in the first phase of the project. That is, initially teachers, facilitators and professional developers planned (out-of-school) intensive opportunities to develop relationships and set mutually agreeable goals, outcomes, protocols and parameters for success. Everyone involved learnt about all aspects of the Effective Teaching Profile, including how this would be observed in classrooms. Instruction and demonstration were followed by opportunities for teachers to perform or practise the new procedures in an authentic classroom context with in-class support.

In Phase 2 we worked with three schools: two secondary (Schools 1 and 2) and one contributing intermediate[2] (School 3). By 2003 nearly 80 percent of the staff in School 1 were involved, having been brought into the project in cohorts of 30 in the first and subsequent years. This level of participation enabled the researchers to formulate a theory and method of professional development for a "whole-school" approach. In contrast, in School 2, 11 teachers (10 percent of the teaching staff) took part in the project in 2002 and 2003 working with two target classes. This latter approach confirmed for us the benefits of teachers working in cross curricular groups, examining and planning for the learning needs of specific target classes. These two approaches—the whole-school focus and working with teachers around specific target classrooms—combined into a comprehensive model that informed the development of the third phase of the project, which commenced in late 2003. As a result of our experiences in the Phase 2 schools, a number of elements of successful professional development of this type became clearer.

---

2 Intermediate schools are public schools for students in Years 7 and 8, or those aged between 10 and 12 years.

Firstly, creating, trialling and evaluating a professional development programme that can assist and support teachers to develop what Gay (2000) terms a culturally responsive context for learning has benefits in terms of changes in teachers' classroom practice, their level of satisfaction with teaching and students' behaviours and learning outcomes. However, it is important to note that the development of a specific context for learning will not necessarily bring about changes in the academic achievement of Māori students. As Timperley and Wiseman (2003) warn, *professional communities* of teachers who focus solely on themselves and their teaching may not necessarily see improvements in student outcomes. Rather, there is a need to develop *professional learning communities* that focus on improving student learning and achievement. In many ways, what we learnt in Phase 2 was that the preoccupation of the professional development team with sequence and working with teachers, and the context for learning they created, resulted in the development of professional communities focused on the needs of the profession rather than professional learning communities focused on learning.

We also learnt that we needed to strengthen one of the reform activities, the *co-construction meetings*, as places where teachers of a variety of subjects are facilitated to focus on the learning needs of the students they teach in a common target class. In this way the teachers can critically reflect on student data gathered for formative purposes relating to student participation (attendance, engagement) and achievement, and then identify what changes in practice are necessary to ensure progress. In addition, we further developed the process of teacher observation, feedback and individual goal setting to feed into these collegial co-construction meetings. At the meetings, facilitators supported teachers to reflect on a range of evidence and engage in co-constructing goals for improving the learning outcomes of a class of students in line with the evidence viewed, rather than focusing solely on curriculum areas. Co-construction meetings were followed by in-class *shadow coaching* aimed at supporting teachers to achieve their goals of changing their instructional practice to further monitor and improve student learning.

It became clear at this point that sustaining the process of reform would involve institutionalising the pattern of reform activities within the school. These activities would involve annual school-based professional development staff induction hui (meetings held within Māori cultural settings) to progressively introduce new staff to a continuous programme of critical reflection on their "discursive positioning" (see Chapter Three) in relation to Māori students. These hui would be followed by in-class observation, feedback, evidence-based co-construction meetings and shadow coaching. This would involve trained and proficient in-school facilitators providing feedback, in its broadest sense, to teachers and participating in co-constructing with teachers how they could change their practice in ways that would enhance Māori students' learning and achievement. In turn, the in-school facilitators would be supported by research and professional development staff whose task was to support the school to maintain the integrity of the programme in the schools.

Once again the value of teachers challenging their own and others' deficit theorising was highlighted. One of the major findings of the first phase of the Te Kotahitanga project was that the major influence on Māori students' educational achievement lies in the minds and actions (positioning within a discourse) of their teachers. The narratives of experience on which this project was based (Bishop & Berryman, 2006) clearly identified that teachers who explain Māori students' educational achievement by positioning themselves within a deficit discourse that explains achievement in terms of the students' deficiencies (or deficiencies of the structure of the school), are unable to offer appropriate solutions to these problems and abrogate their responsibilities for improving the achievement levels of Māori students (Shields et al., 2005; Valencia, 1997). Such deficit theorising blames others and results in low teacher expectations of Māori students, creates self-fulfilling prophesies of failure and leaves teachers bewildered as to how to make a difference for Māori students. Changing this theorising by having teachers reposition themselves within alternative discourses—including different practices as well as theorising—is therefore a necessary condition for improving Māori student educational engagement and achievement. (This concept is developed further in Chapter Three) The development of an institutionalised means for teachers to collaboratively reflect on and change their practice in light of a range of evidence of student participation and achievement, from a range of measures, provides the sufficient condition.

Te Kotahitanga Phase 3

In late 2003 Te Kotahitanga entered its third phase of implementation, this time increasing the scale of the project to include 12 secondary schools with the kind of range as when we first talked to the students: large to small; urban to rural; single sex to co-ed; high decile to low decile; and those with a high proportion of Māori students to a low proportion of Māori students. The professional development continued to apply what the research and development team had learnt to be most effective from the two previous Te Kotahitanga phases. In this third phase, the in-school professional development for teachers was again undertaken by in-school facilitators, who were provided with professional learning opportunities by the research and development team to learn how to best support teachers to implement the Effective Teaching Profile in their classrooms through a sequence of professional development activities. The professional development for teachers followed a series of formal and informal introductory meetings, where the project was outlined to each school's leader and staff.

Once schools undertook to participate in the project, they selected a facilitation team, which consisted of school staff released for the task, augmented by staff from the Schools' Advisory Services and RTLB support teams. These teams were provided with focused professional development by the research and development team to undertake a series of baseline data-gathering activities and teacher-specific professional development in their schools. The professional development to operationalise the Effective Teaching Profile in classrooms involves applying the acronym GEPRISP as the initial implementation model, and PSIRPEG (see Figure 1.1) as the classroom implementation and evaluation model, initially through group-focused activities external to classrooms, followed by an ongoing cycle of activities working in classrooms with teachers.

GEPRISP is a acronym that reminds teachers that this project is focused on the *goal* of improving Māori students' educational achievement, and that the means of doing so commences with an examination of Māori students' *experiences* of schooling and of teachers' discursive *positioning* in relation to the goal and Māori students' experiences. The importance of *relationships, interactions, strategies* and *planning* that can be used to reach the goal is then detailed. To implement what has been learnt at the induction hui, the order of GEPRISP is reversed to PSIRPEG, where teachers focus on their need to undertake classroom and lesson *planning* that will use a range of *strategies* to promote discursive *interactions* in their classrooms, which in turn will develop caring and learning *relationships*, and thus reinforce teachers' agentic discursive *positioning*. Together, these all work towards improving Māori students' educational *experiences* and promote the *goal* of improving Māori students' educational engagement, participation and achievement.

The professional development process

The professional development activities commence with the hui whakarewa (a three-day staff induction workshop), at which the narratives of experience (Bishop & Berryman, 2006) are used to create a learning context in which teachers are able to reflect critically on their own discursive positioning in relation to Māori students. The application of the Effective Teaching Profile is then explained, as are strategies and modes of planning for the implementation of the Profile in their classrooms. How facilitators will observe in classrooms is also detailed, and the return to classrooms is planned for. This initial hui is then followed by the in-school term-by-term cycle of four specific but interdependent activities that have emerged from the previous phases. These involve:

- individual teacher observations using the Te Kotahitanga Observation Tool (trialled and developed in Phases 1 and 2)
- individual teacher feedback and co-construction sessions reflecting on specific events observed in the formal observation, along with individual goal setting
- group co-construction meetings for teachers of a common class reflecting on student participation and achievement evidence and the co-construction of focused group goal setting
- targeted shadow-coaching sessions in order to move towards targeted goals (both individual and group, from feedback and co-construction sessions).

In addition, staff are involved in "new knowledge", "new strategy" or "new assessment" professional development sessions, which tend to be run by the school leaders on an as needed basis. This total programme is called the Te Kotahitanga Cycle Plus, which refers

Figure 1.1 The Implementation and Evaluation Process: GEPRISP and PSIRPEG

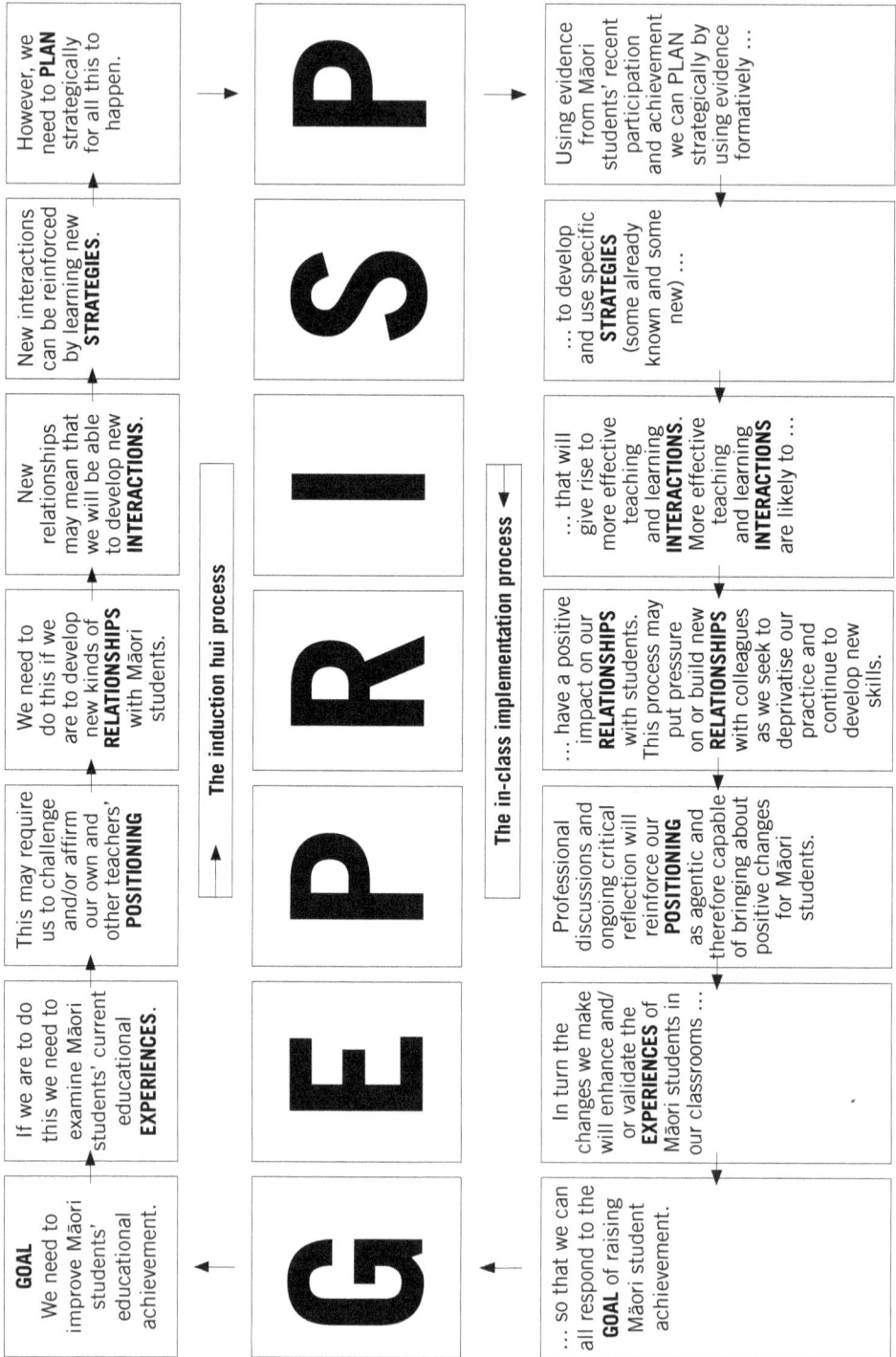

GEPRISP (top row, left to right):

G — **GOAL** We need to improve Māori students' educational achievement.

E — If we are to do this we need to examine Māori students' current educational **EXPERIENCES**.

P — This may require us to challenge and/or affirm our own and other teachers' **POSITIONING**

R — We need to do this if we are to develop new kinds of **RELATIONSHIPS** with Māori students.

I — New relationships may mean that we will be able to develop new **INTERACTIONS**.

S — New interactions can be reinforced by learning new **STRATEGIES**.

P — However, we need to **PLAN** strategically for all this to happen.

The induction hui process

The in-class implementation process

PSIRPEG (bottom row, left to right):

P — Using evidence from Māori students' recent participation and achievement we can PLAN strategically by using evidence formatively ...

S — ... to develop and use specific **STRATEGIES** (some already known and some new) ...

I — ... that will give rise to more effective teaching and learning **INTERACTIONS**. More effective teaching and learning **INTERACTIONS** are likely to ...

R — ... have a positive impact on our **RELATIONSHIPS** with students. This process may put pressure on or build new **RELATIONSHIPS** with colleagues as we seek to deprivatise our practice and continue to develop new skills.

P — Professional discussions and ongoing critical reflection will reinforce our **POSITIONING** as agentic and therefore capable of bringing about positive changes for Māori students.

E — In turn the changes we make will enhance and/or validate the **EXPERIENCES** of Māori students in our classrooms ...

G — ... so that we can all respond to the **GOAL** of raising Māori student achievement.

to the term-by-term cycle of observations, followed by feedback, co-construction meetings and shadow coaching, along with the "Plus" of new approaches sessions.

By 2005 we had developed the model as a series of feedback loops (see Figure 1.2) between the major participants in the project. The diagram illustrates both vertical and horizontal connections between participants, indicating that supportive feedback can be sought from and provided by peers in other settings, as well as from knowledgeable "others". Such a network of relationships is termed by G. Hall (personal communication, October 2007) an "output" model, as compared to the more traditional "input" model that seeks to transmit predetermined knowledge. By this it is meant that outputs—in the form of evidence of thinking, theorising and explanations—are used by the recipient to provide feedback or feedforward to the learner. More commonly, from our experience we find this feedback loop approach creates a learning relationship where co-construction of learning takes place, and where both parties collaborate to determine how practice at all levels of the model might be modified in the light of evidence of current performance.

Figure 1.2 The evidence and feedback cycle central to the project

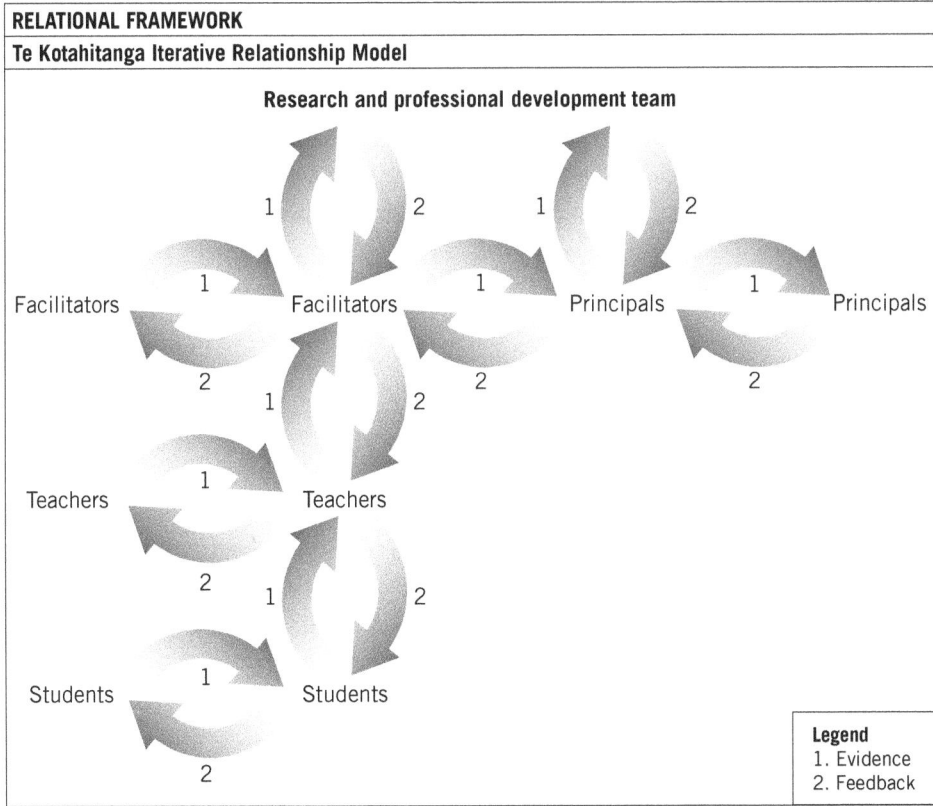

RELATIONAL FRAMEWORK

Te Kotahitanga Iterative Relationship Model

Research and professional development team

Facilitators   Facilitators   Principals   Principals

Teachers   Teachers

Students   Students

Legend
1. Evidence
2. Feedback

The project set out to involve eventually all or most of the 12 schools' staff in the project, and after four years of implementation signs of success—in terms of a wide range of variables, including the primary goal of raising Māori student achievement—were apparent. Details of the first two years of this phase of the project are contained in Bishop et al. (2007); the next two in Bishop, Berryman, Cavanagh, Teddy, Clapham, Lamont et al. (2008).

Evidence of successful change

Three major indicators of successful change were identified during Phase 3: Māori students' experiences; teaching practice; and Māori student achievement.

Māori students' experiences

The first indicator was the outcomes of the ongoing monitoring of Māori students' experiences during all phases of the project. In 2001 (Phase 1), the Māori students (70) we spoke to talked about what would engage them in education. We found time and again during many of these initial interviews (Bishop & Berryman, 2006), that negative deficit thinking on the part of teachers was fundamental to the development of negative relationships and interactions between the students and their teachers, resulting in frustration and anger for all concerned. The students, their whānau (extended families), the principals and the teachers gave us numerous examples of the negative aspects of such thinking, the resultant problematic and resistant behaviours and the frustrating consequences for both students and teachers. The teachers spoke of their frustration and anger; the students spoke of negative relations being an assault on their very identity as Māori people. Students told us of their aspirations to participate in learning, and in what the school had to offer, but they spoke in terms of these actions being an all out assault on their identity, on who they are, on their very basic need to be accepted and acceptable. This in turn precluded them from being able to participate in what the school had to offer.

In the Phase 2 interviews in 2003, Māori students (17) reported positively on their experiences in the classrooms with teachers participating in Te Kotahitanga (Bishop et al., 2007). Although there were still underlying concerns with negative stereotyping and generalisations regarding the ability and behaviour of Māori students, these behaviours seemed to emanate from non-Te Kotahitanga teachers. The students interviewed at this time commented on the benefits of good relationships with their teachers; that is, their teachers made concerted efforts to pronounce their names correctly, related to the students personally and used humour and more personal interactions to motivate and inspire them. These students reported that being Māori in the classroom was about being treated well by teachers, challenged in terms of their learning and listened to as individuals.

The Phase 3 interviews, conducted in 2004 and 2005, focused on the experiences of Years 9 and 10 Māori students (320) from the 12 schools in Phase 3 of the project, who were in the classrooms of teachers who were identified by students, facilitators and principals as being effective implementers of the Effective Teaching Profile. The experiences of these Māori students strongly confirmed the hypothesising of the Phase 1 students; that is, the Phase 3 students clearly affirmed that teachers who engage in the entire range of relationships and interactions found in the Effective Teaching Profile are effective teachers for Māori students. The Phase 3 students talked freely about how they had benefited from being with these teachers. In the conversations with these students, copious examples of the elements of the Effective Teaching Profile were easily recognisable. In fact, taking all of their interview transcriptions into account, apart from their discussions about less effective teachers, whom they spoke of as not adhering to the elements within the Profile, there was little else.

Clearly, from these conversations the Effective Teaching Profile does indeed have real strengths for raising the achievement of Māori students. The professional development these teachers received from their facilitators has changed their approach to teaching, making them exponents of the Effective Teaching Profile and thus more effective for Māori. Subsequently, new cohorts of Māori students are benefiting from the Profile, based on the suggestions from the Phase 1 student narratives.

Students in Phase 3 have strongly confirmed the importance of teachers being agentically positioned and of developing mutually respectful, caring relationships with them and their peers. Their talk clearly indicated the importance of discursive classroom interactions, and they were clear about how this leads to their increased participation and learning. It was also evident that as Māori students begin to feel more secure in themselves and with their teachers, their identities are also affirmed and secure. As a result, they could get on with learning and be far less concerned about the cultural manifestations of their identity. When their identity as Māori was secure, the conversations of these students focused largely on their being engaged with learning, and they were better able to be self-determining.

Teaching practice

The second indicator of success was the pattern of changing teachers' practices in association with students' outcomes. Because Te Kotahitanga is focused on raising the achievement of Māori students through changing teacher practice, we adopted Elmore's (2002) model for demonstrating improvement by measuring increases in teacher practice and student performance over time. This model demonstrates improvement by measuring the quality of teacher practice and student performance on the vertical axis and time on the horizontal axis. Improvement is shown by movement in a consistent north-easterly direction (see Figure 1.3).

Figure 1.3 Improvement in teacher practice and student performance during Phase 3 of Te Kotahitanga

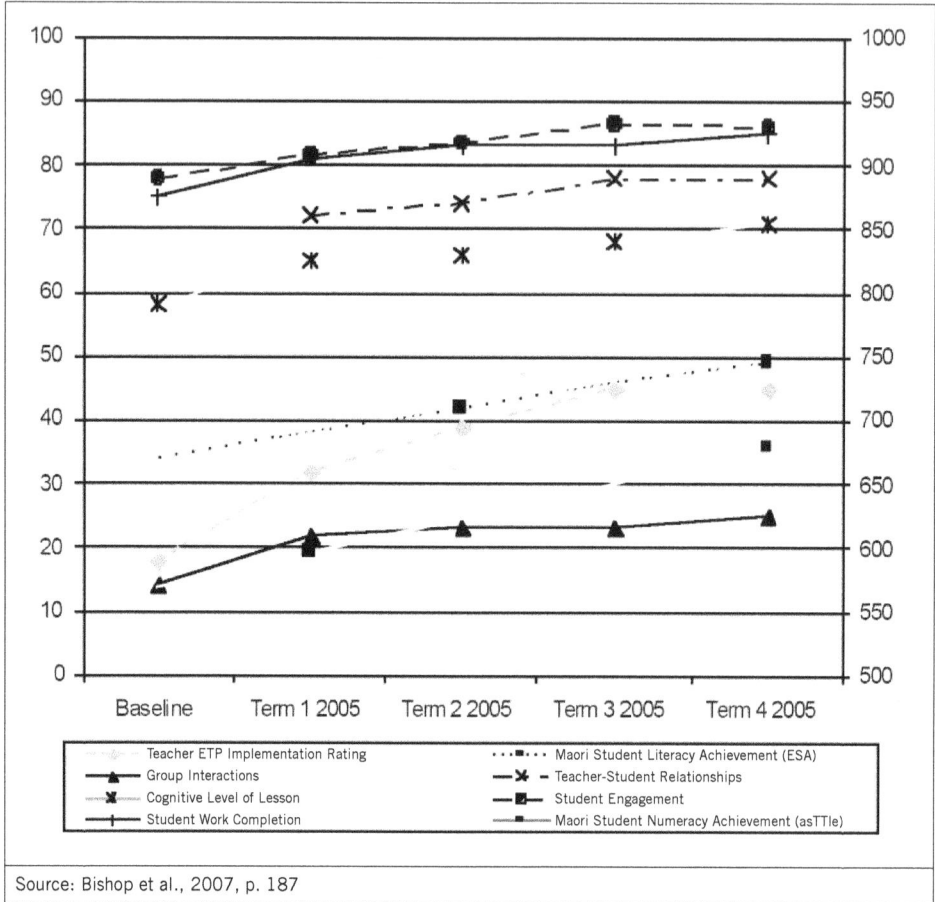

Legend:
- Teacher ETP Implementation Rating
- Group Interactions
- Cognitive Level of Lesson
- Student Work Completion
- Maori Student Literacy Achievement (ESA)
- Teacher-Student Relationships
- Student Engagement
- Maori Student Numeracy Achievement (asTTle)

Source: Bishop et al., 2007, p. 187

Data for Figure 1.3 are taken from the Observation Tool, which monitors teacher–student interactions, teacher Effective Teaching Profile implementation rating, teacher–student relationships, group interactions, the cognitive level of the lessons, Māori student engagement and Māori student work completion. Evidence of student achievement is taken from the Assessment Tool for Teaching and Learning (asTTle) for numeracy and the Essential Skills Assessment (ESA) for literacy. The results for the Observation Tool and ESA were recalculated as percentages for this illustration so that there was a common unit of measurement.

The results (Figure 1.3) are shown on the left; asTTle scores are shown on the right. The positive trends indicated by these eight sets of quantitative results in relationship to each other, supported by the results of all the qualitative data analysed, clearly indicate that there is a relationship between Māori student performance and how well

Te Kotahitanga teachers implement the elements of the Effective Teaching Profile in the project teachers' classrooms.

Figure 1.3 demonstrates, through multiple indicators (Guskey & Sparks, 1996), that as Te Kotahitanga teachers have improved in their use of the Effective Teaching Profile, thus changing the learning contexts in their classrooms, their Māori students have improved in numeracy and literacy achievement. This model demonstrates that teachers across multiple Phase 3 Te Kotahitanga schools have built their knowledge, skills and capacities in their classrooms through the implementation of the Effective Teaching Profile, and simultaneously that their Māori students have experienced continuous improvement in numeracy and literacy performance.

Māori student achievement

The third indicator of successful implementation of the project was improved Māori student achievement (see Table 1.1 below, from Timperley et al., 2007). "In 2006 the first

Table 1.1 Numbers and Percentages of Year 11 students in Te Kotahitanga schools, 2005 and 2006, gaining NCEA Level 1, and percentage-point increases, by ethnicity

	Te Kotahitanga schools							National cohort (decile weighted)
Ethnicity	Year 11 students on roll (number)		Year 11 students gaining NCEA level 1					
			Number		Percent		Increase (percentage points)	
	2005	2006	2005	2006	2005	2006	2005/06	
NZ Māori	973	952	312	461	32.1	48.4	16.4	8.9
European	1210	1302	756	899	62.5	69.0	6.6	4.1
Pacific Islands	292	282	69	110	23.6	39.0	15.4	6.1
Other	263	231	181	175	68.8	75.8	6.9	8.1
Source: Timperley et al., 2007, p. 263								

full cohort of students from the participating schools reached Year 11, this providing an opportunity to assess the impact of Te Kotahitanga on National Certificate of Educational Achievement (NCEA) Level 1 results" (the first level of standardised external qualifications in New Zealand). An independent analysis of the 2006 results by the New Zealand Qualifications Authority (NZQA) statisticians showed that the increase in the percentage of Māori ... students gaining NCEA Level 1 from Te Kotahitanga schools" (a 16.4 percentage point gain, or pp) "was greater than the increase for students from non-Te Kotahitanga schools" (8.9 pp) "(comparing 2006 results with 2005 results and weighting for decile) (Timperley et al. 2007). Table 1.1 also shows that Pasifika students made similar gains (15.4 pp) compared to Pasifika students in a non-Te Kotahitanga decile-weighted comparison group (6.1 pp). These findings indicate that teachers implementing the Effective Teaching Profile may also benefit other previously marginalised students, as well as Māori.

Te Kotahitanga Phase 4

In 2005 the project reached a point where it appeared to be suitable for replication or expansion to sites other than those where the reform was still being developed and tested. As a result, 21 new schools were invited to participate in the project alongside the 12 Phase 3 schools that had entered in 2003.

However, as we continued to work with the original 12 schools, a new set of considerations came into play. These new considerations concerned how a reform might be sustained, given that sustaining reform projects in schools is extremely difficult, even if initially well implemented, because of the tendency of reform projects to founder once initial external support and funding are withdrawn (Coburn, 2003; Sarason, 1996). We therefore had to return to the literature to ascertain just how this could be achieved. This book is the result of that search. It sets out to identify a model of sustainability that draws on a wide range of local and international literature, covering both theoretical and practical issues. It seeks to identify just what is needed to sustain large-scale reform projects such as Te Kotahitanga beyond the initial implementation phase alongside what is needed to successfully scale up sustainable reforms.

Towards a model for scalability

A significant stepping-off point in this search was the large meta-analysis conducted by Cynthia Coburn (2003). Significantly, for our purposes, she noted that few studies consider issues of sustainability: only 18 of 44 projects she studied "involved investigations of schools that had been involved in the reform for 4 or more years" (p. 6). Most of the studies she reviewed were of schools in their first few years of implementing a new, externally generated reform. Of particular significance to us was her concern that only one of the 44 projects she found looked at schools involved in reforms for which "an implementation period with additional resources and attention had officially ended" (p. 6). Couple these concerns with the title of Sarason's (1990) book, *The Predictable Failure of Educational Reform*, and the incentive to develop a model that would ensure the gains made by the Phase 3 schools in raising Māori students' achievement were not just a flash in the pan, became very strong.

Therefore, a major question that is not well addressed in the literature concerns how schools that have successfully initiated an educational reform sustain this reform in the face of the withdrawal of, or change in, external funding and personnel, competing priorities for resources, changing demands on schools and teacher and leadership turnover. This in turn leads to the larger question of how sustainable reforms might be taken beyond those in the initial project. Coburn (2003) suggests that externally funded reforms are particularly vulnerable to this problem "because implementation typically involves a short-term influx of resources, professional development, and other forms of assistance to facilitate implementation that dissipates over time as external developers turn this attention to other sites" (p. 6). Yet Timperley et al. (2007) argue that external developers are a crucial ingredient in the successful development and implementation of effective professional development and the provision of professional learning opportunities for teachers.

Coburn (2003) provides a model in her paper, and this model proved to be a useful starting heuristic for considering how to take a project to scale in a large number of classrooms in project schools, how to sustain the gains made in these classrooms and schools and how to take the project to other schools once it had proven to be successful in the initial schools. Coburn indicates four main components:
1) pedagogy
2) sustainability (essentially meaning institutionalisation)
3) spread
4) ownership.

However, in light of our experiences in Te Kotahitanga and the literature we reviewed for this book, we have developed this model by adding three more components:
5) the need for an unrelenting focus on improving Māori (or any target) students' educational achievement
6) the need for leadership that is proactive, responsive and distributed
7) the need to develop further evaluation and monitoring instruments, along with the need to raise the capacity and capability of staff in the schools to undertake this evaluation and monitoring.

The following model (Figure 1.4) was developed in a parallel study funded by Ngā Pae o te Māramatanga (Bishop & O'Sullivan, 2005).

Earlier we looked at the GEPRISP/PSIRPEG acronym used for the implementation and evaluation process. The theoretical model in Bishop and O'Sullivan (2005) uses GPILSEO as a acronym device for the essential elements of a reform initiative. This model suggests that in order to ensure the reform initiative will be sustainable and scalable, the following elements (shown in Box 1.2) should be present in the reform initiative *from the very outset*. Each element includes a clear focus.

Figure 1.4 GPILSEO: A reform initiative must have these elements from its inception

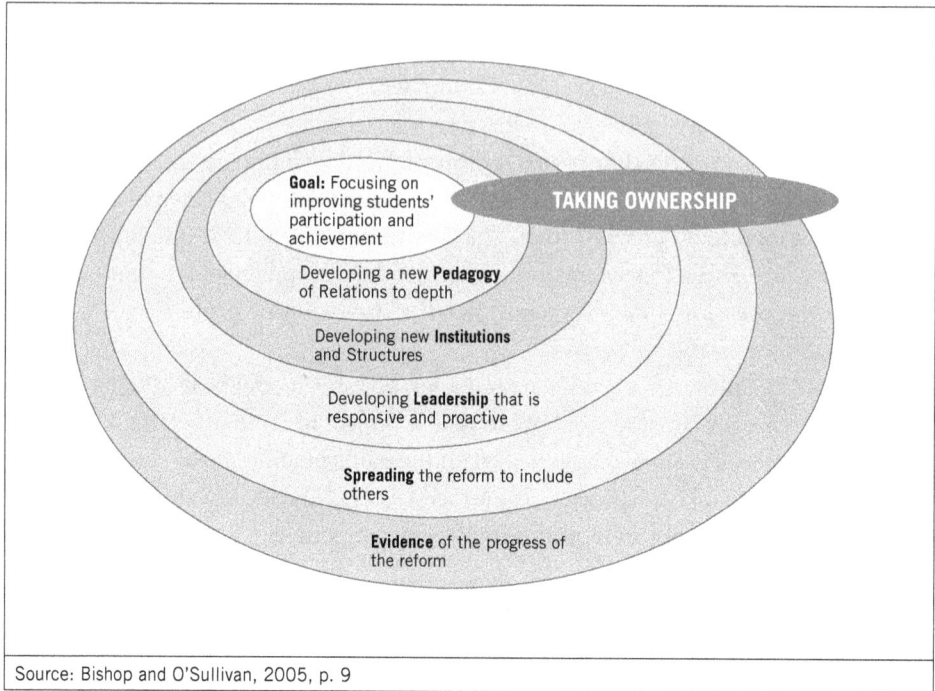

Goal: Focusing on improving students' participation and achievement

TAKING OWNERSHIP

Developing a new **Pedagogy** of Relations to depth

Developing new **Institutions** and Structures

Developing **Leadership** that is responsive and proactive

Spreading the reform to include others

Evidence of the progress of the reform

Source: Bishop and O'Sullivan, 2005, p. 9

Box 1.2 GPILSEO: Elements and foci

- GOALS: establishing *goals* and a vision for reducing disparities through improving targeted students' educational achievement in its widest sense.
- PEDAGOGY: embedding a new *pedagogy* to depth in order to change the core of educational practice.
- INSTITUTIONS: developing new *institutions* and organisational structures to support in-class initiatives.
- LEADERSHIP: developing *leadership* that is responsive, proactive and distributed.
- SPREAD: *spreading* the reform to include all teachers, parents, community members and external agencies.
- EVIDENCE: developing and using appropriate tools and measures of performance to provide *evidence* to monitor the progress of targeted students and the reform in the school/s as a means of modifying core classroom and school practices.
- OWNERSHIP: creating opportunities for all involved to take *ownership* of the reform in such a way that the original objectives of the reform are protected and sustained.

It is important to emphasise that although each element is presented as if it should be implemented in an orderly, linear fashion, this is not how it works in reality. Rather, each element is interdependent and interacts with the others in a variety of ways and in a variety of settings. How this might look is shown in Table 1.2, again as an ideal type, which in practice would be far more complex in terms or interrelatedness and outcomes.

Table 1.2 GPILSEO: Details of each element

Establishing **GOALs** and a vision for improving targeted student participation and achievement	The reform must contain a means whereby individual teachers, schools and policy makers can set specific, measurable goals for improving student participation and achievement in their widest sense. Targeted student achievement must be the focus of the reform, because nonspecific education-for-all approaches simply maintain the status quo: while all students may increase their achievement, the disparities remain.
Developing a new **PEDAGOGY** to depth	The reform must contain a means of embedding the conceptual depth of the reform into the theorising and practice of the classroom teachers, school leaders, principals and national administrators. Coburn (2003) suggests that teachers and schools that have a deep understanding of the underlying theories and principles, and can implement appropriate practices, are better able to respond to the new demands and changing contexts in ways that will sustain and deepen the reform over time. Reform without depth of understanding will trivialise the initiative, and teachers and schools will revert to old explanations and practices in a short time. From their detailed synthesis of best evidence regarding what constitutes effective professional development and learning for teachers, Timperley et al. (2007) also found that sustainability appears to depend on whether teachers acquire an in-depth understanding of the underlying theoretical principles so that they can use their learning flexibly in their classrooms when new situations and challenges arise. Such understanding is relevant to all levels of the education system.
INSTITUTIONALISING the elements of the reform	Connections to and collaboration with other teachers, including teachers in other schools engaged in similar reform, is essential, and the institutionalisation of a means to ensure this happens in a systematic manner is an essential element of sustaining change. Such institutionalisations need to be prioritised so that they are seen to be supportive of the efforts of teachers and are aligned with—and indeed can inform—national policies. Similarly, structural and organisational arrangements need to be modified to accommodate new institutions and staffing (re)allocations.
Developing proactive, responsive and distributed **LEADERSHIP**	Proactive, responsive and distributed leadership is essential for the sustainability of a reform in a school. Leaders at all levels— classroom, school and system—need a sound understanding of the theoretical foundations of the reform and of what that theoretical basis means for classroom practice, school structure and culture, and national policies. Above all, leadership activities need to focus on and accept responsibility for student learning outcomes.

SPREADING the reform	The reform needs to contain, from its very inception, a means of spreading within existing teachers' classrooms, and from there to teachers in other schools, and to community and national policy makers. This element is necessary to align the new norms of the reform within the school, within the norms of supporting institutions and within communities associated with the school to ensure sustainability. Extending the reform to other sites is based on implementing the same flexible, responsive reform in new partnerships.
Using **EVIDENCE** to engage in individual and collaborative problem solving and decision making	The reform needs, from the very outset, a means of engaging teachers in individual and collaborative evidence-based problem-solving activities. Evidence can range from narratives of students' experience, through to the results of norm-referenced standardised tests. Whatever the case, it is vital that the capacity of the staff is raised so that they can gather and use appropriate evidence of student performance. As the reform grows and develops in each school, systemic and institutional developments are necessary to support the changes taking place in the classroom. An area that needs to be developed is that of accurately measuring student attendance data, stand-downs, suspensions, early-leaving exemptions, retention rates and achievement data. This has two purposes: to allow teachers the opportunity to collaboratively reflect on these data to inform ongoing practice; and to use the same data for summative purposes to identify if there is a relationship between the implementation of the educational reform in question and positive changes in student participation and achievement. To ensure these objectives are met in the sequence of formative preceding summative purposes, it is important that the project schools are able to undertake the task of data gathering and processing in real time. To do so they will need to continue to develop the use of electronic student management systems so that the schools can use the data for formative purposes in collaborative settings, and the data can be aggregated for summative purposes.
OWNERSHIP of and authority for the goals of the reform must shift to the school	The last consideration is that ownership of and responsibility for the reform must shift from the external originators to within the school. This is necessary to ensure ongoing changes to the culture of the school are located in the hands of those most responsible for student learning and outcomes. As a result, one of the key considerations of reform is the creation of conditions within the project itself that will ensure that in-depth knowledge of and authority for the project shift from external actors to teachers, schools and policy makers. This shift in ownership ensures the reforms become self-generative while at the same time maintaining the integrity of the reform so that the aims of the reform are met. The shift also ensures new situations are addressed from an in-depth understanding of the reform's aims and approaches rather than from past practice. This shift in ownership is crucial—despite being the least-reported aspect in the literature on sustainability—because it is not the reform itself that needs to be preserved but rather the goal; in this case, the long-term, ongoing reduction of educational disparities through the raising of student achievement.

Application of the model to a variety of settings

This model can be applied to a variety of levels within education—classroom, school and system wide (see Table 1.3 below). It is important to emphasise that although this model presents sustainability and scalability as discrete entities, this is only for the purposes of clarity. In reality, the emphasis is on the interdependence of each of the elements within and between the various levels of the system: the classroom, the schools and the system as a whole.

GPILSEO at the classroom level

For a reform initiative to bring about sustainable change in classrooms, and which can then be extended to other classrooms, there must from the very outset be:

- a focus on improving targeted students' engagement, participation and achievement in the classroom
- a means of implementing a new pedagogy to depth, so that students and teachers can understand and competently implement new practices, and new theories of practice, in their day-to-day classroom relationships and interactions
- a means of developing new institutions in the classroom, such as those developed using co-operative learning approaches
- a means of developing distributed leadership within the classroom so that students can be initiators of, and take responsibility for, their own learning and support the learning of others
- a means whereby the new classroom relationships and interactions will include all students
- a means of gathering and examining evidence to monitor the progress of all students to inform changes in instructional practice
- above all, teacher and student learning that are central to classroom relations and interactions, and teacher learning that is based on analyses of patterns of student learning.

Evidence from the classrooms of the teachers in Phase 3 of Te Kotahitanga showed that all of these elements are developing in the classrooms in the project schools—some faster than others, but nevertheless developing. There is clear evidence in Bishop et al. (2007) and from a wide range of sources that, in terms of this GPILSEO model, teachers are:

- focusing on improving Māori student achievement
- using the new culturally responsive pedagogy of relations to implement the Effective Teaching Profile (including developing understanding of antideficit theorising and agentic positioning)
- changing the institutional structures in their classrooms
- distributing leadership through the development of power-sharing relationships

- spreading the reform to include all students in the benefits of participation in the conversation of learning
- formally and informally monitoring and evaluating Māori students' (and others') progress to inform their changing practices
- above all, taking ownership of the aims and objectives of the project.

GPILSEO at the school level

At a school level there needs to be:
- a focus on improving all targeted students' achievement across the school
- a culturally responsive pedagogy of relations developed across all classrooms, which is used to inform relations and interactions at all levels within the school and community
- time and space created for the development of new institutions within the school, and structures such as timetables, staffing and organisational structures need to support this reform
- leadership that is responsive to the needs of reform, proactive in setting targets and goals and distributed to allow power sharing
- a means whereby all staff can join the reform, and parents and community are also included
- a means whereby in-school facilitators, researchers and teachers are able to use appropriate instruments to monitor the implementation of the reform to provide data for formative and summative purposes
- a means whereby the whole school, including the board of trustees, can take ownership of the reform.

Ownership is seen when there has been a culture shift so that teacher learning is central to the school, and when systems, structures and institutions are developed to support teacher learning. In this way, the reform seeks to address both culturalist (the need to change the culture of the school) and structuralist (the need to change power and resource allocations within the classrooms and schools that reflect the wider society) concerns at the school level.

GPILSEO at the system level

The third level in Table 1.3 concerns the need for system-wide reform. At this level there needs to be a national policy focus and resource allocation for those least well served by education systems (Ministry of Education, 2008). This needs to be sufficient to realise the potential of these group members by raising their overall achievement and thereby reducing historical disparities. The reform should provide:
- a means whereby inservice professional learning opportunities and professional development for teachers is onsite, ongoing and involves feedback loops, and whereby

preservice teacher education is aligned with inservice professional development so that each supports the other in implementing new culturally responsive pedagogies of relations

- the development of supportive policies and infrastructure that provide incentives for teachers and the ability to revisit funding so that, for example, salaries for in-school professional developers are incorporated into schools' staffing allocations and schooling organisations to provide ongoing, interactive and embedded reform
- national-level support and professional development for leaders to promote proactive, responsive and distributed instructional/pedagogical leadership models
- collaboration between policy funders, researchers and practitioners in an iterative process of interaction, feedback and adaptation
- national-level support for the production of appropriate evidence that will enable collaborative formative problem solving and decision making that is ongoing and interactive, and from which supportive policies for standards, assessments and the mix of accountability and capacity building grow
- national-level support for integrated research and professional development that provides data for formative and summative purposes
- national ownership of the problem and the provision of sufficient funding and resources to see solutions in a defined period of time, in an ongoing, embedded manner.

This model therefore encompasses the need to address both culturalist and structuralist positions (see Chapter Three) at the three levels of classroom, school and system by creating a means of changing the classroom, the culture of the school and the education system itself. Cultural change concerns are addressed through goal setting, the development of appropriate pedagogies to depth and the taking of ownership of the whole reform at each level. Structural concerns are addressed by the development of new institutions, responsive and distributed leadership, the spread of the reform to include all those involved, the development of data management systems within the school to support the reform and the taking of ownership by the teachers, school and policy makers of both the cultural and structural changes necessary to reform education to address educational disparities, thereby removing the key contributing factors to poverty among Māori in Aotearoa New Zealand and other minoritised peoples in other parts of the world. Structural concerns are also addressed at a system-wide level when schools are supported, at a national level, to implement these structural changes.

Table 1.3 Sustainability and scalability at classroom, school and system-wide levels

	Sustainability / going to scale	Classroom	School	System
Goal	Goals need to focus on reducing disparities by raising targeted students' achievement in its widest sense.	Goals need to focus on improving targeted students' participation, engagement, and achievement in the classroom.	Goals need to focus on improving all targeted students' achievement across the school.	Goals need to focus on developing policies and allocating resources to ensure that those least well served by the system see overall achievement gains, thereby reducing historical disparities.
Pedagogy	New pedagogy needs to be embedded in order to change the core of educational practice.	A culturally responsive pedagogy of relations needs to be embedded so that students and teachers can understand and competently implement new practices and new theories of practice in their day-to-day classroom relationships and interactions.	A new pedagogy of relations needs to be embedded in all classrooms, and needs to inform relations and interactions at all levels in the school and community	Inservice professional learning opportunities and professional development for teachers need to be onsite, ongoing and involve feedback loops; and preservice teacher education needs to be aligned with inservice professional development so that each supports the other in implementing new culturally responsive pedagogies of relations.

	Sustainability / going to scale	Classroom	School	System
Institutions	New institutions and organisational structures are needed to support in-class initiatives.	Developing new ways of relating and interacting in classrooms needs to be systematically organised and institutionalised.	Time and space for the development of new institutions within the school need to be allowed; structures such as timetables, staffing and organisational structures need to support the reform.	Supportive policies and infrastructure are needed that, for example, provide incentives for teachers, and revisit funding to allow salaries for in-school professional developers to be incorporated into schools' staffing allocations and organisation.
Leadership	Leadership needs to be responsive, proactive and distributed.	A means of developing distributed leadership within the classroom is needed so that students can be initiators of, and take responsibility for, their own learning and support the learning of others.	Leadership needs to be responsive to the needs of the reform, proactive in setting targets and goals, and distributed to allow power sharing.	National-level support and professional development for leaders is needed to promote proactive, responsive, and distributed instructional/ pedagogical leadership models.
Spread	A means of spreading the reform is needed to include all teachers, parents, community members and external agencies.	Inclusive classrooms are needed in which new classroom relationships and interactions include and engage all students in learning.	All staff need to join the reform, and parents and community also need to be included.	Policy funders, researchers, and practitioners need to collaborate in an iterative process of interaction, feedback and adaptation.

	Sustainability / going to scale	Classroom	School	System
Evidence	A means of developing and using appropriate tools and measures of progress is needed in order to monitor the progress of targeted students towards the goals and the reform in the school/s as a means of modifying core classroom and school practices and policies.	Teachers and students need to be able to gather and examine formal and informal formative assessment measures in order to improve their practice and learning through informing changes in instructional practice.	In-school facilitators and researchers need to be able to use appropriate instruments to monitor the implementation of the reform in order to provide data for formative and summative purposes.	National-level support is needed for the production of appropriate evidence that will enable collaborative formative problem solving and decision making that is ongoing and interactive, and from which supportive policies regarding standards, assessments and the mix of accountability and capacity building grow.
Ownership	A means of creating opportunities for all involved to take ownership of the reform is needed, in such a way that the original objectives of the reform are protected and sustained.	Ownership is seen when teachers' and students' learning needs are central to classroom relations and interactions, and when teachers' learning needs are based on analyses of patterns of student learning.	Ownership is seen when the whole school, including the board of trustees, takes ownership of the reform, when teacher learning is central to school systems and structures, and when institutions are developed to support teacher learning.	National ownership of the problem and provision of sufficient funding and resources is needed in order to see solutions within a defined period of time and in an ongoing, embedded manner.

Source: Bishop et al., 2007, p. 197

Coda

Guskey (1995) cautions against searching for the "one right answer" in trying to identify the essential elements of a successful professional development programme. Instead, he suggests that we need to establish criteria against which success might be measured; for example, children's engagement with learning and achievement in association with the reduction of disparities. In this way, Guskey argues that one might avoid "prescriptions of general practices that are described in broad and nebulous terms" (pp. 116–117). Further, prescriptions of general practice risk ignoring contexts, which in turn promotes culturally devoid prescriptions and frameworks within which children provide a multitude of "right answers". Sustaining a project and taking it to scale—that is, ensuring depth of the transfer of knowledge, spreading the reform and transferring ownership of the project, institutionalising reform components and developing effective leadership—require, in Guskey's terms, a minimalising of prescription. The best that can be offered are *procedural guidelines* that appear to be critical to the professional development process. These guidelines reflect a framework for developing the optimal mix of professional development processes and technologies that will work best in a specific context at a particular point in time (Guskey, 1995, p. 118).

In this book we present a set of procedural guidelines based on Table 1.3 that can be used when seeking to implement and sustain a professional development project, and when taking a project to scale. We illustrate these with findings from our research before highlighting how they might apply to other settings. We start by looking, in Chapter Two, at the goal of targeted student achievement.

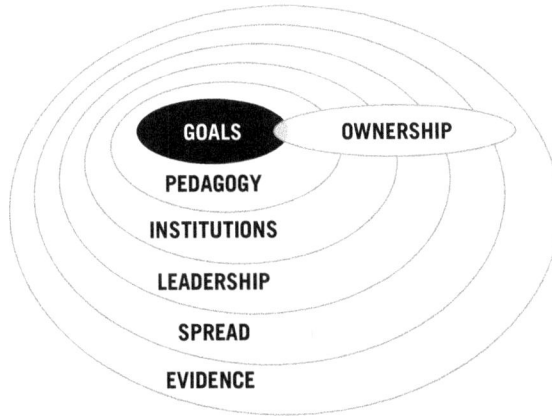

GOALS

OWNERSHIP

PEDAGOGY

INSTITUTIONS

LEADERSHIP

SPREAD

EVIDENCE

CHAPTER TWO

Goals—Targeted Student Achievement as the Focus of Educational Reform

As the main institution for fostering social cohesion in an increasingly diverse society, publicly funded schools must serve all children, not simply those with the loudest or most powerful advocates. This means addressing the cognitive and social needs of all children, with an emphasis on including those who may not have been well served in the past. (Fullan, 2003, p. 3)

Introduction

The widely accepted educational goals for Māori established at the first Hui Taumata Matauranga (national Māori education summit) held in 2001 are that Māori ought to be able to live as Māori, actively participate as citizens of the world and enjoy both good health and high standards of living (Durie, 2001). Together with government goals of equipping learners with 21st century skills and reducing systemic underachievement in education, these goals inform the new 2008–2012 Māori Education Strategy, *Ka Hikitia—Managing for Success* (Ministry of Education, 2008, p. 11), which has as its main strategic outcome "Māori students enjoying education success as Māori". Within this framework there are four student outcomes for Māori: learning to learn; making a distinctive cultural contribution; contributing to te ao Māori (the Māori world); and contributing to Aotearoa/New Zealand and the world.

However, as was illustrated earlier, currently the educational achievement and associated social positioning of Māori do not match these aspirations. Further, while these outcomes are most clearly exhibited in secondary schools, the foundations for these problems are to be seen in the primary school years. Indeed, there are indications (Crooks, Hamilton, & Caygill, 2000; Wylie, Thompson, & Lythe, 1999) that although there are achievement differentials evident in children entering primary school, it is by Years 4 and 5 that these differentials begin to stand out starkly. In addition, Phillips, McNaughton, and MacDonald (2001) have identified that achievement differentials are to be seen at the interface between early childhood centres and the first years of schooling, hence the need for system-wide reform.

Decades of educational reforms in New Zealand, policies such as multiculturalism and biculturalism and models of reform that have emphasised the deficiencies of homes in terms of literacy resources (Nash, 1993), or, more recently, the neurophilosophy claims about deficiencies of the brain (Clark, 2006), have meant that for the large proportion of Māori students who attend mainstream schools, apart from minor changes there has been little if any shift in these disparities. As a result, along with Fullan (2003) we wish to emphasise that it is not just overall student achievement that needs to be the goal of educational reform, but targeted student achievement, and the target needs to be those students who are least well served by the education system (Ministry of Education, 2008).

We take this position, which is one that the *Ka Hikitia* policy also promotes, because focusing on improving the achievement of all students will not realise the potential of those previously not well served. Until recently, the focus of educational policy has been on educating all students, which in theory was fine. Unfortunately, this has meant that the education system primarily became one of social reproduction for members of the dominant majority culture (Bourdieu & Passeron, 1973), rather than having a focus on equitable outcomes. In reality, therefore, educational reform that focuses on all students actually maintains the status quo of educational disparities, because any innovation tends to focus on how it can benefit children of the majority culture more than how it can benefit children of minority cultures. An associated problem is that initiatives that promote the social reproduction of the majority culture often reinforce notions of deficiency that majority-culture teachers have about minority-culture children.

The position we take in this book is that past and current policies and practices have done little to reduce educational disparities in this country, and that continuing with approaches that focus on improving achievement for all students without focusing on reducing disparities is futile. Rather than continuing to look to the majority culture for solutions, we suggest that the answers to Māori educational achievement and disparities actually lie in the sense-making and knowledge-generating processes of the culture the system marginalises. As Paulo Freire (1970) stated many years ago in *Pedagogy of the Oppressed*:

> This then is the great humanistic and historical task of the oppressed: to liberate themselves and their oppressors as well. The oppressors, who oppress, exploit and rape by virtue of their power, cannot find in this power the strength to liberate either the oppressed or themselves. Only power that springs from the weakness of the oppressed will be sufficiently strong to free both. (p. 21)

The imposition of a model of change from outside the experiences, understanding and aspirations of the community group has failed to acknowledge matauranga Māori (Māori ways of knowing) (G. H. Smith, 1997), and in Irwin's (1992) terms, "has left it marginalized and in a precarious state" (p. 10). Further, as has been argued by Smith, and by Bishop (2005), locating solutions within Māori cultural ways of knowing does actually offer workable solutions to what have long been seen as immutable problems.

Kaupapa Māori-generated initiatives, programmes and approaches developed by Māori people—such as the kaupapa Māori educational institutions of kōhanga reo, kura kaupapa Māori and wānanga in Māori-medium settings, Te Kotahitanga in English-medium settings and those that resonate with Māori philosophical understanding and aspirations—are examples of educational reforms that target the reduction of educational disparities within New Zealand through specifically targeting raising the achievement of Māori students. Evidence from the New Zealand Qualifications Authority (see Chapter One) has demonstrated that targeting Māori students in the Te Kotahitanga programme saw their academic achievement raised, along with the achievement levels of Pasifika students, and also European/Pākehā students to a lesser extent.

In summary, the position we are taking in relation to targeting students who are currently missing out on the benefits that education has to offer contrasts with the more common call for educational reform for all students. Our experience is that this latter position has been the status quo in New Zealand since mass secondary schooling was established following World War II, and there has not been any discernible change in the statistics of disparities since then. In other words, programmes that target all students promote the achievement of those already doing well. Evidence shows that programmes that target Māori also benefit other minoritised students (and nonminority students as well), which leads us to suggest that what is good for Māori is also good for others. Such an approach addresses the ongoing systemic underserving of Māori children by truly creating a foundation for inclusiveness. In other words, a system where no one misses out, where Māori are included in sharing the benefits that education has to offer at last and non-Māori students continue to prosper. However, it is important to remember that what is good for all has not necessarily been good for Māori in the past, and we do not see why it should be so in the future.

The experiences of other minoritised peoples in New Zealand

The situation of involuntary and most voluntary migrant groups in New Zealand is also of concern because their experiences are similar to those of Māori people. Over successive generations they tend to lose their language and culture. This pattern was identified among Pasifika peoples and Greek, Chinese and Korean migrants by Holmes (1982), who saw that despite the aspirations of these cultural groups to retain their distinctive languages and cultures, the effect of the education system was to homogenise these students into English-speaking Kiwis. The problem is that the dominant cultural practices of the education system do not see cultural and linguistic diversity as an asset, but as a problem to be removed or dealt with. One major outcome of this approach is that most groups find that over approximately three generations their home language begins to disappear from among their community, to be replaced by English (Holmes, 1982).

The level of bilingualism in New Zealand is low, particularly among first-language speakers of English. Where bilingualism occurs it is mainly found in minority language groups among Māori speakers, and among minority ethnic communities, including new-settler language speakers but, as noted above, these languages are often under threat. The low incidence of bilingualism among first-language speakers of English is being fostered by the somewhat erroneous impression that English is *the* international language and is therefore "all that we need". As a result it is felt that New Zealanders on the whole have little need to learn other languages other than for purely utilitarian (economic and trade) reasons. Hence much is made of the benefits for trade and tourism of learning the languages of our trading partners, the Japanese, Koreans and Chinese. Increasingly, within the New Zealand business community bilingualism is seen to benefit the entrepreneur desirous of entering the competitive international marketplace. This is seen as an essential ingredient in promoting and developing economic and trade relationships. Similarly, on the rapidly diversifying domestic scene, bilingualism of English plus an economic/trade language is an increasingly sought-after skill in teaching, tourism, journalism, interpreting, translation and social work.

The nonutilitarian reasons for language learning such as intellectual benefits, personal pleasure, access to cultural and international understanding, and language and cultural maintenance are not easily promoted from a monolingual/utilitarian approach. Yet research by Cummins (1989) and Lo Bianco (1987, cited in Waite, 1992), indicates that there are intellectual benefits to bilinguals in the form of increased control over their ability to manipulate language, more divergent thinking and greater mental flexibility, as well as the fostering of tolerance and respect for the world view of others. Included among this greater range of mental flexibility is the ability to gain a greater insight into the value systems of another culture, its knowledge bases and preferred lifestyles.

Such benefits not only increase intercultural understanding, but also greatly enhance one's ability to understand one's own cultural world view and its relationships to others. Indeed, as Durie (2005) emphasises, knowledge of one's own language is central to one's identity, hence the emphasis placed by Māori people on the revitalisation of te reo Māori (the Māori language). For this reason, gains in intercultural understanding through a deeper understanding of one's own culture and its relationship to others would be of benefit if incorporated into education programmes in New Zealand. This may help to reduce conflict between New Zealand and migrant students at school, and may promote other benefits, principally and most significantly the movement from the current predominance of deficit theorising towards a more positive approach to minority children.

In addition, there is now extensive research (Waite, 1992; along with Holmes, 1982; Metge, 1990; Wong-Filmore, 1991) that demonstrates "that children who have a well established home language do as well if not better at school than children whose parents switch to English in the mistaken belief that this will be helpful" (Waite, 1992, p. 26). Such research supports the contention that instruction in the home language will facilitate the learning of another language. It also supports the contention that any reading skills acquired in the home/mother language can transfer to learning to read a new language, given the proviso that reading transference may be limited by the similarity of script between the home language and English. A major shift is required from viewing the child who has two or more languages as having deficiencies and needing "remedial" intervention in the language of instruction, to viewing the education system as needing to engage in systemic change. The notion of an education system that capitalises on the valuable treasures that children bring to the school, has powerful and far-reaching implications.

Addressing educational disparities

Fullan (2003) suggests that focusing on student achievement in order to reduce disparities is actually a moral imperative that needs to be addressed at all levels of education: the classroom; the school; and the wider education system as part of a wider social justice agenda. That is, schooling needs to have an overall *moral purpose*, which is to directly or indirectly reduce educational disparities through improving student outcomes. In practical terms, this moral purpose is seen in a system where all students learn, where the gap between high and low performance is greatly reduced, where there is a focus on those least well served by the system and where "what people learn enables them to be successful citizens and workers in a morally based knowledge society" (Fullan, 2003, p. 29). In an American Education Research Association (AERA) presentation, Hargreaves (personal communication, 2008) supported and expanded this notion by suggesting that "a compelling and inclusive moral purpose steers a system, binds it together and draws the best people to work it".

Shields et al. (2005), in their analysis of the impact of deficit theorising and pathologising practices on the achievement of minoritised students, also identified the need for new discourses for academic excellence and equity. These writers stressed that we are not so naive as to expect that such change will result in the magical achievement of all minoritised children to the same high level. Shields et al. emphasised their awareness, as practising educators, that there are—and always will be—considerable differences in skill, motivation and ability within each group of students. The argument, however, is about *between-group equity*, for "we believe firmly that no group of children, regardless of the reason for its marginalization, is inherently less able than any other, more included group" (p. 141). Shields et al. continued:

> Put another way, in a socially just education system, if we were to place the scores of the total population, the scores of the dominant group, and those of a minoritized group on a graph, they would be coincident. There would not be a lower range of scores for the minoritized group. Neither would there be higher drop-out rates among minoritized groups, lower school leaving grade point averages, higher rates of suspension or disciplinary incidents, or disproportionate numbers of students who fail to go on to higher levels of education. (2005, p. 142)

Addressing educational disparities for Hargreaves and Fink (2006) is a matter of improving learning for those currently missing out on what education has to offer. In other words, "the prime responsibility of all educational leaders is to sustain learning" (p. 3) for *all* students, meaning "learning that matters, that lasts and that engages students intellectually, socially and emotionally" (ibid.). It is not temporary gains in education that are needed—as happens when teachers and schools "teach to the test"—but rather learning and learning about learning, the aim of which is to create and develop lasting improvements in learning that are reflected in measurable student achievement with an overall goal of reducing educational disparities. Unless this happens, we are merely maintaining the status quo, which is seeing increasing disparities between the haves and have nots.

These findings clearly point to the need for educational reform that promotes the inclusion of young people who are clearly not benefiting from the opportunities that education and the wider society have to offer them.

In New Zealand this problem of addressing educational disparities is at the centre of the Government's strategic agenda document (Ministry of Education, 2004) for education. The New Zealand Government is concerned that international measures of student achievement, such as the Programme for International Student Assessment (PISA) at a secondary level, and Trends in International Mathematics and Science Study (TIMSS) and the Progress in International Reading Literacy Study (PIRLS) at a primary school level, continue to indicate that while New Zealand has an excellent education system, in which students exhibit high average achievement by international standards, New Zealand has one of the world's widest gaps between its highest and lowest achievers. For example, a recent New Zealand Educational Institute Symposium (2008) identified that little progress had occurred in literacy since 2001, despite there having been large-scale educational reform projects implemented during this period to improve literacy outcomes. Indeed, during the period from 2001 to 2006 New Zealand's ranking fell from 1st to 4th, to 13th to 24th. This fall occurred despite a generally good performance of the system and is due to the fact that "we have a system in which too many students, especially those from low socio-economic backgrounds or who are Māori or Pasifika, are not receiving the value from education that they should, and are not doing as well as they should" (Ministry of Education, 2004, p. 5). As a result, the New Zealand Government's policy "is to raise achievement and reduce disparity across the whole education system on a sustainable basis" (ibid.). In other words, the aims are for sustained excellence with improved equity.

The disparities between the low achievers and the rest, combined with the relatively large number of low achievers, according to the Parliamentary Committee on Education and Science (2008), "causes this group to be referred to as 'the long tail'" (p. 5). This sort of analysis suggests the need to "narrow the gaps" between "New Zealand's top and bottom performers" (ibid.). In contrast, Hattie (2008) challenges the concepts of the "tail" and the "gaps" as leading to inaccurate depictions of the policy problems and their solutions, particularly in reference to Māori and Pasifika achievement issues. He suggests that "we have neglected the majority of underperforming students by using the wrong language and metaphors" (p. 1). He explains that:

> These metaphors conjure pictures that are misleading—and lead to seeking solutions to the wrong problem. Too often the 'tail' is interpreted as more Maori and Pasifika at the lower-end tail of the achievement distribution [Figure 2.1]; or that we have to close or narrow the gap by pouring more resources into helping these lower achieving students, who are predominantly Maori and Pasifika students [Figure 2.2]. (p. 1)

Figure 2.1 The tail **Figure 2.2 Narrowing the gap**

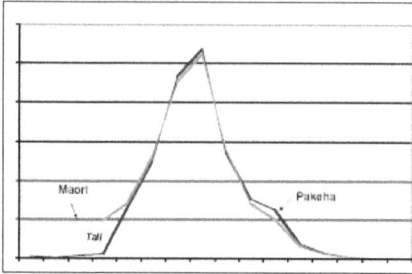

Figure 2.1 The tail

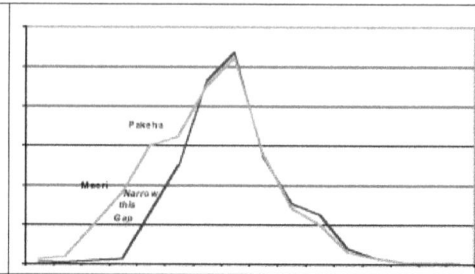

Figure 2.2 Narrowing the gap

Hattie explains that neither of these metaphors addresses the complexity of the New Zealand picture:

> NZ has one of the largest 'spreads' or dispersions of student scores in the world. We have a *flatter* achievement curve compared to many other countries. This greater dispersion is often presented as a 'tail' and in one sense it is but it is a greater spread of scores or a flatter distribution and not more Maori or Pacific students clustered in the left-hand tail. (p. 1)

He continues by explaining that:

> [u]sing the asTTle norming data … Figures [2.3] and [2.4] depict the distribution of scores for Maori, Pasifika, Pakeha, and Asian students in Reading and Mathematics. It is the case that there are greater proportions of Pakeha and Asian than Maori and Pasifika students above the overall median (55% vs. 39% for Reading and 59% vs. 33% for Mathematics). The major message, however, is that there are two gaps (above and below the median), the tail is less of a problem than the gaps both sides of the middle. (p. 1)

Figure 2.3 asTTle Reading scores **Figure 2.4 asTTle Numeracy scores**

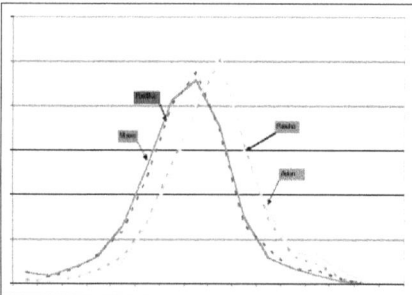

Figure 2.3 asTTle Reading scores

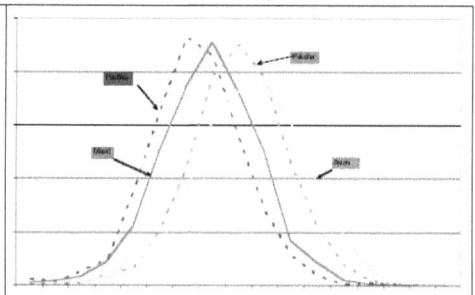

Figure 2.4 asTTle Numeracy scores

The main message from this analysis is that we need to reduce the disparity everywhere, not focus on the bottom 10 or 20 percent, because this is not where most Māori students are located. As was noted earlier (Shields et al., 2005), the issue is that the two distributions need to be superimposed, one on top of the other, rather than be disparate, as in the above figures. Hattie (2008) concludes:

We need a metaphor that points to moving Maori and Pasifika students *above* the middle higher as well as moving those *below* the middle upwards. In a crude sense, we need to move the Maori and Pasifika 40%ers and 60ers% up simultaneously, but the wrong metaphors (i.e., gaps, tails) means that we focus on the bottom 10%ers and ignore these [other] students. (p. 1)

Where New Zealand fits into the international scene

New Zealand is not alone in the world in addressing this problem of educational disparities. Figure 2.5 (below) shows that countries like New Zealand that have significant proportions of ethnic/cultural minorities within their populations, such as the United States of America (USA), Australia, the United Kingdom (UK) and Belgium, are more likely to have inequitable education systems than those countries whose populations are more predominantly monocultural.

Figure 2.5 Overall performance: New Zealand's high average and large variance [1]

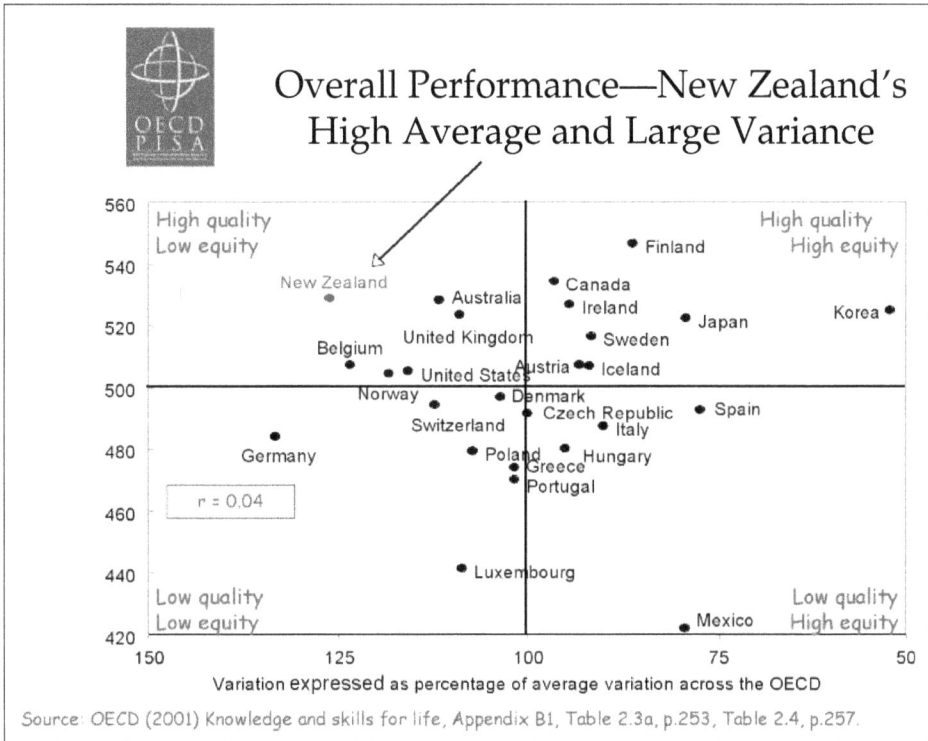

Source: OECD (2001) Knowledge and skills for life, Appendix B1, Table 2.3a, p.253, Table 2.4, p.257.

1 This graph, although dating from 2001, remains an accurate picture of New Zealand's position relative to the variables in the graph. The fact is that New Zealand's location on these indices has not changed appreciably since this time.

The vertical axis on Figure 2.5 is an internationally accepted measure of excellence in reading achievement scores. The horizontal axis is also an internationally accepted measure, but this time of equity. The interaction between these two variables identifies four broad types of education system: upper right *high quality, high equity*; upper left—*high quality, low equity*; lower right *low quality, high equity*; lower left *low quality, low equity*.

We can see from this figure that Korea, Finland, Japan, Spain and Sweden are among those located in the upper-right quadrant, the "excellent plus equitable" quadrant. The aspiration of the New Zealand Government is to move New Zealand to the upper-right quadrant to join this group of countries. However, these countries with high-quality and high-equity systems tend to be predominantly monocultural, with very low proportions of their populations from ethnic/cultural minority groups. In these countries, social reproduction-based education systems work well to address the needs of the majority of the population. In contrast, the group of countries that New Zealand belongs to have significant ethnic/cultural minority groups whose members feature strongly in statistics of deprivation and educational disparity. Within these countries, traditional social reproduction education systems do not address the needs of ethnic and culturally diverse populations.

The solution is not as simple as extending what suits the children of the majority culture to ethnic and cultural minorities, because this has patently not worked in the past. The problem we face in New Zealand—along with the USA, the UK and Australia—is that we are just not able to extend the benefits of the current education system to students who are ethnically and culturally dissimilar to the majority of teachers in the system. The solution to New Zealand's aspiration to move from the upper-left to the upper-right quadrant is one where all levels of the education system (policy makers, schools and teachers) target the improvement of ethnic minority students by making a paradigm shift to an equity-based education approach. This will require a paradigm shift from social reproduction systems to equity-based systems and schooling practices, rather than looking to the countries in the upper-right quadrant for solutions. This paradigm shift to equity-based systems is one that more and more countries will have to face as their populations become more and more ethnically diverse following current international migration and population growth patterns.

The answers outlined in this book suggest that targeting ethnic minority groups at all levels of the education system, from the level at which policies and resourcing are defined to where practice is implemented in schools and classrooms, is necessary to address these problems. In other words, system-wide and school goals need to be oriented to an equity-based agenda, rather than reproducing those conditions that suit the majority culture.

The power of goal setting

Focused and purposeful educational goal setting is proposed in this chapter as an essential part of the process to address ongoing educational disparities by creating contexts in which people are motivated and supported to think and act in ways that will improve the educational achievement of those students previously not well served by the education system.

What is a goal?[2] According to Latham and Locke (2006), a goal is "a level of performance proficiency that we wish to attain, usually within a specified time period" (p. 332). Latham and Locke's meta-analysis of some 1,000 studies on 88 different tasks "involving more than 40,000 male and female participants in Asia, Australia, Europe and North America show[s] that *specific high goals are effective in significantly increasing a person's performance*—regardless of the method by which they are set" (p. 332, emphasis added). It is the process of goal setting from the very inception of the reform that is so important for successfully embedding the process of paradigm shifting that is fundamental to educational reform.

Robinson, Hohepa, and Lloyd (2009) argue that "[g]oal setting works by creating a discrepancy between what is currently happening and some desired future state" (p. 96). Similarly, Timperley et al. (2007) suggest that goal setting is actually a discrepancy-creating process, in that setting a goal acknowledges our discontent with the status quo. Or as Latham and Locke (2006) suggest, "the goal creates constructive discontent with our present performance" (p. 332). Commitment to the goal is vital, however, as any discrepancy or discontent with current practice needs to be experienced in a constructive manner rather than in negative terms. If discontent is positively conceptualised, then the teacher will be motivated to undertake "goal-relevant behaviour. Goals focus attention and lead to more persistent effort than would otherwise be the case" (Robinson et al., 2009, p. 96). For example, when a teacher sets a goal for their class of raising specific students' achievement in certain tests within specified time frames, they will critically reflect on their own performance more readily and will seek out more effective teaching practices that will be more likely to see the goal achieved than those being used presently.

In other words, goal setting channels one's energies into determining ways in which the goals will be achieved and allows one to prioritise actions in the face of multiple demands on one's time. This increased focus and sense of purpose "increases enjoyment of tasks and willingness to take on challenges" (Robinson et al., 2009, p. 96). Robinson et al. (2009) also stress that goals will only have the effect of motivating teachers to be critically reflective and to modify their behaviour if three conditions are met:

> Teachers, parents or students need to feel they have the capacity to meet the goal from either their current resources or from the expertise and support they will receive while pursuing the goal. People need to be committed to goals and this requires that they understand and value them. As long as this is the case, it does not matter whether or not they participate in the actual setting of the goals … Specific rather than vague goals are required because specificity makes it possible to judge progress and thus adjust one's performance. Self-regulation is impossible if the goal, and therefore progress towards it, is unclear. (p. 96)

---

2 We will identify the role of leadership in developing and realising goals in Chapter Five.

Schmoker (1999) is critical of many schools' goal-setting practices, because in his experience school goals are rarely linked to student achievement. He says that many of the initiatives of the school improvement movement, for example, while having high ideals, multiple approaches, vision statements and mission statements, occurred in the "near absence of any written or explicit intention to monitor, adjust, and thus palpably increase learning or achievement" (p. 2). He further suggests that experience alone does little to inform us about the quality or effectiveness of the education we are providing. Yet in many cases this is the touchstone for measuring the effectiveness of activities, while at the same time keeping educators from other sources of information, such as "formal research on best practices or their consequences" (ibid.). As a result, Schmoker is adamant that sustainability is predicated on the adequate establishment of measurable goals, monitoring of the outcomes of the innovation in reference to the goals, followed by adjustment of the reform to suit the particular circumstances of the schools and the students:

> History has demonstrated that translating theory into practice, though important, is not enough. We also need an ongoing concern with the real impact we are having. Otherwise, after all our training and fanfare, even the most promising innovation often dissipates into insignificance, as we have seen with so many beneficial programs. (p. 5)

Finally, Schmoker suggests that educators at all levels should set short- and long-term goals, because one of the most important ingredients he identifies as being necessary for long-term, system-transforming change is short-term results; that is, "even though long-term, cultural transformation should always be the goal of all reform efforts, it must rely upon short-term, measurable successes" (p. 5).

In terms of leadership, of which more will be said in Chapter Five, Robinson, Lloyd, and Rowe (2007) found that:

> Goal setting, like all the leadership dimensions described here, has indirect effects on students by focusing and coordinating the work of the school community. With student background factors controlled for, leadership made a difference to students through the degree of emphasis placed on clear academic and learning goals. (p. 9)

Other meta-analyses by Witziers, Bosker, and Kruger (2003) and Marzano, Waters, and McNulty (2005), both cited by Robinson (2007), concurred with this finding, showing that "the direction-setting role of the leader had more direct impact on student outcomes than any of the other six dimensions of leadership" (p. 10). Robinson (2007) also argued that in schools with high achievement levels or those making achievement gains, academic goals were both a feature of leadership and a quality of the school's organisation. In other words, "if goals are to function as influential coordinating mechanisms, they need to be embedded in school and classroom routines and procedures" (pp. 9–10). Many of the studies in Robinson et al.'s (2009) meta-analysis also supported the notion that leaders in high-performing schools give emphasis to community goals and expectations, both informing the community of outcomes and promoting staff consensus about school goals.

Short- and long-term goals: Who sets these?

Te Kotahitanga is a means whereby schools and individual teachers are supported to undertake a major paradigm shift in their theorising about their practice of teaching, which involves developing a new *theory of practice* that will support equity-based educational practices. Part of this paradigm shift involves the introduction and development of a method whereby schools and individual teachers can set interdependent goals that will address their personal and collective desire to improve the educational achievement of Māori students. The Te Kotahitanga professional development programme then seeks to provide a means whereby teachers and schools can reach and measure these goals.

However, it appears that a number of high-performing individuals and teams gradually develop expertise in the new ways of teaching and learning and begin to look for *new* goals and strategies. This situation raises a question: What do high-performing individuals do once they have mastered the strategies associated with an innovation? The answer to this question appears to be twofold. First, the high-performing teams and individuals should be congratulated for embedding the new practices into their daily activities and on attaining their goals. They should receive recognition in some agreed form. Second, they should be encouraged to set their own new goals, along with strategies for attaining them. Probably the goals will be able to focus on further developing expertise in classroom instructional practices. In other words, capacity building to ensure that educators can set, evaluate and reset goals should be part of professional development for sustainable educational reform. These goals will be especially powerful the closer they are aligned to the wider goals of the school with regard to student achievement, and to the strategies the school and professional development teams are using to implement the new paradigm shifts.

For example, a school might see as relevant and timely a five-year goal of "a 20 percentage point increase in retention and achievement of Māori students at Years 11 and 13, respectively". Further, it may specify that "this goal would be attained by ensuring a 90 percent staff participation rate by year three of the project". In the fifth year of the project they may decide to set a further five-year goal that is inclusive of all students; for example: "There will be a 20 percentage point increase[3] for all groups of students, in terms of retention and attainment, who are attaining below the decile-weighted average,[4] to be retained and achieve at or above that average." Or, it could be more generic, such as: "There will be an increase in retention and attainment by a specified amount of all

---

3 This would effectively see the attainment gap closed in most schools. Individual schools may need to adjust this figure to suit their own attainment figures; see Education Counts (http://www.educationcounts.govt.nz) for specifics.

4 This is a measure based on the average attainment of all students attending a comparable set of schools.

students currently not being retained or achieving to or above our decile-weighted average in Year 11 and Year 13 at years three and five, respectively." These goals have the advantage of being specific and measurable. They are also adjustable and modifiable in relation to the evidence of attainment. Or, a goal might be to move students along the achievement scales in particular standardised tests such as asTTle and Progressive Achievement Tests (PATs). They could also be experiential in terms of examining and reporting on the schooling experiences of various targeted groups of students. Whatever the case, the goal must be specific, with a focus on student outcomes/achievement in its widest sense, and be measureable, achievable, relevant and time framed—in other words, a *smart* goal.

Conclusion

As Latham and Locke (2006) argue, school-wide goals allow individuals, whether they be policy makers, teachers or students, to establish their own specific goals and means of attaining these goals in a manner that allows them to build on their immediate past successes rather than having to start from scratch and sort out a way to address what has seemed to be an immutable problem. In this way, individuals are able to take ownership of the goal of improving achievement and reducing disparities, signalling the importance of educational reform as a collective activity.

It needs to be stated that any educational reform project such as Te Kotahitanga is really only a means to an end rather than an end in itself. The desired end for educational reform is that schools and interdependently linked teachers will be able to take ownership of the goal in a manner that can reasonably be expected to be successful and ongoing in that:

- the paradigm shifts necessary to bring about change will be embedded in their classroom and school-wide practices
- teachers will have a clear understanding of the theory of practice necessary to maintain this paradigm shift so that they can flexibly respond to the learning needs of their students
- the students and teachers will be able to set their own goals and means of monitoring their progress towards these goals.

Goldsmith and Reiter (2007), however, warn of the danger of goal obsession, about getting so caught up in our drive to achieve that we lose sight of why we are working so hard, and that relations among school staff and the wider community need to be addressed. Of course this puts emphasis on the leader of the reform in the school to ensure that while it is preferable that leaders are the initiators (Hall & Hord, 2006), who set clear, decisive, long-term policies and goals, they also need to be able to bring their staff to participate in the innovation in a manner that allows them full agency and commitment.

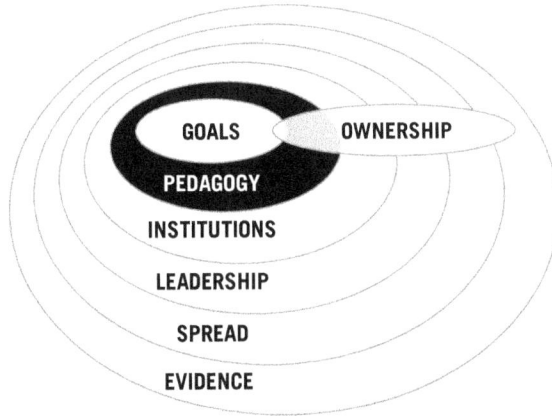

GOALS OWNERSHIP
PEDAGOGY
INSTITUTIONS
LEADERSHIP
SPREAD
EVIDENCE

CHAPTER THREE

Developing a New Pedagogy to Depth

Teachers who have a deep understanding of the pedagogical
principles of a reform are better able to respond to new demands
and changing contexts in ways that are consistent with underlying
principles of reform, then sustaining and, at times, deepening
reform over time. (Coburn, 2003, p. 6)

Introduction

In the previous chapter we looked at the crucial importance of goal setting that targets student achievement. The second main consideration for sustaining and extending an educational reform is that it must contain what Alton-Lee (2006) terms a deep, complex "explanatory theory of how different ways of managing the classroom and creating activities are related to student outcomes" (p. 618). That is, the reform must be built upon a theory of pedagogy that teachers can take to depth. In this way, the theory can provide teachers with an ongoing means of addressing new demands on their practice, rather than simply providing them with a set of practices they are expected to replicate, regardless of context.

How useful are current educational theories? The culturalist versus structuralist debate

Hattie's (2003a) meta-analyses of the different explanations for student achievement have led him to conclude that "almost all things we do in the name of education have a positive effect on achievement" (p. 4). However, not all effects are equal. With Hattie's caution in mind, our research (Bishop et al., 2003, 2007) considered the relative importance of influences on student achievement such as whānau, home and community; classroom relationships and pedagogy; teachers, schools and school systems; the students themselves; and a multitude of other contributing and confounding factors relating to learning and achievement, including external socioeconomic contexts and systemic and structural conditions. In these studies we spoke with and listened to students talk about their schooling experiences in secondary schools, and the meaning these experiences of schooling in mainstream settings (where over 90 percent of Māori students participate) had for them and for other young Māori people. Both groups of students, in 2001 and again in 2004 and 2005, identified that the development of caring and learning relationships between the teacher and the students was the crucial factor in their being able to effectively engage in education.

Importantly, in both sets of interviews, students (and their whānau) understood themselves to be powerless to develop positive, caring and learning relationships where they did not already exist. They felt that it was the teachers who had the power to bring about the necessary changes. Similarly, the teachers who positioned themselves within the relational discourse in 2001, and again those teachers interviewed in 2005, emphasised the importance of relationships at all levels of the project: within the classroom, between facilitators and themselves and between themselves and their leaders, parents and community members.

Large meta-analyses by Hattie (1999, 2003a, 2003b) and Alton-Lee (2003) support the beliefs of these young Māori people, their families and some of their teachers by telling us that the most important systemic influence on students' educational achievement is the teacher. Hattie (2003a), using reading test results prepared as norms for the asTTle formative assessment programme, found that achievement differences between Māori and Pākehā remained constant regardless of whether the students attended a high- or low-decile school. Hattie concluded that it is not socioeconomic differences that have the greatest impact on Māori student achievement. Instead, he suggested that "the evidence is pointing more to the relationships between teachers and Māori students as the major issue—it is a matter of cultural relationships not socio-economic resources—as these differences occur at *all* levels of socio-economic status" (p. 7).

Similarly, Alton-Lee (2003), citing the 2000 PISA study, showed that New Zealand literacy achievement differs more markedly *within* schools than *between* schools, which is not what we would expect if the socioeconomic argument were to hold. Her analysis also indicates that the quality of classroom relations and interactions within schools has more to do with the creation of educational disparities than does the decile ranking of the schools.

This finding means that although we cannot ignore the impact of structural impediments, such as socially constructed impoverishment, we cannot allow this analysis to disempower teachers from action. Hattie (2003a) and Alton-Lee (2003) are clear that teachers have the potential and ability to change the educational outcomes of Māori students. Several other studies have also indicated that the quality of teaching is the single most significant systemic influence on children's achievement: the quality of teaching has been found to account for 16 to 60 percent of the difference in achievement (Bosker & Witziers, 1995; Cuttance, 1998), compared to the variance attributable to schools of between 0 and 20.9 percent (Cuttance, 1998). Further:

> Recent research on the impact of schools on student learning leads to the conclusion that 8–19% of the variation in student learning outcomes lies between schools with a further amount of up to 55% of the variation in individual learning outcomes between classrooms within schools. In total, approximately 60% of the variation in the performance of students lies between schools or between classrooms, with the remaining 40% being due to either variation associated with students themselves or to random influences. (Cuttance, 2000, pp. 1158–1159)

This analysis is supported by the Victorian Quality Schools Project, where Cuttance (2001) extended his earlier conclusion to suggest that the range for the teacher/class effect in fact accounted for up to 60 percent of the variance.

These conclusions suggest that reform must commence with the classroom rather than with the school, and that "pedagogy and learning practices" are "key educational policy levers" (Organisation for Economic Co-operation and Development, 2002, p. 3). Research by Phillips et al. (2001) would concur with this. In a study that indicated how Māori and Pasifika new entrant students' reading scores could be improved by addressing teachers' expectations of their learning, they found that:

low rates of progress in literacy are neither inevitable nor unchangeable in low decile schools. Educators working in these environments can help bring children up to speed—to expected levels of achievement. (p. 10)

Similar findings emerged from a study by Rubie-Davies, Hattie, and Hamilton (2006) of 21 primary school teachers at 12 Auckland schools and their 540 students, in relation to their expectations for their students' achievement in reading. Teacher expectation for end-of-year achievement, teacher judgement of achievement at end of year, actual achievement for the beginning of the year and actual achievement for the end of the year were compared. The study found that teacher expectations for Māori were lower than their expectations for Pasifika, Asian and New Zealand European students. Not only were teacher expectations lower for Māori, their expectations were significantly lower than the actual achievement of Māori students, despite the fact that at the beginning of the year there were no statistically significant differences between actual achievement of Māori and any other ethnic group: Māori achievement levels were on a par with other groups. However, by the end of the year, the achievement of Māori and Pacific students was significantly below that of their Asian and New Zealand European counterparts. In other words, teacher expectations had created a self-fulfilling prophecy about low achievement of Māori and Pasifika students. Effect size gains for reading achievement were lower for Māori than for any other group. Research in the USA by Weinstein, Gregory, and Strambler (2004) parallels these findings for African-American and Latino students.

This is not to deny that other broad factors such as the prior learning and experiences the child brings to school, the socioeconomic background of the child and their family, the structures and history of the school and the socially constructed impoverishment of Māori created by the processes of colonisation are not important. It is just that teacher effectiveness stands out as the most easily alterable factor within the school system. It is what transcends influences external to the classroom and the school that is the focus of the majority of work that seeks to improve the educational futures of all students. Further, as Hattie (2003a) suggests, this is the most useful site for the provision of professional learning opportunities for teachers when seeking to change the learning culture in schools and to reduce the persistent disparities in educational achievement. This position is supported by numerous international scholars, including Elmore (2004), Fullan (2003), Hargreaves (2005) and Sidorkin (2002), who advocate that changing classroom practices and modifying school structures to accommodate and support these changes are the strategies most likely to improve student performance.

Using G. H. Smith's (1997) terms, it is clear that these positions are "culturalist" approaches, which propose that changing the culture of the school will bring about improvements in educational inequalities. Such positions stand in contrast to the more "structuralist" notions of Chapple, Jefferies, and Walker (1997). Nash (1993) and Thrupp

(2001, 2008), who advocate a social stratification (low social class, low socioeconomic status and resource/cultural deprivation) argument that being poor or poorly resourced inevitably leads to poor educational achievement. Much research in this area looks at the associations between variables (such as socioeconomic status, ethnicity and other family attributes) and achievement in ways that suggest that such variables predetermine, or at least strongly influence, achievement outcomes. Advocates of this position argue that schools and classrooms are agents of the wider society. This means that it is important to acknowledge how patterns of discrimination and inequality that exist in the wider society may well be reflected in the arrangements of the school (McLaren, 2003) and the classroom (Bishop & Glynn, 1999). The solutions to educational inequalities offered by members of this group at best offer a qualified "yes" to the question "Can teachers make a difference?".

Thrupp (2008) is one who is critical of the "overemphasis on the power of quality teaching" (p. 13), and who demonstrates the structuralist position by saying that "for student underachievement, I don't really think that it is plausible to assert that teachers have so much power to make the difference. I think that teachers can do a lot, but not as much as they are being asked to do" (p. 2). He goes on to suggest that, as a result, "the key is for teachers to refuse to accept too much responsibility for student achievement in the first place" (p. 13), although he does not define what he means by "too much responsibility". However, essentially, the overall structuralist/contextualist position is more that the "real solution to educational inequalities is political change that reduces inequalities of power and resources" (M. Thrupp, personal communication, May 2008). Such a position is clearly put by Anyon (1997, cited in Thrupp, 2001), who speaks for this group when she states:

> Unfortunately educational 'small victories' such as restructuring of a school or the introduction of a new pedagogical technique, no matter how satisfying to the individuals involved, without the long-range strategy to eradicate underlying causes of poverty and racial isolation, cannot add up to large victories in our inner cities with effects that are sustainable over time. (p. 20)

Nonetheless, both sets of arguments pose problems for educational practitioners in their search for improvement. The culturalist arguments tend to ignore or downplay the impact of structural impediments on student achievement, whereas the more structuralist positions tend to promote the argument that teachers do not have agency in their practice, in that there appears little that teachers can achieve in the face of overwhelming structural impediments such as school mix and structural poverty.

Although often seen in opposition to each other, both the culturalist and the structuralist or contextualist arguments provide necessary—but not sufficient— conditions for educational reform; the former downplays external considerations, the latter downplays internal relationships and interactions along with teacher agency.

Culturalists quite rightly point to the need for pedagogic reform and changes to school culture as being necessary, and promote a *universalist* approach, a *pedagogy for all*, such as the Quality Education movement in Australia, with its focus on providing quality education for all as a means of addressing the emerging diversity and increasing disparities of the schooling population. However, they tend to ignore the lived reality of Māori people, which Ballard (2007) identifies as current New Zealand society being a "racialised social context", and the impact this context has on Māori students' educational participation and achievement.

Structuralists—while quite rightly arguing that those children who do not achieve well in schools come from cultural groups that are minoritised (Shields et al., 2005) by the dominant culture, and that social inequality affects individuals and schools—tend to forget that schools have long called the shots over what constitutes learning, how relationships between home and schools will be established and the type of interactions that will take place, both between the home and the schools and within schools and classrooms. In short, schools have long pursued a social reproduction agenda; that is, they have replicated and reproduced the social and cultural divisions in the wider society.

However, neither group of theorists adequately identifies how power differentials that are part of the wider society are played out in classrooms on a day-to-day basis, and the part teachers, school leaders and policy makers may play (albeit unwittingly) in the perpetuation of power imbalances and educational disparities. Ironically, Māori students and their families are only too aware of how these power imbalances are played out (Bishop & Berryman, 2006), whereas members of the majority culture appear not to be aware of it, and this includes some academic theorists. As Alton-Lee (2003) and Timperley et al. (2007) argue—along with G. H. Smith (1997) and other kaupapa Māori theorists in New Zealand, and Freire (1997), Kincheloe and Steinberg (1997), McLaren (2003) and Valencia (1997)—the product of long-term power imbalances needs to be examined by educators at all levels, including their own cultural assumptions and a consideration of how they themselves might be participants in the systematic marginalisation of students in their classrooms, schools and the wider system.

G. H. Smith (1997) has warned that neither culturalist nor structuralist analyses can satisfactorily account for Māori language, knowledge and cultural aspirations as major components of existing and developing educational interventions for Māori. To Smith, what is needed is a model that locates culture at the centre of educational reform in the face of deeper structural limitations, in the same manner as that practised by the kaupapa Māori educational initiatives of kōhanga reo and kura kaupapa Māori. To Smith, these later institutions have developed "our forms of resistance and transformative praxis which engage both culturalist and structuralist concerns" (p. 222). From this understanding developed in Māori-medium schooling, the English-medium sector needs a model that addresses both the concerns and limitations of the culturalist and structuralist positions, yet also includes a means whereby educators at all levels of the education system can critically reflect on the part they might play in the wider power plays that mediate Māori participation in the benefits that education has to offer.

Harker (2007) demonstrates such positioning when reconsidering the large data sets of the Smithfield (1994) studies and the Progress at School (1991) studies. He concludes that:

> It is clear from the data presented here that any uni-causal explanation based on socio-economic circumstances is inadequate to explain ethnic differences, thus supporting the caution expressed in Biddulph's BES (Biddulph, Biddulph, & Biddulph, 2003). The most likely explanation would seem to lie in the interaction between school environments and the values, attitudes, and motivations that underpin the school 'culture' and the culture of the home and community environments and the values, attitudes and motivations on which they are based. (p. 17)

Harker goes on to suggest that:

> While it is important (even necessary) for the family and community culture of the students to be understood and supported by schools, it is also important (even necessary) for the culture of the school to be understood and supported by families and communities. (p. 17)

Harker is promoting an analysis that is not based on either a schools/teachers barrier culturalist argument or a home/society barrier structuralist argument; he is in fact identifying the discursive shift that has been taking place in New Zealand's educational theorising recently when he suggests moving from positioning oneself within either a structuralist or a culturalist mode of explanation towards drawing from more interactive, relational discourses. In this latter mode, as Harker suggests, we can see that the arguments about whether schools or family make the difference are really not useful. It is more a function of the interactions between these two sets of players that offer us explanations of variation in achievement and, more importantly, provide us with solutions to problems of educational disparities.

Such a relational theory is central to Te Kotahitanga, as detailed by Bishop (2007) and Bishop et al. (2007), where Māori aspirations for self-determination are placed at the centre of the theoretical framework. Self-determination, in Durie's (1995) terms, "captures a sense of Māori ownership and active control over the future" (p. 16). Nevertheless, despite self-determination meaning the right to determine one's own destiny, to define what that destiny will be and to define and pursue the means of attaining that destiny, there is a clear understanding among Māori people that this autonomy is relative, not absolute; that it is self-determination *in relation to others*. It is a call for all those involved in education in New Zealand to reposition themselves in relation to these emerging aspirations of Māori people for an autonomous voice and successful participation in the mainstream of society (Bishop, 1994; Durie, 1998; G. H. Smith, 1997). In other words, a kaupapa Māori position seeks to operationalise Māori people's aspirations to restructure power relationships to the point where partners can be autonomous and interact from this position, rather than from one of subordination or dominance, and this should take place at all levels of education.

Young (2004) explains that indigenous peoples' aspirations for self-determination are relational, acknowledge interdependence and "are better understood as a quest for an institutional context of non-domination" (p. 187). That is, being self-determining is possible if the relations in which people and individuals stand to each other are nondominating. To ensure nondomination, "their relations must be regulated both by the institutions in which they all participate and by the ongoing negotiations among them" (p. 177). The implications for educational institutions and classrooms from this position are that they should be structured and conducted by the participants in these institutions in such a way as to seek to mediate these potential tensions by actively minimising domination, co-ordinating actions, resolving conflicts and negotiating relationships. In Young's terms, this is an education where power is shared between self-determining individuals within nondominating relations of interdependence.

Discursive (re)positioning in the classroom

To illustrate how useful it is to theorise from a relational discourse, compared to a culturalist or a structuralist discourse, we can examine the problem presented to us by many teachers in our 2001 and 2005 interviews (Bishop et al., 2003, 2007) about why they, with the best intentions in the world, were frustrated in their attempts to reach Māori learners. The reason was that many of the teachers drew from *deficit discourses*, either about the children and their homes or about the structures of the school and/ or the education system, to explain their experiences with educating Māori students. Indeed, the students, their whānau, the principals and the teachers gave us numerous examples of the negative aspects of such thinking, the resultant problematic and resistant behaviours and the frustrating consequences for both students and teachers. The teachers spoke of their frustration and anger as they fought to change the children and/or their homes or took on the system and structures of the school; the students spoke about negative relations being an assault on their very identity as Māori people.

This illustrates the usefulness of the concept of discourse. By discourse, we mean the meanings we have adopted and which we manifest in positioning thoughts, words and actions that are shaped by power relations, and which provide a complex network of images and metaphors that determines, in large part, how we think and act in relation to a given topic. In other words, by drawing on particular discourses to explain and make sense of our experiences, we are positioning ourselves within these discourses and acting accordingly in our classrooms. If the discourses offer deficit explanations, then we will act accordingly in our relations and interactions with those whom the discourse deems to be in deficit. The discourses already exist, they have been developing throughout our history, are often in conflict which each other through power differentials and—importantly for our desire to be agentic—in terms of their practical importance some discourses hold solutions to problems while others do not.

Bruner (1996) explains that the differing theories of practice that teachers hold as they enter the reform has a major impact on how they will relate to and interact with students. He argues that when teaching occurs, progress is decided upon and practices are modified as "a direct reflection of the beliefs and assumptions the teacher holds about the learner" (p. 47). This means that "our interactions with others are deeply affected by our everyday intuitive theorizing about how other minds work" (p. 45). In other words, our actions as teachers, parents or whoever we are at that particular time are driven by the mental images or understanding that we have of other people. Senge (2000) makes a similar point when he says that "every organisation is the product of how its members think and interact" (p. 19). Or, to put it another way, the problems that schools face are "always deeply influenced by the kinds of mental models and relationships at large in the system" (ibid).

In effect, if we think that other people have deficiencies, then our actions will tend to follow our thinking, and the relationships we develop and the interactions we have with these people will tend to be negative and unproductive. So, despite our being well meaning, and with the best intentions in the world, if students with whom we are interacting as teachers are led to believe that we think they are deficient, they will respond to this negatively. We were told time and again by many of the interview participants in 2001 (Bishop & Berryman, 2006) and again in 2007 (Bishop et al., 2007) that negative deficit thinking on the part of teachers was fundamental to the development of negative relations and interactions between the students and their teachers, resulting in frustration and anger for all concerned.

Bruner (1996) explains that understanding this has major implications for educational reform and reformers because:

> in theorizing about the practice of education in the classroom … you had better take into account the folk theories that those engaged in teaching and learning already have. For an innovation that you, as a 'proper' pedagogical theorist, may wish to introduce will have to compete with, replace, or otherwise modify the folk theories that already guide both teachers and pupils. (p. 46)

Senge (2000) supports this notion by suggesting that before a reform initiative is introduced, let alone identified as being suitable for sustaining, it is people's thinking and interacting that are worth examining, and progress may need to involve what Cochran-Smith (2004) terms "unlearning" taking place.

Such understanding has major implications for teachers hoping to be agentic in their classrooms and for educational reformers. Elbaz (1981, 1983) explains that understanding the relationship between teachers' theories of practice about learners and learning is fundamental to teachers being agentic. The principles teachers hold dear and the practices they employ are developed from the images they hold of others. To Foucault (1972), the images that teachers create when describing their experiences are expressed in the metaphors that are part of the language of the discourse around education. The metaphors are part of the language of specific discourses that allow teachers to make sense of and see things in certain ways. It is through these metaphors that we organise our relationships and our work, our research and our pedagogy, and they have a powerful influence on how we, and those with whom we interact, understand or ascribe meaning to particular experiences and what eventually happens in practice.

Danaher, Schirato, and Webb (2000) explain that "these discursive windows or explanations shape our understanding of ourselves, and our capacity to distinguish the valuable from the valueless, the true from the false and the right from the wrong" (p. 31).

This means simply that teachers draw from a variety of discourses to make sense of the experiences they have when relating to and interacting with Māori students. Therefore, rather than it being anything inherent or biological within the students, or even the teachers, it was the discourses that teachers drew upon to explain their experiences that kept them frustrated and isolated. It was not their attitudes or personalities; it was what Foucault (1972) termed their positioning within discourse.

This situation can be problematic when, as Scheurich and Young (1997) note, the foundational elements of knowing are derived from only one particular social history, and this is seen as normal and authoritative. Issues of power imbalances come into consideration and the means of addressing power imbalances within classrooms needs to be considered. Teachers' actions and behaviours and how they relate to and interact with students are, therefore, governed by the discourse in which they position themselves and how they understand and position the other people in the relationship, this positioning being a product of power relations. As a result, Coburn (2003) warns that unless reform initiatives address this situation, as teachers draw on their own prior learning and experiences to interpret and implement reforms they may graft new approaches to the old, maintain old routines and practices and leave unchallenged their prior beliefs and undertakings. Reform initiatives must therefore include a means whereby teachers can critically reflect on their discursive positioning and, where necessary, (re)position themselves from drawing on discourses that limit change to other discourses that promote and foster change.

The crucial implication from this analysis is that it is the discursive positions that teachers take that are the key to their being able to make a difference, or not, for Māori students. Therefore, prior to in-class-type professional development to promote new, high-quality classroom practices, such as culturalist theorists promote, teachers need to be provided with learning opportunities where they can critically evaluate where they discursively position themselves when constructing their own images, principles and practices in relation to Māori students in their own classrooms. Such an activity is necessary so that they can critically reflect on the part they might be playing in the wider societal power plays that mediate Māori participation in schooling.

When we commenced Te Kotahitanga in 2001 in secondary schools, the majority of teachers we spoke to were positioned in discourses that limited their agency and efficacy. In particular, the discourses were those that suggest the deficiencies posed by students, families, schools, the education system and society create situations and problems that are far beyond the power of teachers to address in the classroom. As a result, the learning opportunities offered to teachers in the professional development programme needed to provide them with an opportunity to undertake what Davies and Harre (1997) call *discursive repositioning*, which means they need to be offered an opportunity to draw explanations and subsequent practices from alternative discourses that offer them solutions instead of reinforcing problems and barriers. This approach is supported by Mazarno et al. (2005), who have argued that most educational innovations do not address the "existing framework of perceptions and beliefs, or paradigm, as part of the change process—an ontological approach" (p. 162), but rather assume "that innovation is assimilated into existing beliefs and perceptions" (ibid.). They go on to suggest that reforms that are more likely to succeed are those that are fundamentally ontological in nature, providing participants with an "experience of their paradigms as constructed realities, and an experience of consciousness other than the 'I' embedded in their paradigms" (ibid.). Or, as Sleeter (2005) suggests:

> [i]t is true that low expectations for students of color and students from poverty communities, buttressed by taken-for-granted acceptance of the deficit ideology, has been a rampant and persistent problem for a long time … therefore, empowering teachers without addressing the deficit ideology may well aggravate the problem. (p. 2)

According to Burr (1995, p. 146), we are all able to reposition ourselves from one discourse to another because, while we are partly the product of discourse, we have agency that allows us to change the way we see and make sense of the world by drawing from other discourses. We are free agents and we have agency; what is crucial to understand is that some of the discourses we draw on limit our power to activate our agency.

In Te Kotahitanga, we use narratives of the experiences of all the people most closely involved with the education of Māori students, including the young people themselves, to provide teachers with the opportunity to reflect on the experiences of others involved in similar circumstances, including, perhaps for the first time, the students (Bishop et al., 2003, 2007). Sharing these vicarious experiences of schooling enables teachers to reflect on their own understanding of Māori children's experiences, and consequently on their own theorising/explanations about these experiences, their consequent practice and the likely impact of this theorising and practice on Māori student achievement. In other words, we are seeking to open the "Black Box" that Timperley et al. (2007) refer to, as teachers are afforded the opportunity to reflect critically on their own discursive positioning and the implications of this positioning for their own agency and for Māori students' learning. In addition, where necessary, teachers are able to reposition themselves from discourses that limit their agency to those where they can be agentic.

As we began to implement what became Te Kotahitanga, we also learnt that positive classroom relationships and interactions are built upon positive, nondeficit, agentic thinking by teachers about students and their families. Agentic thinking views the students as having many experiences that are relevant and fundamental to classroom interactions. This agentic thinking by teachers means they see themselves as being able to solve problems that come their way, and as having recourse to skills and knowledge that can help all of their students, and they believe that all of their students can achieve—no matter what. We learnt that this positive thinking is fundamental to the creation of learning contexts in classrooms where young Māori people are able to be themselves as Māori, where Māori students' humour is acceptable, where students can care for and learn with each other, where being different is acceptable and where the power of Māori students' own self-determination is fundamental to classroom relations and interactions. Indeed, it was the interdependence of self-determining participants in the classroom that created vibrant learning contexts, which were in turn characterised by the growth and development of quality learning relations and interactions, increased student attendance, engagement and achievement, both in school and on nationally based measures (Bishop et al., 2007).

Of course discursive repositioning, while in itself a necessary condition for educational reform, is not sufficient to bring about educational reform. However, theorising from within a relational discourse addresses the limitations of both the culturalist position (limited consideration of the impact of power differentials within the classroom, school and society) and the structuralist position (limited consideration of the agency of teachers, school leaders and policy makers) at all levels of education, and can be used to develop a model that promotes effective and sustainable educational reform.

Responsive and sustainable classroom practices

Commencing a project by talking with students is not usual, but it can be very useful. From a detailed analysis of the literature, Cook-Sather (2002) identified that this kind of authorising of students' experiences and understanding can directly improve educational practice, in that when teachers listen to and learn from students, they can begin to see the world from the perspective of those students. This in turn can help teachers make what they teach more accessible to students. These actions can also contribute to the conceptualisation of teaching, learning and the ways we study as being more collaborative processes. Further, students can feel empowered when they are taken seriously and attended to as knowledgeable participants in learning conversations, and they can be motivated to participate constructively in their education. Cook-Sather also found that authorising students' perspectives is an important way of addressing power imbalances in classrooms so that students' voices have legitimacy in the learning setting. In short, as Cook-Sather states, "authorising student perspectives is essential because of the various ways that it can improve educational practice, re-inform existing conversations about educational reform, and point to the discussions and reform effects yet to be undertaken" (2002, p. 3).

The narratives of experience of the Māori students (Bishop & Berryman, 2006) resonated not only with the conversations with their families, their principals and some of their teachers, but also with the research of others (Hawk & Hill, 2000; G. H. Smith, 1997; Villegas & Lucas, 2002), our own research into effective teaching in Māori-medium settings (Bishop, Berryman, & Richardson, 2001b), our theoretical position on kaupapa Māori research (Bishop, 2005; L. Smith, 1999) and an examination of appropriate Māori cultural metaphors (Bishop et al., 2007).

From this latter consideration, as is detailed in Chapter One, we suggested that educators need to create learning contexts within their classrooms where:

- power is shared between self-determining individuals within nondominating relations of interdependence
- culture counts
- learning is interactive, dialogic and spiral
- participants are connected to one another through the establishment of a common vision of what constitutes excellence in educational outcomes.

In this way, the pattern is similar to what Gay (2000) and Villegas and Lucas (2002) identify in their concept of culturally responsive teaching, and Sidorkin (2002) and Cummins (1995) identify in their concept of a pedagogy of relations. The merging of these concepts is a useful way to describe the pattern identified from this set of Māori cultural metaphors, as identified by G. H. Smith (1997) and Bishop et al. (2007) as a culturally responsive pedagogy of relations, the practical representation of which we termed the Effective Teaching Profile (see Box 1.1, Chapter One, and Bishop et al., 2003, 2007).

Again, as detailed in Chapter One, teachers' understanding of the need to explicitly reject deficit theorising as a way to explain Māori students' educational achievement levels, and taking an agentic position in their theorising about their practice, is fundamental to creating a culturally responsive pedagogy of relations. The continuum between these two extremes can be seen in teachers' classrooms currently. The aim of Te Kotahitanga is to support teachers to move along the continuum to a point where more of them will feel more in control of their lives and teaching. As they move towards becoming agentic, teachers demonstrate on a daily basis their:

- care for the students as Māori
- high expectations for student performance
- capability to manage their classrooms so as to promote learning

- use of a range of discursive learning interactions with students
- knowledge of a range of strategies that can facilitate learning interactions
- ability to promote, monitor and reflect upon student learning outcomes in order to judge the impact of their teaching on student learning.

The implementation of the Effective Teaching Profile would see the development in classrooms of contexts for learning that were described in Bishop et al. (2001b) as follows:

> We must attempt to create learning relationships within classrooms wherein learners' culturally generated sense-making processes are used in order that they may successfully participate in classroom interactions. Such relationships must promote the knowledges, learning styles and sense-making processes of the learner as 'acceptable' or 'legitimate'. Teachers should interact with students in such a way that new knowledge is co-created. In this way, learners are able to be co-inquirers, interact and exchange notes and take part in the whole process of learning from goal setting to assessment and evaluation. Learning is to be seen as active, close to real-life, problem-based, integrated, critically reflective, creative, and life-long. Teachers seek to create socio-cultural contexts wherein learning takes place actively, reflectively and where learners can not only use a variety of learning styles, but also have the power to determine which learning styles they need to use. In other words, creating contexts where they can safely bring what they know and who they are into the learning relationship. Teachers and community interact and home and school aspirations are complementary. Further, where what students know, who they are, and how they know what they know, forms the foundations of interaction patterns in the classroom. In short, where culture counts. Such a position stands in contrast to traditional positions, where knowledge is determined by the teacher and children are required to leave who they are at the door of the classroom or at the school gate. (p. 7)

Culture is central to effective pedagogy because learning new concepts is aided by creating associative links; that is, connecting prior knowledge, including that obtained outside the classroom, to new classroom learning to counter the proposition that "substantial amounts of classroom time is wasted because the instructional experiences do not match children's memory processes" (Alton-Lee, 2006, p. 618). Culturally responsive pedagogies, therefore, become all the more important the greater the distance between the world of the teacher and that of the child. When there is a cultural mismatch between teacher and child, "it ought to be the teacher who makes the cognitive adjustment" (Bishop, 2003, p. 235). This, in turn, allows student engagement from a self-determining perspective, which Bruner (1996) argues brings commitment, from which comes learning (Applebee, 1996). In practice, this means there will be a pedagogy of power sharing that involves children in decisions about curriculum planning and "the directions that learning will take" (Bishop, 2003, p. 225).

Consequently, Māori language, culture and knowledge become a valid guide, both literally and metaphorically, to classroom interactions so that "Māori children can be themselves" (Bishop, 2003, p. 225). Culture is, in fact, one's sense-making process. Too often (as was seen in Bishop et al., 2007) culture is seen as tikanga or customs, and cultural iconography displayed in classrooms is seen as being sufficient for engaging Māori students with learning. However, if instead it is the child's sense-making process that is "acceptable" and "official", teacher interactions can focus on the co-construction of knowledge. A further benefit of this approach is that it can lessen the distance between the world of the child and that of the school, which in turn increases the likelihood of parental involvement in the child's schooling.

A study of high-performing Hispanic schools in the USA by Reyes, Scribner, and Scribner (1999) provides evidence of the significance of such an approach to teaching to the achievement of minority students. Reyes et al. noticed that in a number of schools where Hispanic children were achieving well, central to their success were dynamic teachers who were able to transcend cultural and linguistic barriers to make a difference in the lives of these children. The high-performing Hispanic schools that were the focus of this study "have been characterised as communities of learners where students were first, learning is fun and everything begins in the classroom" (Reyes et al., 1999, p. 4). Classroom experiences in these schools were characterised by "teachers engaging students in the learning process that maximises excellence and achievement" (ibid.). Teachers were typically antideficit theorists, and as a result understood their own agency in the matter, took responsibility for their students' learning, and did not fall into the trap of allowing lower expectations to lead to self-fulfilling prophecies about student failure. Within these classrooms, teachers were also empowered by the structural and wider cultural arrangements of the school to "adapt, modify, make culturally relevant, and match curricula to the unique needs of Hispanic students" (ibid.). Instruction was interactive, active and student centred. Assessment was primarily formative; that is, "ongoing and advocacy-oriented" (ibid.), and through this process students were encouraged to become responsible for their own learning.

Such findings are supported by an extensive, internationally based meta-analysis of differing effects on schooling (Hattie, 1999). For example, "effective teachers set challenging goals and then structure situations so that students can reach these goals" (p. 16). Indeed, Hattie's meta-analysis concludes that teaching is most effective when "achievement is enhanced to the degree that students and teachers set and communicate appropriate, specific and challenging goals", and "achievement is enhanced as a function of feedback", yet "the incidence of feedback in the typical classroom is usually very low, usually in seconds at best per day" (ibid.). To Hattie, feedback in its widest sense and the setting of challenging goals (which is a function of high expectations) are therefore the two most significant aspects of classroom practice that characterise effective teaching.

Nonetheless, Hattie (1999) and Nuthall (2007) both stress that feedback on its own is insufficient, because teachers must be attentive to how their feedback is interpreted and understood by the child. In short, responding to the different ways in which children receive feedback "requires that teachers care about their students, know where they are coming from, and overly attend to the issue of whether their students are learning" (Hattie, p. 19). Effective professional development, in focusing on the classroom as the site of change, will therefore need to support the introduction and establishment of classroom strategies and interactions that provide cognitive challenges and challenging feedback.

Hattie's (2003a) analysis of what differentiates the expert teacher from the merely competent is also instructive. As was identified earlier, most educational initiatives have a positive effect on learning, but the effects are not equal. Therefore, "the aim needs to be to identify those attributes that have marked and meaningful effect on student learning—not just a positive (greater than zero) effect" (Hattie, 2003a, p. 4). Of the 33 most significant factors explaining variance in outcome, 21 are controlled by the teacher. Of the 11 remaining, "student's prior cognitive ability" is the most significant variable and the only one that rates among the five most important (p. 5). These conclusions are based on an analysis of over 500,000 studies, and the testing of findings of the analysis in over 3,000 classrooms throughout the USA (Bond, Smith, Baker, & Hattie, 2000).

Hattie's five "major dimensions of expert teachers" are teachers who can:
• identify essential representations of their subject
• guide learning through classroom interactions
• monitor learning and provide feedback
• attend to affective attributes
• influence student outcomes (Hattie, 2003a, p. 6).

Expert teachers use their subject and pedagogic knowledge differently from teachers who are simply experienced. They are better able to integrate new material with children's prior knowledge and can make crosscurricular relationships. Experts can alter their lessons and change their goals in response to students' needs. It is their flexibility that further distinguishes experts from the experienced; Luke, Freebody, Lau, and Gopinathan (2005) term this the skill of "weaving". They are flexible and seek out data, rather than rely on what is readily available, when trying to solve problems affecting a particular child.

In a study of effective Māori-medium teachers (Bishop et al., 2001b), we found that the pedagogic characteristics of expert teachers included depth of professional and cultural knowledge, passion and dedication, a clear philosophy of teaching and clear teaching goals. Expert teachers were committed to developing children's understanding and intellectual growth, their behaviour management strategies were nonconfrontational, they were genuinely interested in children and they provided high-quality academic feedback. These effective teachers continually reflected on their work and had high academic and behavioural expectations of children. Their classroom management was high quality, and they incorporated students' prior learning into their teaching strategies and used materials that were related to the children's world view and experiences. They matched strategies and materials to children's ability, and monitored children's progress. They encouraged high levels of academic engagement and close links to whānau, and created a:

culturally appropriate and responsive context for learning by providing a visibly culture rich environment, enabling the children to bring their own culturally-generated meaning-making processes to learning. In this way, cultural identities were affirmed and a high degree of academic engagement is assured. (Bishop et al., 2001b, pp. viii–xii)

Conclusion

As Timperley et al. (2007) and Coburn (2003) found in their respective meta-analyses of the relevant literature, sustainability appears to be dependent on whether teachers acquire an in-depth understanding of the underlying theoretical principles of the reform so that they can use their learning flexibly in their classrooms when new situations and challenges arise. Sustainable educational reform does not just provide teachers with new instructional strategies, although these may well be part of the overall package; rather, sustainable educational reforms are theory- or principle-based so that teachers can address future problems by critical reflection from a base of theory rather than practice.

Such theories can be encapsulated in what Robinson et al. (2009) term "smart tools," such as the GEPRISP/PSIRPEG model, which provides teachers with the theory of Te Kotahitanga classroom practice in a acronym, or the GPILSEO model for classroom, school and system reform. These two smart tools provide teachers and other leaders with a means of critically reflecting, especially within the rapid pace that most classroom interactions take place. Huberman (1983, cited in Fullan, 2007, p. 24) terms this the "classroom press", meaning the press for immediacy and concreteness within a context of multidimensionality and simultaneity; in other words, doing many things at once, with a number of people, where conditions can change unpredictably from day to day and from year to year, where teachers undertake numerous interchanges every day (200,000 per annum according to Huberman), attending to the conditions that create relational trust and that promote caring and learning relationships. As Luke et al. (2005) argued, the best metaphor to describe these actions and thought is "weaving".

The challenge for sustainable educational reform is to provide teachers with a means of improving their practice in a way that they can deepen over time, hence the need for theory and theory-based smart tools. Just as the old adage says, "Give someone a fish and you feed them for a day; give them a net and they can feed themselves for more than a day", so, too, sustainable educational reforms need to provide the net for the long term, not the fish for one meal.

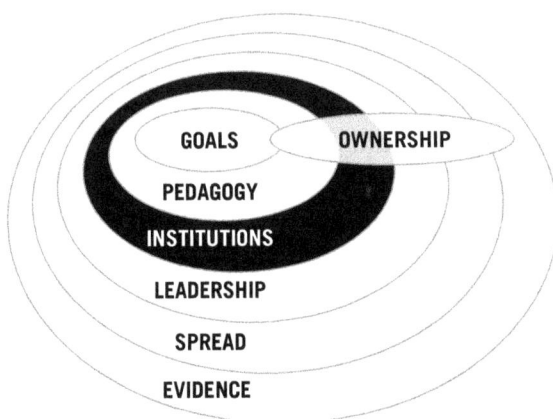

GOALS   OWNERSHIP

PEDAGOGY

INSTITUTIONS

LEADERSHIP

SPREAD

EVIDENCE

CHAPTER FOUR

Institutionalisation of the Reform Within the School

The main reason that change fails to occur in the first place on any scale, and does not get sustained when it does, is that the infrastructure is weak, unhelpful, or working at cross purposes. By the infrastructure I mean the next layers above whatever unit we are focusing on. (Fullan, 2001, p. 18)

Introduction

So far we have looked at two main considerations for sustaining and extending educational reform: goal setting that targets student achievement (Chapter Two) and the need for the reform to be built upon a theory of pedagogy that teachers can take to depth (Chapter Three). The third major consideration is that the initiative must contain a means, from its very inception, that will ensure the reform elements become institutionalised within school structures and organisational arrangements in both the original and subsequent schools. Once the initial thrust and interest die down, unless the reform elements are embedded as part of the school's core business as usual, the reform will suffer from competing priorities, changing demands, and "teacher and administrator turnover" (Coburn, 2003, p. 6). The result will be that the reform will not survive far beyond the initial period of implementation, which typically involves short-term influxes of high-energy professional developers, extra resources and funding, along with high levels of interest from neighbouring schools.

Although it is clear that classrooms are the most effective initial sites for educational reform (Alton-Lee, 2003; Elmore, Peterson, & McCarthey, 1996; Hattie, 1999, 2003a), teachers who work in isolation are unlikely to develop and maintain to any significant extent "new teaching strategies spontaneously and on their own" (Elmore et al., 1996, p. 7). Therefore, Hattie (2003a) and Marzano (2003) support Coburn (2003), who suggests that teachers are better able to sustain change when there are "mechanisms in place at multiple levels of the system to support their efforts" (p. 6). In other words, teachers are strengthened in their capacity to sustain change if they are supported by a broader systemic focus on reform within the school and at national policy levels (Hattie, 1999). To this end, on site ongoing models of reform can be individualised to each teacher's needs, with classroom observations, monitoring and evaluation of new teaching techniques being an integrated component of the programme (Timperley, 2003a).

The relationship between teaching practice and structural support

The relationship between teaching practice and structural support was examined by Elmore et al. (1996), who investigated three elementary schools known nationally in the USA for being engaged "in serious structural change and pursuing ambitious goals for student learning" (p. 13). They identified that these schools were engaged in what is generally accepted as effective school-wide practice: grouping students for instruction; creating opportunities for teachers to share knowledge collaboratively; taking greater responsibility for budget and personnel decisions in their school; and making professional development part of their regular responsibilities. Overall, they were "trying to change teaching and learning by changing the structure of the organization in which they worked" (p. 237).

However, from their analysis of the schools, Elmore et al. concluded that "there probably is no single set of structural changes that schools can make that will lead predictably to a particular kind of teaching practice" (p. 238). By this they mean that simply creating new structures will not necessarily cause teachers to change their practice. This finding challenges a common assumption among reform advocates that making some specific changes in structure, such as reducing class sizes or grouping students, will bring about changes in teaching practice, which in turn will lead to students learning in different ways and knowing different things.

Elmore et al., along with Bruner (1996), suggest that this picture of structural changes leading teachers to change their practice is far too simplistic. Teachers make decisions about how and what to teach not as a result of the structure they are placed within, but rather as the result of a complex internal conversation between their past practices, their judgements about what to teach (which are strongly influenced by their perception of those whom they are teaching), deeply rooted habits of practice and what they think about what and how they should be teaching. Hattie's (1999) large meta-analysis supports this conclusion that changes in structure such as class size, streaming and student grouping practices will not necessarily lead to different kinds of teaching and students learning in different ways. It is what teachers *do* that makes the difference. As Elmore et al. (1996) conclude:

> the transformation of teaching practice is fundamentally a problem of enhancing individual knowledge and skill, not a problem of organizational structure; getting the structure right depends on first understanding that problem of knowledge and skill. (p. 240)

In other words, structural reform works most effectively when the reform creates conditions where changes in practice lead to changes in structure, and where school institutions, structures and organisations evolve in a responsive, flexible manner so as to be supportive of classroom reform. Indeed, the main finding from this detailed analysis of the relationship between structure and pedagogy was that "changing structure did not change practice, it only relabeled existing practices with new names. The schools that succeed in changing practice are those that start with the practice and modify school structures to accommodate to it" (Elmore, 2004, p. 4).

Because Te Kotahitanga seeks to change teachers' skills and knowledge so that they are able to connect curriculum content knowledge to students' prior experiences and cultural understanding, they are provided with support in the form of in-class facilitators. These support staff help teachers to understand how they can bring about change in their classroom practice so as to "understand what students are actually doing when they are actively understanding something" (Elmore et al., 1996, p. 229). This knowledge of practice further ensures "their capacity to create settings in which that understanding occurred consistently for most students" (ibid.). Evidence from the project (Bishop et al., 2007) shows that facilitators have assisted teachers to embed a systematic knowledge of practice in both abstract (theory) and concrete (practice) terms in ways that demonstrate that those teachers are now able to teach in ways that Elmore et al. (1996) term "teaching for understanding".

The provision of a new support person (the in-class facilitator) was seen as important in Te Kotahitanga because, although many teachers are keen to try out new approaches in their classrooms, it is "extraordinarily difficult to get teachers to engage in sustained reflection and criticism of their own work that leads to fundamentally different ways of teaching" (Elmore et al., 1996, p. 233). Nor is it realistic to expect teachers to do so unaided. Therefore, the addition of a group of facilitators of staff learning, whose task is to support staff to implement the Effective Teaching Profile in their classrooms, has been an essential structural/organisational support provided for the teachers, initially by the reform, then gradually, as reform funding diminishes, by the school. As such, staff development becomes a seamless part of the culture of the organisation, and teachers work within an ongoing norm of continuous improvement, building into the school a systemic and systematic way of implementing self-reflection and critique.

Further structural and organisational changes were also seen. In the early phases of Te Kotahitanga the initial implementation of the Effective Teaching Profile in school classrooms was tolerated rather than accommodated by school structures. However, ongoing implementation of the profile and improved student results led to a growth in confidence and enthusiasm by many teachers and school leaders. The teachers began to adapt their classroom spaces and seating arrangements, develop new resources and change their means of delivering the curriculum. This in turn led to their requesting time and space to meet with colleagues to discuss a common group of target students, which in turn led to school leaders responsively changing the school-wide timetable to allow for the new Te Kotahitanga institutions (observations, feedback, co-construction meetings, shadow coaching) to be supported and established in the schools.

The role of the teacher in institutional change

The Change Over Time project (Hargreaves & Goodson, 2006), which compared school reform across eight schools in Canada and the USA, found that "[t]eachers accept or resist particular reforms according to the correspondence or not of the reforms with their generational missions, their academic subject orientations and commitments, and the school's identity" (p. 15). Teacher identity and belief systems are most influenced and shaped in the early career stages (p. 24). It would seem, therefore, that influencing "generational missions" through teacher training programmes is an important systemic accompaniment to the school-based aspects of reform.

Leithwood, Jantzi, and Fernandez (1994) argue for the importance of teachers setting and working towards personal goals to the likelihood of sustainable reform. The implication of this for reform schools is that there must be an alignment of staff goals with the reform pedagogy, and that sustainable implementation of the project requires the recruitment and retention of staff who can provide such alignment. Schools need to institutionalise their recruitment and retention programmes to meet this end and change staffing organisational structures to accommodate the new functionalities (Copas, 2007). Reform goals are more likely to be achieved if they are clearly understood and if teachers are convinced that the reform objectives are achievable. The extent to which the school's goal-setting process is perceived as "participatory" and "dynamic" is also a useful predictor of sustainable change (Leithwood et al., 1994, p. 90).

The entrenchment of the reform into school culture in this way is also likely to strengthen the goal of improving Māori students' achievement against changes in government policy and resistance from outside (Copas, 2007), so that success can be normalised (Durie, 2006, p. 15). Strengthening the capacity of teachers to set the agenda for change is necessary because it is intended that the primary ongoing source of professional advice is not the outside (usually government-funded) expert but the teacher's professional colleagues in the workplace.

Therefore, the sustainability of the reform depends in part on teacher willingness to engage seriously in ongoing development of new pedagogic knowledge. It requires sound and deep theoretical understanding of different approaches to classroom practice and a commitment to ongoing professional interactions. If the reform and its associated meetings and commitments are peripheral to everyday school life, then the project will never be sustainable. If, however, they are the centre of the school routine, then they are well placed to have a significant impact. It is therefore essential when considering the schools into which the reform might expand that primary consideration be given to the school's capacity and willingness to organise its administration and develop a culture around the project. Central to this consideration is the quality of leadership within the school and its board of trustees.

Collaborative approaches to school change can reduce resistance because teachers are less likely to feel detached or isolated from change. Nevertheless, Guskey (1995) cautions that "elaborate needs assessments, endless committee and task-force debates, and long and tedious planning sessions often create confusion and alienation in the absence of any action" (p. 121). It is therefore important that support provided to teachers is "linked to established norms of continuous improvement and experimentation, and these norms then guide professional development efforts" (Guskey, 1995, p. 121). The translation of newly learnt concepts into classroom practice under "unique on-the-job conditions, is an uneven process requiring time and extra effort, especially when beginning". Guskey further points to the importance of time:

> Support coupled with pressure ... is vital for continuation. Support allows those engaged in the difficult process of implementation to tolerate the anxiety of occasional failures.

Pressure is often necessary to initiate change among those whose self-impetus for change is not great. (p. 123)

He continues:

What makes the early stages of implementation so complicated is that the problems encountered at this time are often multiple, pervasive, and unanticipated ... regardless of how much advanced planning or preparation takes place, it is when professionals actually implement the new ideas or practices that they have the most specific problems and doubts. (p. 123)

Even when all these conditions are met, reformers need to be mindful that developing reform projects in schools in this manner may well result in the development of what Timperley, Phillips, and Wiseman (2003) term professional communities of teachers who solely focus on themselves and their teaching. If, for example, the preoccupation of the project is solely with sequence and working with teachers and the contexts for learning they create, there is no guarantee that students' educational achievement will improve. Timperley et al. (2003) caution that "teachers' levels of motivation to implement new programmes, satisfaction with student achievement and feelings of success are unreliable indicators of the realities of student achievement" (p. 128). Further, they argue that high-quality professional development can assist teachers to acquire new skills and knowledge, but it is the school-based factors that "determine whether that knowledge will be focused on bringing about significant changes in student achievement" (ibid.).

As a result, the Te Kotahitanga professional development programme consists of a series of institutionalised practices that provide supportive feedback on both individual teachers' changing classroom practices, as well as on how collectively they could modify their practices in light of evidence of Māori students' progress with learning. The initial induction workshop and the facilitated observations that are followed by targeted feedback sessions are designed for individual teachers. In the induction workshop the opportunity for individual teachers to reflect critically on their discursive positioning and the part they are playing in the learning outcomes of Māori students is followed by a term-by-term sequence of observations and feedback sessions (which rapidly become co-constructed sessions), so that individual teachers can critically reflect on their classroom practices. The programme then provides groups of teachers who teach a common class with the opportunity to put their new learning into practice in a collegial setting, where teachers are supported by a facilitator to reflect critically on evidence of student learning and collectively modify their practice (in line with their new learning) so as to further enhance student learning. This leads to the responsive development of school-level structural support:

For [Te Kotahitanga] schools the drive to have all the teaching staff Te Kotahitanga trained and supported provides another opportunity and further impetus to design new school-wide systems and processes that support the programme's focus on developing effective teachers via the structured ongoing professional development cycle of peer learning and support. (Copas, 2007, p. 13)

Professional learning communities

Sustainable educational reform therefore begins with individual teachers, but requires organisational change to ensure that school routines do not simply accommodate the professional development, and that the reform becomes a central component of the routine. An organised school-wide system for improving teachers' learning and classroom practice is therefore necessary for the development of what Timperley et al. (2003), Stoll and Seashore Louis (2007) and Nieto (2000), among others, term "professional learning communities", where evidence-based learning, participation and achievement are the goals, and the former does not outweigh the latter. This reflects the argument that sustainable professional development is not just an individual process: it requires a momentum of its own, a momentum that is more powerful than the individual and is not solely dependent on any one individual for its success.

Schools are traditionally dominated by norms of privacy. The cultural change from schools being a collective of relatively isolated practitioners to one of a collegial, professional learning community is therefore significant and requires systematic and ongoing attention to be effective. In addition, the procedures for the institutionalisation of the school as a professional learning community must contain their own means of sustainability so that teacher learning becomes continuous and not dependent on the "outside expert".

Timperley et al. (2003), Stoll and Seashore Louis (2007) and Nieto (2000) identify the following characteristics as being instrumental in the development and sustaining of effective professional learning communities:

1. Communities engage in reflective dialogue, whereby teachers examine research and link this to practice, developing a shared language, deepening their instructional knowledge, and using this research to evaluate and challenge their own assumptions and practices, and their consequences. Such communities acknowledge that what we think will affect what we do, and how well we will do in the future.

2. Communities maintain a collective focus on student learning and achievement, where data are used to reflect on the effectiveness of teaching, to discuss individual rates of progress, to benchmark and to make decisions about the next learning steps.

3. Communities collaborate and teachers share expertise in order to critically examine practices and evidence of student participation and achievement, and develop skills and knowledge to engage in joint planning of future goals and strategies.

4. Practices are deprivatised, and teachers learn from peer coaching, structured observations and the sharing of classroom data from dialogue, interaction and feedback from colleagues.

5. Values and expectations about learning and achievement are shared. In other words, there is a body of collectively agreed professional beliefs so that there is a collective vision of where they are going, what is important, how to achieve what is important and who is responsible for achieving those goals.

In effect, therefore:

A professional learning community is one in which teachers update their professional knowledge and skills within the context of an organised, school-wide system for improving teaching practices. Teachers' efforts, individually and collectively, are focused on the goal of improving student learning and achievement. (Timperley, 2003b, p. 129)

The ongoing nature of professional learning communities allows them to support sustainable professional development and to take a long-term view of achievement. Successful professional learning communities are also characterised by their ability to identify clear indicators of children's progress, to create and sustain a culture of meeting achievement goals within the school and to ensure that it is achievement (Timperley et al., 2003) not fashion or assumptions that determine pedagogy (Guskey, 1995). Successful learning communities make "achievement the touchstone" of a professional development initiative, and they do so in a collaborative manner (Timperley et al., 2003).

In Timperley et al.'s (2003) study of what constitutes sustainability in a programme for improving the teaching of reading to five- and six-year-olds, data were used to prompt change in teaching practice where it was found that a particular teaching method was not working for a child. In this study, Timperley et al. found that achievement information was used by classroom teachers to inform their teaching practice because it allowed constant monitoring of their effectiveness as teachers. When necessary, teachers were able to adjust their methods to ensure that the learning needs of the child were being addressed. By using both formative and summative assessment to guide the single objective—improving children's achievement—teachers received timely and regular information on the effect of their efforts. In this way, if teachers are able to see a direct positive impact on achievement outcomes of new approaches to teaching, then the prospect of sustainability is enhanced because "successful actions are reinforcing and likely to be repeated ... [and] practices that are new and unfamiliar will be accepted and retained when they are perceived as increasing one's competence and effectiveness" (Guskey, 1995, p. 121).

The professional learning community gives the teacher a context for evaluating and improving practice informed by evidence rather than just the teacher's own experience. Elmore et al. (1996), along with Bruner (1996) and others, argue that without the benefits of such a supportive context, how teachers teach is a combination of their judgements about what they ought to be teaching and to whom, and "deeply rooted habits that are often at odds with their own expressed views of what they ought to do" (p. 239). A strong professional learning community is also a context in which there can be stronger professional accountability. Teachers who keep themselves up to date on current research in their areas of expertise, and who do their best to apply known best practice, are, in an important sense, more accountable to their profession than teachers who shut the door and teach what they have always taught, as they have always taught it. Similarly, professional accountability is at play when teachers share their knowledge with others, invite review of their instructional strategies and willingly speak out when their professional judgement tells them they must (Goldberg & Morrison, 2003, p. 79).

Little (1999) argues that "teacher learning is supported in schools that institutionalise teachers' individual and collective responsibility for student achievement and well-being, and make inquiry into student learning a cornerstone of professional development" (p. 235). In the Timperley et al. (2003) study, these schools held regular structured meetings to focus on teaching strategies for students whose progress was not at the expected rate. These meetings were held with a sense of urgency and were supported and facilitated by senior teachers working with others in their classrooms to help them to develop new teaching strategies. School-wide commitment to the urgency and centrality of structured and focused meetings of the professional learning community was found to be essential.

Rosenholtz (1989) identified facilitated goal setting at both the individual and group levels as a central criterion for improving school performance and as essential to teachers' learning. Goal setting and learning are inextricably linked, because clearly articulated goals "underscore norms of school renewal—that teachers are expected to learn on a continuous basis" (p. 72). In this context, teacher learning is guided by children's needs, and teachers should use data that are available to them about students to guide their own professional learning needs, thus creating learning as the focus of schooling at all levels, so that goals direct teacher learning towards identified gaps in effective practice. To Rosenholtz, structured teacher collaboration is essential for the organisation of teachers' learning opportunities. Collaboration is important because it helps teachers overcome what can be a "professionally orphaned life", "with norms of self-reliance militating against requests for, and offers of, assistance, teachers' opportunities for growth in isolated settings are limited almost entirely to trial-and-error learning" (p. 73). Currently, without structured intervention, teachers' "opportunities for learning are circumscribed by their own ability to discern problems, develop alternative solutions, choose among them and assess the outcome" (ibid.). Sustained whole-school improvement in teaching cannot, therefore, be an individual enterprise, nor can it be the sum of each teacher's individual enterprise. Instead, "analysis, evaluation, and experimentation in concert with colleagues are conditions under which teachers improve instructionally" (ibid.).

Rosenholtz (1989) has also argued that school-wide goal setting for teacher learning is beneficial because it establishes for each individual the direction of his or her improvement efforts. Goal-setting activities provide a context for review and reflection and for the creation of a unity of purpose. Such an approach also supports, and is supported by, the professional learning community because "shared goals about teaching render legitimacy, value and support, or, if need be, collective pressure to conform to school norms" (p. 79). Rosenholtz found a positive correlation between schools that demonstrated "learning-enriched conditions" and teachers' identification of colleagues as their most important source of teaching new ideas. Conversely, teachers in "learning impoverished" environments did not see their colleagues as useful sources of new ideas (p. 96). Professional reading and participation in professional conferences were further characteristics of learning-enriched schools, which contrasted with the reliance on more easily accessible professional development, such as workshops and short courses, favoured by teachers in learning-impoverished environments.

Where professional development is given a structured, institutional, collegial context and focus, it can support whole-school development because it is capable of involving a substantial number—if not all—of the school staff in problem-solving, student-learning-focused, professional learning community meetings. In terms of sustainability and taking a reform to scale, it is clear that administrative arrangements conducive to an ongoing professional learning community are a non-negotiable requirement for the sustained implementation of the reform in any school.

Infrastructural support

The New American Schools project found that the potential for sustained change is enhanced when the "culture of school systems" is integrated with the objective of change, and when the focus of professional development is not on "the quick fix of the day" but on "practices driven by results and continuous improvement" (Berends, Bodily, & Nataraj Kirby, 2004, p. 155). The three main lessons offered by New American Schools are that:

- sustainability depends on continuous evaluation and dissemination of best practice ideas
- schools and teachers need assistance and help in changing
- investing in schools is a "necessary but not sufficient requirement for sustained improvement" (Berends et al., 2004, pp. 161–162).

Sustainability is further dependent on diverting public financial support away from short-term-focused traditional programmes and towards projects of a longer term focus. Vested stakeholder interests in the perpetuation of traditional professional development need to be challenged to facilitate sustainability and minimise future resistance. In other words, financial and other resources need to be reprioritised as a necessity for schools and policy makers.

The reform must also contain within itself a means of enhancing systemic capacity to sustain and motivate high-quality, career-long teaching that requires "norms of continuous improvement" to entrench themselves in the school culture. To Rosenholtz

(1989), the focus of improvement must be continuous, because teaching "cannot be standardized. It is through informed experiments, pursuing promising directions, and testing out and refining new arrangements and practices that we will make the most headway" (p. 98).

The culture of the school can tend towards encouraging ongoing teacher learning and a rejection of the view Rozenholtz (1989) found in learning-impoverished schools, whereby teacher learning is "terminal", culminating in the acquisition of a set of easily defined skills and an easily defined stagnant knowledge base (p. 98). In contrast, reforms need to encourage teachers "to define professional growth as sustained, where new skills and practices may be filed into an ever-expanding portfolio that pliantly accommodates diverse student needs as contextual differences arise" (ibid.). Structural impediments to change can be more quickly identified and solutions determined at the point of implementation:

> School organization, while by no means the only influence on how teachers teach, is seen by many advocates of teaching for understanding as a key variable in determining teachers' capabilities to engage in new, more ambitious practices. (Elmore, 1996, p. 6)

It therefore makes sense to argue that:

> Existing infrastructure mechanisms must be modified in ways that guarantee new policy directions are translated into appropriate daily operations. Well-designed infrastructure mechanisms ensure local ownership, a critical mass of committed stakeholders, processes that overcome barriers to stakeholders effectively working together, and strategies that mobilize and maintain proactive effort so that changes are implemented and there is renewal over time. (UCLA Center of Mental Health in Schools, 2006, p. 110)

Organisational change

In a detailed analysis of attempts by the Te Kotahitanga project team to develop a model for sustainable school-wide practices in the project schools, Copas (2007) suggested that although the GPILSEO model, as it stood then, clearly identified what sustainable change might look like in Te Kotahitanga schools, it did not provide a theory for how schools might go about achieving structural and organisational change. Copas quotes Ackerman-Anderson and Anderson (2001), who argue:

> Traditionally, most leaders have thought of 'planning for change' as 'planning for implementation'. If leaders think only of implementation, it is no wonder that their well-intentioned efforts founder. When they neglect activities such as … building an integrated change strategy and preparing the organization to receive and participate in the transformation, then change efforts struggle. (p. 4)

Copas (2007) identified that Te Kotahitanga had commenced with the provision of theory for the implementation of the project in the classroom along three main fronts:

- *ideas*: movement along the continuum from nonagentic (deficit) to agentic (nondeficit) discursive positioning

- *practices*: movement from domination by transmission models of classroom interactions to a more even balance between transmission and discursive interactions
- *outcomes*: movement from the current status for Māori students of attendance, engagement and achievement patterns, to being on a par with others.

However, she argued that missing from this scenario was a critical fourth dimension, organisational change, by which she meant:

[t]he funding, strategies and infrastructure required to support implementation and development from temporary, peripheral (and sometimes contested) acceptance as an improvement project, to routine legitimacy embedded within the organization as part of the school's core business. (p. 4)

Copas (2007) has argued that current best organisational practice (Ackerman-Anderson & Anderson, 2001; Cohen, 2005; Hall & Hord, 2006) maintains that "the foundation for successful organizational change occurs systematically and upstream" (p. 4). This means that organisations need to prepare themselves for a wide range of organisational responses. Schools need to plan for the fact that their participation in large-scale, theory-based reforms will not only involve changes to the core instructional practices in the classrooms, but will also involve changing infrastructural and organisational support systems within the school. How this will look will differ from school to school, as each setting differs markedly from each other, and theory-based reforms acknowledge this diversity. In fact, theory-based reforms promote flexibility, which means the reform can be appropriate to and owned by practitioners in a wide range of settings and circumstances.

As we stated in the Introduction to this book, it is crucial that the local participants at the school level, as much as at the classroom level, be able to adapt and modify the actual activities in line with the reform principles to make the reform relevant to their own setting. Theory-based reforms are designed to be sustainable and extendable in the face of competing interests and agendas by the provision of an appropriate theory that school leaders can call upon when new situations and challenges arise.

A theory of organisational change

Gallos (2006) proposes that Bolman and Deal's (2003) four-frame model offers a systematic and manageable way to "approach and examine a full range of organizational possibilities" (p. 351). The four frames are:

1. *structural frame*: the need to organise and structure groups to achieve results
2. *human resources frame*: the need to tailor organisations to satisfy human needs, improve human resource management and build positive interpersonal and group dynamics
3. *political frame*: the need to cope with power and conflict, build coalitions, develop political skills and deal with internal and external politics

4. *symbolic frame*: the need to shape a culture that gives purpose and meaning at work, states organisational arrangements for internal and external audiences and builds team spirit through ritual, ceremony and story.

1. The structural frame

The structural frame includes considerations of how leaders might:

- reorganise the timetable to allow the new aspects such as observation, feedback, co-construction and shadow coaching, which are fundamental to the reform, the opportunity to become a normal part of the daily operation of the school
- provide office and teaching space for professional development staff
- write project goals into school plans and outcomes into reports
- position staff developers within the organisational chart of formal responsibilities and authority
- include the lead staff developer in senior management decision making
- include the reform in routine reporting mechanisms
- develop student data-management systems so that teachers have "real-time" evidence of student attendance, engagement and achievement for collaborative decision making and problem solving
- develop vertical and horizontal co-ordinating mechanisms.

As Gallos (2006) states:

[e]xisting infrastructure mechanisms must be modified in ways that guarantee new policy directions are translated into appropriate daily operations. Well-designed infrastructure mechanisms ensure local ownership, a critical mass of committed stakeholders, processes that overcome barriers to stakeholders effectively working together, and strategies that mobilize and maintain proactive effort so that changes are implemented and there is renewal over time. (p. 12)

An important aspect of sustaining reform is the development of a culture of change so that the reform is accepted by teachers as a core aspect of the school's daily operations (Hattie, 1999), or what Davies (2007, p. 8) terms the development of an "achievement culture that lasts". As Guskey (2005) warns, reform must be distinguishable from the many fashions that come and go under the guise of professional development. The needs of the new pedagogy and supportive institutions, for example, determine school routines and timetables so that school-based professional development can acquire the capacity to respond immediately to newly identified classroom needs. Linking all professional development to the school's annual plan, with the reform at its core, would signal its importance to teachers and its priority to those allocating the professional development budget. All other professional development should support the reform and be linked to its objective: reducing disparities through increasing the achievement of the targeted students. Again, to emphasise publicly its importance, the reform's outcomes could also be noted in the school's annual report (Copas, 2007).

In an analysis of structural supports for sustaining Te Kotahitanga, one school principal has described the Te Kotahitanga co-construction meetings as the "engines of sustainability in our school" (Copas, 2007). Co-construction meetings are formal opportunities for teachers of a common class to collaboratively determine the future direction of their collective teaching efforts, despite teaching different subjects, on the basis of evidence of students' progress. They are timetabled and structured into the organisational plan of the schools and are becoming an expected and ordinary part of the development of these schools as professional learning communities. One Te Kotahitanga facilitator told Copas that "Co-construction meetings occur in school time and the school pays for relief for teachers. We find this far superior to after school meetings when people often have other priorities, engagements and commitments" (Copas, 2007, p. 7). This means that reform is seen as part of the school's core business, and other professional priorities, engagements and commitments are not prioritised over the reform.

2. The human resources frame

The human resources frame of analysis emphasises the fit between the individual and the organisation:

> An underlying assumption is that organizations exist to serve human needs. Tailoring the organization to meet individual needs at the same time as training the individual in the relevant skills to meet organizational needs is seen as the path to organizational effectiveness. (Gallos, 2006, p. 347)

St John (2002) suggests that an effective infrastructure would include permanent positions for professional developers (and coaches) who can work with outside experts (intermediary organisations) and administration and teachers in their respective schools. These roles must be recognised as distinct and permanent, which would usually require a reconceptualisation of roles and structures in schools—valuing improvement on the same level as curriculum. In other words, the person in charge of improvement (the professional developer) would hold a permanent position of equivalent rank to, and be a member of, the senior management team because "an improvement infrastructure supports the maintenance and continual upgrading of the infrastructure" (St John, 2002, p. 4).

At present, senior management teams in New Zealand secondary schools are dominated by curriculum and student behaviour responsibilities/roles, among which staff development responsibilities are located as part of an already overloaded portfolio. Rather than staff development being a central task for a senior staff person, it is included along with other tasks, thereby creating a workload issue that most often pushes staff development requirements low down on the agenda. Clearly, substantive school improvements require site team members who are committed each day to ensuring effective systemic change and who have enough time and ability to attend to the details (UCLA Center of Mental Health in Schools, 2006, p. 12).

Copas (2007) has observed that Te Kotahitanga schools are staffed with dedicated, hard-working teachers and teaching support staff, who, for the most part, combine running the school (i.e., teaching, administration, etc.) with improving it (i.e., Te Kotahitanga work). This structural situation creates an almost insurmountable capacity issue:

> Many beleaguered schools barely have the capacity to operate the system … [Yet] in education we assume that we can provide money to people who are running the schools and that they will have the time, expertise and incentives to take on the second job of improving schools as well as running them. This phenomenon is often described as trying 'to change the tires on the car while it is moving'. (St John, 2002, p. 5)

St John notes that in most businesses it is one person's task to run the company and another person's job to improve it. The key to understanding why sustaining change in educational organisations is so difficult lies in the location of those who are responsible for implementing and maintaining change in practice. St John suggests that most businesses invest heavily from their own funds to maintain their capacity for ongoing improvement of their products. He cites drug companies, aeroplane manufacturers and software developers as examples of companies that invest their own funds into expensive research and development, and into building the capability of their own staff to conduct what to them is absolutely necessary ongoing evaluation and revision of their core business. Whereas in education "the resources and expertise for improving instruction lie outside the system. And they are supported almost entirely by 'soft money' provided by foundations and government agencies" (p. 5). Hence the problem: the improvement infrastructure that is necessary to constantly revise the core business of education is not part of the enterprise. Is lies outside, and is therefore vulnerable to being withdrawn according to factors over which the school has no control. It is also probably not as valued by the schools as it would be if it were provided from their own funding.

In most reforms, schools are expected to prepare themselves for the inevitable withdrawal of external project funding that was used to establish and implement the reform. As the project morphs from a project into a programme, and then into business as usual, it is expected that school governance and management teams will face the brutal fact that they will need to find the money themselves from already tight budgets. The advice they receive is that preproject funding models were developed for a different time and different needs, and some elements of these models will just have to cease and the funding and staffing will need to be reallocated. Whatever the case, the reallocation of resources needs to be seen within a context of limited expenditure on research and development within schools, and is something that St John (2002) suggests needs to be addressed by policy makers at a national level.

3. The political frame

The political frame of reference addresses national and local positioning in relation to divergent interests, scarce resources and various power distributions, alliances and networks. In particular, managing the perception of and resistance to a programme is a key consideration within an organisation that seeks to take on a school-wide reform. Because reform programmes involve changing teachers' practice, schools need to make preparations to manage such issues at a number of levels, including how to handle matters when the reform challenges teachers' discursive positionings. Comments from teachers in Te Kotahitanga highlighted in Copas's (2007) study included: "I'm here to teach all the kids" and "Why aren't we treating all students equally" in response to the focus of the project to primarily address Māori students' educational needs. Some schools also experienced community backlash along similar lines. In one area, a Ratepayers Association group sent letters of complaint to the local paper asking, "Why the focus on Māori kids, what about the rest?" In another, a teacher who had left the school received a detailed hearing in the local newspaper covering their concerns about the project in the school.

Another issue identified by Copas (2007) was participation: should it be voluntary or compulsory? Copas found that principals who made participation in the programme compulsory were encountering compliance and resistance issues with staff who were reluctant conscripts, whereas principals who made the programme voluntary were finding that some key staff were opting out, jeopardising the success of the whole programme. Other principals were concerned that a programme that focuses on Māori students should be voluntary, whereas professional development programmes that focus on literacy and numeracy are expected to involve all staff, without question. Engaging all staff in a reform such as this remains a problematic issue, especially when teachers' unions lead the resistance.

In this climate, according to Bolman and Deal (2003), it is vital that schools are well prepared for these issues. Although they will be programme specific, each project will engender similar problems, whether they are ethnic based or focused on the introduction of national testing, for example (another contentious issue). What is needed is for schools to network with others so that they are prepared, as much as possible, to deal with such issues, otherwise much energy will be wasted on maintaining a coherent direction for the school in the face of seemingly insoluble problems. These matters are soluble; it just takes time, patience, communication and co-operation, preferably based on an analysis of how similar schools have addressed similar issues previously.

Changes in status among staff members as a result of the implementation of a project also cause problems. Within Te Kotahitanga, the establishment of a cadre of professional developers within the school who work closely with the principal has challenged existing relations, and has had an impact on traditional power and status patterns within the schools. Traditional power structures in secondary schools tend to follow curriculum and discipline responsibilities: the principals are the overall leaders, their deputies look after the day-to-day running of the school, including discipline, and the next most senior people are staff who have the responsibility for a specific curriculum area. The changes that occur with the introduction of a group of facilitators of teacher learning who have regular access to the principal need to be managed by the schools' leaders. Otherwise, those currently holding positions of authority and who have control over the allocation of what are often seriously scarce resources may feel resentful, with consequent effects on their participation and co-operation in the process of the reform.

Unless schools build clear organisational processes and infrastructure to support the changes required to implement the reform, difficulties will arise as emerging institutions confront established relational processes and established power structures. Other status issues may be encountered if the "rank" of the facilitator is not seen as being sufficient by, for example, senior staff who are expected to be "coached" to change their instructional practice. There have also been reports of workplace bullying of some high-achieving, high-profile Te Kotahitanga teachers from other members of staff who are less than happy with their relative change in status among the staff and students.

4. The symbolic frame

The key aspects of Bolman and Deal's (2003) symbolic frame of reference include the creation of a common vision, shared meanings, relevant rituals and symbols. This frame emphasises the importance of the vision and values of the reform having common acceptance, and school leaders working towards and creating organisational structures to this end. The importance of the goals and vision of the reform being central to the school's organisational structure cannot be overstated. It is this centrality of the reform to what the school seeks to achieve as an institution that will promote what is acceptable in terms of attitudes and values, and that will influence what is taught (via the curriculum); indeed, what constitutes acceptable and official knowledge and what becomes acceptable as instructional practice—in Elmore's (2004, p. 8) terms, the "core of educational practice".

It is therefore important that the goals and vision of the school, along with outcomes and successes, are made visible to all involved with the school through the school's website, newsletter and reports, among other activities. One of the groups that needs to be reached is the local community, who are often at a loss as to what is actually happening within their local schools, especially those whose children do not fare well in the school. The celebration and promotion of "good news stories" is one way of promoting the outcomes of the reform to community members, as well as to other schools and to policy makers. Copas (2007) reported that one principal held off giving information to Māori parents until she could give them good news because "they have had bad news for eons". Although initially criticised by some staff for taking this stance, it proved effective in gathering momentum and achieving community buy-in for Te Kotahitanga, because once the community began to see the positive results they became very supportive of the school's initiative. The Te Kotahitanga schools have devised a variety of ways (electronic and visual) of celebrating Te Kotahitanga successes within their organisations and communities, engendering support for their goals.

Conclusion

Sustainability of reform initiatives and taking reform to scale means that change must be sustainable in both the original and subsequent schools. Reform initiatives therefore need to include, as part of the reform process, a means of institutionalising the elements of the reform within the school, and structural reforms need to occur to allow this to happen. The reform must commence with this understanding clearly at the forefront. The reform must not be promoted or seen as an adjunct to existing systems, but rather as a means of reforming the integral elements of the structure of the school, so that they become part of the everyday life of the institution and the institution would be diminished by their removal. In this way, the reform will include a means whereby the benefits can remain once the reform matures and the initial energy, personnel and funding are removed. At the same time, organisational structures can support and guide teachers towards a desired outcome and, as numerous studies illustrate, seemingly immutable problems can be overcome.

CHAPTER FIVE

Knowledgeable and Supportive School Leadership

In many ways, however, the question of how much impact school leaders have on student outcomes is a flawed one, because the answer surely depends on what it is that leaders do. The contribution of leadership research should be to identify the types of leadership that have relatively more or less impact on students, so that they can be emphasised in leadership preparation and development programmes and be better supported by education policies and infrastructure. (Robinson, 2007, p. 5)

Introduction

So far in this book we have identified the central importance of changing classroom relationships and interactions to bring about change in student achievement and disparity levels. We have argued that such changes on their own are not sufficient to bring about sustainable school-wide changes. Institutional, organisational and structural changes are necessary to create contexts in which classroom learning can be responded to, supported and enhanced so that student achievement can improve and disparities can be reduced. It is leaders who drive these changes.

We now turn to the question of "what leaders need to know and do to support teachers in using the pedagogical practices that raise achievement and reduce disparities" (Robinson et al., 2007, p. 2). This focus on leadership is central to the GPILSEO model because, as Leithwood, Seashore Louis, Anderson, and Wahlstrom (2004) concluded from a detailed review of leadership literature, "leadership is second only to classroom instruction among all school-related factors that contribute to what students learn at school" (p. 7). In the GPILSEO model, effective leadership of sustainable educational reform:

- establishes and develops specific measurable *goals* so that progress can be shown, monitored and acted upon
- supports the development and implementation of new *pedagogic* relationships and interactions in the classroom
- changes the *institution*, its organisation and structures
- *spreads* the reform to include staff, parents, community, reform developers and policy makers so that a new school culture is developed and embedded
- develops the capacity of people and systems to produce and use *evidence* of student progress to inform change
- promotes and ensures that the *ownership* of the reform shifts are within the school.

Leadership has an overall purpose

It is important to reiterate that these leadership activities have an overall purpose, which is to directly or indirectly reduce educational disparities through improving student outcomes. Fullan (2003) sees this as having a *moral purpose*, which at the school level means:

> that all students and teachers benefit in terms of identified desirable goals, that the gap between the high and low performers becomes less as the bar for all is raised, that ever-deeper educational goals are pursued, and that the culture of the school becomes so transformed that continuous improvement relative to the previous three components become built in. (p. 31)

Elmore (2004) supports this purpose and argues that the primary purpose of educational leadership is the "guidance and direction of instructional [pedagogical] improvement" (p. 13). Robinson et al. (2009) found, in the empirical part of their best evidence synthesis of leadership studies, that pedagogic or instructional leadership that involves a "close involvement of leadership in establishing an academic mission, monitoring and providing feedback on teaching and learning and promoting the importance of professional development" (p. 55) has nearly four times the impact on student outcomes as the other commonly promoted form of leadership, transformational. However, they also warn against dismissing the qualities of transformational leadership through creating false dichotomies between these two types of leadership.

In effect they are suggesting that leadership needs to exhibit characteristics that encompass the broad rubric of pedagogic or instructional leadership, with its unequivocal focus on improving student outcomes, as well as incorporating those aspects of transformational leadership, and what Shields (2003) terms "transformative leadership", into the mix of what constitutes effective leadership. In other words, the leadership mix or distribution in schools needs to include instructional leaders' unequivocal focus on improving student outcomes through the provision of support for teaching and learning, transformational leaders' concerns with the collective interests of the group—the "ability to inspire and motivate others and develop group commitment to a common vision" (p. vii)—and transformative leaders' focus on creating the conditions or contexts that release others' capacity for self-determination in a manner that promotes the establishment of collaborative relationships for attaining the desired end.

Along with Robinson et al. (2009), from our experience we would suggest that creating dichotomies in leadership styles can promote the notion that there is a distinction between tasks and relationships; that is, between "leading through progressing tasks and leading through relationships and people" (p. 8). There is also a danger that we talk about there being a sequence of, first, developing relationships, then developing tasks; in other words, get the relationship right then pursue the common task, the educational challenges, the goal setting and such like. In contrast, Robinson et al. argue that "relationship skills are embedded in every dimension" (p. 8). In goal setting, for example, "effective leadership involves not only determining the goal content (task focus), but doing so in a manner that enables staff to understand and become committed to the goal [relationship focus]" (p. 8). So whether we are focusing at the level of the classroom, school or system, relationships are part and parcel of everyday activities that seek to improve student outcomes.

At the classroom level we learnt from detailed interviews with 350 Māori students in 2004 and 2005 that the teaching approaches they preferred—and, indeed, within which they could achieve—were not a matter of teachers being either task or relationship oriented, but both simultaneously (Bishop et al., 2007). These Māori students clearly understood that when both were happening at the same time they were able to engage effectively with learning and see their achievement levels improve. They were able to describe a range of scenarios. The first was when a teacher was task oriented but did not clearly show that they cared for the learning of their students: learning did not occur. Second, if the teacher demonstrably cared for the learning of the students but was unable to engage them in meaningful learning interactions, again they were unable to learn. It was only when their teachers were task *and* relationship oriented simultaneously—that is, they were able to demonstrate on a daily basis that they cared for the learning of their students, set high expectations for performance and classroom management (including their own subject content knowledge), as well as being able to use a range of discursive interactions and strategies, including formative assessment—that they knew they were going to learn and achieve. One student commented: "She's dedicated to what we do in our class. I think it's just her passion, that she likes seeing kids achieving instead of failing. Feels cool, that we've got someone who's gonna help us get through school".

Fullan (2003) notes that this task–relationship intersection is based on what Bryk and Schneider (2002) term "relational trust", which their research showed was fundamental to improved student achievement. Just as at the classroom level, relational trust is also fundamental to creating an effective school culture. Robinson et al. (2009) suggest that practical steps for developing relational trust include:

> establishing norms of integrity, showing personal regard for staff, parents and students; demonstrating role competence and personal integrity through modeling appropriate behaviour, following-through when expectations are not met, demonstrating consistency between talk and action, and challenging dysfunctional attitudes and behaviours. (p. xv)

We would add to this list, from our experiences in working with educational reform for indigenous students, those qualities created in classrooms and across schools where teachers and leaders create learning relationships wherein learners' culturally generated sense-making processes are used and developed so that they may successfully participate in problem-solving and decision-making interactions. Such relationships must promote the knowledge, learning styles and sense-making processes of the participants as "acceptable" or "legitimate". Leaders should interact with others in such a way that new knowledge is co-created within contexts where all can safely bring what they know and who they are to the learning relationship; and where what participants know, who they are and how they know what they know form the foundations of interaction patterns. In short, where culture counts (Bishop & Glynn, 1999).

Bryk and Schneider (2002) stress that developing relational trust is effective because it reduces feelings of vulnerability among teachers faced with new and somewhat daunting tasks associated with the reform initiative. The development of relational trust facilitates collaborative problem solving that allows for curriculum alignment and collaborative decision making based on evidence of student learning; supports internal in-school accountability that all students learn; and reduces the tendency to look for external agencies to blame. Relational trust is also fundamental to addressing the need for balancing the inevitable tension between individual autonomy and self-determination and the need for collective and collaborative action towards a common goal. Bryk and Schneider conclude that relational trust provides the moral resource that is needed to sustain "the effort of the long haul", which is needed for school reform. Teachers need to feel they are working in a context where their strong personal commitments to the organisation and its goals are respected, valued and reciprocated. Just as the students in the example above were willing to give their best efforts when they felt they were with a teacher who ensured their success at school, so too when school/reform leaders create a context based on relational trust, all school participants are "more willing to give extra effort even when the work is hard" (Fullan, 2003, p. 43).

As this illustration shows, leadership is not just confined to principals, although much of what we say in this chapter will clearly resonate with them. Rather, we are talking about all leaders—the school's trustees, the principal, members of the senior management team, heads of departments and syndicates, developers and facilitators of professional development, educational policy makers and analysts, teachers, parents and students—since all of these people exercise leadership in some form during their daily interactions.

Distributed leadership

The model of leadership we are promoting is one termed "distributed" by Elmore (2000) and is also one of collective responsibility, mainly because no one person can be responsible for all the leadership activities detailed above. It is our belief that the strength of the school will be greatly enhanced when these leadership activities are undertaken by all those involved in a collaborative way. This is particularly important in large secondary schools for, as Robinson et al. (2007) note, "size, more differentiated structures and specialist teaching culture" (p. 21) limit the degree to which the principal can be directly involved in the pedagogic process. This points clearly to the need for leaders other than the principal to be prominent in many of the activities. For example, it may be appropriate for heads of departments or knowledgeable and skilled professional developers to be involved in providing feedback to teachers in their classrooms in secondary schools, whereas this may well be a task that principals of primary schools may be willing and able to cover.

Like the New American Schools project (Berends, Bodily, & Kirby, 2003), the Chicago Annenberg Challenge (Smylie, Wenzel, & Fendt, 2003) found that although principal leadership is critical, it becomes ineffective if it is leadership to the exclusion of all others. In-school leadership is best not left to just one person. The Inner London Education Authority's Junior School Project's key factors of school effectiveness that were within the school's own sphere of influence included:

- the head teacher's leadership of assessment and professional development
- the deputy head teacher's involvement in policy decisions
- the involvement of teachers in curriculum development
- budgetary priorities and policy development (Mortimore & Whitty, 1997).

Without diminishing the role of the principal, this supports the notion of shared "pedagogic leadership" proposed in the New Zealand Ministry of Education's best evidence syntheses (Alton-Lee, 2004, p. 2).

Although distributed leadership can contribute to a coherent sense of direction and strengthen the basis for reform to sustain itself, it remains true that if the principal is not instrumental in setting the vision for reform and ensuring the necessary responsive cultural and organisational environment, as Hall and Hord (2006) argue, space is created for individuals or cliques to take over the leadership of the reform or to destabilise the reform. We have also found that when there is a change in principal, this can be a time when the reform's aims are seriously challenged to the point of being annihilated by the new principal determining a new direction for the school.

We now turn to a detailed investigation of the qualities of effective leadership, organised in terms of the GPILSEO model. A summary is then provided in Table 5.1.

The qualities of effective leadership

1. Effective leadership establishes and develops specific measurable goals so that progress can be shown, monitored and acted upon

Effective leaders establish explicit academic goals that are "vital for maintaining a coherent and stable student-centered vision" (McDougall, Saunders, & Goldenberg, 2007, p. 53). Robinson (2007) explains that:

> Goal setting works by creating a discrepancy between what is currently happening [and] some desired future state. When people are committed to a goal, this discrepancy is experienced as constructive discontent that motivates goal-relevant behaviour. Goals focus attention and lead to more persistent effort than would otherwise be the case. (p. 10)

Leithwood and Jantzi (2006) argue that people are motivated to set goals and work towards them when individual:

> evaluation of present circumstances indicates that it is different from the desired state, when the goals are perceived to be hard but achievable, and when they are short term but understood within the context of longer term and perhaps more important, more obviously valuable purposes. (p. 206)

For an individual to motivate others, however, the individual must possess a high level of self-efficacy or agency. Leadership, therefore, ought to be based on the assumption that "the school improvement process must be conceived of as relating to the school, subgroups and individuals simultaneously, yet still leading ... to a coordinated, positive set of results" (Lindahl, 2007, p. 321).

Effective principals lead individuals and groups as well as institutions (Lindahl, 2007). Principals need to inspire collective efficacy, which means they must see themselves as having a clear sense of purpose. Holloman, Rouse, and Farrington (2007) argue that a major impediment to implementing large-scale reforms is that "[t]he culture of today's school does not promote permanent fixes. In fact, the cynicism that many educators feel today is a result of years of cyclical changes in programmes and innovations"

(p. 437). Leadership, therefore, begins with a convincing and authoritative introduction to the reform, especially to influential school staff members (Hall & Hord, 2006). The principal sets the school's tone, and the authority vested in the principal makes the office instrumental to reform. Equally, a new principal unconvinced by the reform's objectives or methodologies has considerable power to undermine reform, even where a school board of trustees directs otherwise.

The school's capacity to effect change is not simply the sum of individuals' capacities. No individual can work effectively in a vacuum, which is why leadership must attend to the co-ordination of all individual activities towards a shared goal. But ultimately the specifics of change should be demonstrably linked to the reform's wider vision:

> Leaders matter. What leaders think, say, and do—and who they are when they come to work each day—profoundly affects organizational performance, the satisfaction they and those with whom they interact derive from their work, and their ability to sustain engagement with their work over the period of time necessary to oversee significant improvements. (Sparks, 2005, p. 7)

Leadership, in what the Education Review Office (2002) calls good practice schools for Māori, involves a commitment to improving Māori achievement that is driven by a vision that is shared by the board of trustees, principal and teachers. In this context it is incumbent upon school leadership to (a) understand what is being promoted by reform initiatives, and (b) be simultaneously responsive and proactive in promoting and supporting the reform through institutional and structural change.

Leadership needs to be proactively directed towards a common goal of establishing the school as a high-performing institution where high levels of student achievement and learning are normalised. This means that "[i]f goals are to function as influential co-ordinating mechanisms, they need to be embedded in school and classroom routines and procedures" (Robinson, 2007, pp. 9–10). Leaders of high-achieving schools are more likely to see that their goals and expectations are well understood and to see that academic achievement is recognised and conveyed to the community. Staff consensus about goals is more likely to characterise high-performing schools (Robinson, p. 10). Goals need to be specific, because specificity allows self-regulation: "it's possible to judge progress and thus adjust one's performance ... Goal-setting increases performance and learning" (Robinson, p. 11). As Leithwood and Riehl (2003) argue, effective leaders understand the importance of leadership that sets relevant examples for staff and others to follow that are cohesive and in line with the school values and goals.

The professional development staff need in order to develop the capacity to set goals

It is important that leaders of educational reform initiatives, such as professional development facilitators, themselves set—and support teachers to set—specific goals rather than unspecified changes or developments. This is because "the potency of leadership for increasing student achievement hinges on the specific classroom practices which leaders stimulate, encourage and promote" (Leithwood & Jantzi, 2006, p. 223). Achieving these goals requires leadership that looks beyond short-term solutions to immediate problems: a mixture of long-term and short-term goals is necessary. Schmoker (1999) promotes the setting of short-term goals as being motivational, but Hargreaves and Fink (2006) warn that setting short-term goals may promote the practice of teaching so that students can pass the next test. Focusing on long-term learning gains is necessary and will focus teaching activities on sustainable long-term change designed to eliminate barriers to achievement. Short-term goals are, however, necessary to monitor progress towards the long-term goals.

Goal setting is encouraged at a number of levels in Te Kotahitanga: school wide, among groups and individual teachers, and within classrooms. Boards of trustees and principals are supported to set specific measurable goals for those students not currently being served well by the school. Teachers are supported to set individual goals in feedback sessions following formal observations in their classrooms, and group goals during collaborative co-construction meetings. Students are supported to set goals based on examinations of their performance.

2. The need to promote and support pedagogic reform

Effective leadership for sustainable educational reform promotes and is responsive to the development and implementation of pedagogic relationships and interactions in the classrooms that promote the reduction of educational disparities through improvements in student learning and achievement. Effective leaders do this by providing and/ or supporting the means/process of professional learning for teachers that allows embedding the conceptual depth of the reform into the theorising and practice of classroom teachers, principals and national policy makers. Teachers' conceptual depth of the theoretical principles that underlie the reform is a major indicator of sustainability.

As we identified in Chapter Three, teachers and school leaders who have a deep understanding of the underlying theories and principles and who can implement appropriate practices are better able to respond flexibly to new demands and changing contexts in ways that will sustain and perhaps deepen the reform over time. Reform without depth of understanding will trivialise the initiative, and teachers and schools will soon revert to old explanations and practices. Two of the dimensions of leadership identified by Robinson et al. (2009) support this understanding. The first is that which "involves leadership of effective teaching, including how to improve and evaluate it, along with skills in developing collegial discussions on instructional matters" (p. x). Their empirical analysis shows this dimension to have a moderate impact on student outcomes. It includes such activities as:

• leaders being actively involved in collegial discussions on how teaching practice affects student achievement

- an active oversight and co-ordination of the teaching programme
- involvement in teacher observation and feedback
- leading staff to systematically monitor student progress to inform their ongoing teaching programme.

Coupled with this dimension is a focus on promoting and participating in teacher learning and development. This dimension includes actions such as leaders using their own knowledge to help staff solve teaching problems, and working directly with teachers or subject department heads to plan, co-ordinate and evaluate the impact of teachers and teaching on student learning and achievement through the monitoring of student progress in relation to what is being taught and how it is being taught.

It is also important that leaders are seen to be learners themselves as an integral part of the whole learning process. The evidence gathered by Robinson et al. (2009) showed that:

> leaders who are actively involved in professional learning gain a deeper appreciation of what teachers require to achieve and sustain improvements in student learning, which enables them to discuss the changes with teachers and support them in making appropriate adjustments to class organisation, resourcing and assessment procedures. (p. xi)

In short, the more leaders focus their relationships, their work and their learning on the core business of teaching and learning, the greater their influence on student outcomes will be.

The New American Schools project (Berends et al., 2003) found that principals' involvement in planning, co-ordinating and supporting teaching was the single most significant contributing factor to project implementation by the classroom teacher. Principals take an active role in classroom-level implementation of reform through ensuring the effective use of formative assessment. They also facilitate curriculum coherence, which in Robinson's (2007) terms means that "common objectives and assessment tools make it easier for teachers to focus on teaching problems and make a more sustained effort to develop or acquire the expertise needed to solve them" (p. 15). Principals help teachers to judge their own performance relative to goals through classroom observations and feedback. Among the characteristics of effective principal leadership were the clear expression of expectations, supported by adequate resources, a personal interest in the project's professional development and a willingness to engage in pedagogic discussion with teachers. The project found a positive correlation between teacher implementation and teacher perception of principal leadership. There were further positive correlations between these factors and improved levels of children's achievement. Implementation was, however, impeded by high principal turnover, even where the new principal was supportive of the project (Berends et al., 2003).

Effective principals in this project ensured there was immediate and accessible advice available to teachers (Berends et al., 2003). Teachers also reported that the in-school professional development facilitators were more likely to gain professional respect from their colleagues than were outside advisers, because as immediate colleagues they had already demonstrated their professional credibility. Teachers were more likely to accept their advice and also regarded them as a source of motivation. Similarly, Farrell (2003) found that in his Comprehensive School Reform programme, called Expeditionary Learning, the single most significant predictor of success was the principal's understanding and commitment to the programme. In successful schools, commitment was demonstrated by a willingness to remain in the school and lead the project for five years or more.

Creating, promoting and developing professional learning communities

According to Robinson (2007), "[s]uccessful leadership influences teaching and learning through both face-to-face relationships and by structuring the way that teachers do their work" (p. 10). Creating and sustaining effective school-wide professional learning communities would appear to be a critically important function of leadership. A professional learning community in this sense is an inclusive group of people, motivated by a shared learning vision, who support and work with each other and who find ways—inside and outside their immediate community—to inquire about their practice and together learn new and better approaches that will enhance all pupils' learning (Stoll, & Seashore Louis, 2007).

The Chicago Annenberg Challenge (Smylie et al., 2003) found that professional learning communities of teachers foster successful project implementation by providing opportunities for reflection, inquiry, collaboration and productive "intellectual tensions". Successful schools exhibited orderly conduct, strong school–community relationships, a well placed and co-ordinated curriculum that extends beyond basic skills to "challenging intellectual work", and where "instructional time is protected from interruption" (pp. 142–143).

The professional learning community will not develop of its own accord, and is necessarily a product of leadership. It must be consciously created, and thoughtfully and systematically sustained. Consideration needs to be given to ways of incorporating meetings into school routine without additional cost and without closing the school for the duration of the meeting (DuFour, 1998). This emphasises the need for the reform to be placed at the centre of school routine, such that the necessity of each school meeting can be assessed against its contribution to the reform. Schools might then consider prioritising meeting agendas in terms of their contribution to reform goals. In order to do this, Holloman et al. (2007) suggest that they "[m]ake sure that there are no committees [or meetings] within your school's organizational structure that have no purpose. Aimless committees [and meetings] represent a lack of organization and can promote misalignment" (p. 440).

Robinson and Timperley (2007), referencing Bolam, McMahon, Stoll, Thomas, and Wallace's (2005) work, warn that there is little evidence that professional learning communities have a strong impact on student outcomes unless they promote "the type of teacher learning that makes a difference to their students" through "an intensive focus on the relationship between what the teacher had taught and what the students had learned" (p. 11). By this it is meant that in these professional learning communities leaders not only supply or demonstrate how teachers can obtain evidence of student participation and learning, but also lead collaborative problem-solving and decision-making discussions about the relationship between teaching practice and student outcomes based on collaborative analysis of this evidence. In other words, leaders focus "the group on how to move beyond analysis of the data to identifying specific teaching practices to help a particular student or group of students" (Robinson & Timperley, 2007, p. 12). In this role leaders are facilitators of student learning rather than leaders of collegial discussions.

3. The need to redesign the institutional and organisational framework

Leaders need to create opportunities for connections to, and collaboration with, other teachers engaged in the reform. As we have seen, the institutionalisation of a means to ensure that this happens in a systematic way is an essential element of sustaining change. Such institutionalisations need to be prioritised so that they are seen to support the efforts of teachers and are aligned with, and indeed can inform, school policies and strategic plans. Effective leadership that aims to sustain an educational reform needs to strategically promote and align organisational and structural changes with the need to embed the reform within the everyday practices of the school. This will include changing timetables, meeting times and agendas, staff recruitment procedures, staff promotion criteria, the provision of support and space for in-school professional development staff, the establishment of permanent positions for professional development staff in the school, the reshaping of the role of the heads of departments and the reshaping of the composition of the senior management team to include senior professional developers, among others.

New Zealand schools are self-managing. Responsibility for operational decisions, including the provision of professional learning opportunities for the staff of the school, has been devolved to the governance of boards of trustees. This includes the provision and allocation of funds from schools' budgets for the ongoing provision of professional learning opportunities for staff. The prioritising of the allocation of a significant amount of funding that could be directed towards sustaining the reform, once the externally generated support and funding are withdrawn, is thus in the hands of New Zealand schools.

Current evidence from the Te Kotahitanga programme (Bishop et al., 2007), based on our five-year study of facilitating teachers to implement changes in classroom relationships and interactions, shows that gains in teacher competence in the practices that are fundamental to the implementation of the Effective Teaching Profile continue to be made over time. It follows that if these gains are to continue and remain, it is important to maintain the facilitated activities that support these gains: the formal term-by-term cycle of observations, feedback, co-construction meetings and shadow coaching, supplemented by ongoing content and strategy workshops.

These conditions mean that, for Te Kotahitanga, once the external support has been withdrawn from the school, the professional development, Cycle Plus,[1] needs to be maintained within the schools, with its attendant staffing and organisational support. For leaders, this means they will need to (re)prioritise and rationalise resource expenditure. For some this will involve conflict as previous resource allocations are challenged, but alignment of resource allocation to the visions and goals of the school is necessary, and unless resource procurement and allocation are strategically handled, the reform will face great challenges and will probably remain as a "project" on the periphery of the school's activities rather than being centralised, as is necessary for success.

4. The role of effective leaders in spreading the reform

Effective leadership that aims to sustain an educational reform needs to develop a means to spread the reform so that parents, whānau and community are engaged in a way that addresses their aspirations for the education of their children. Through these actions we would expect to see a reconnection of parents and families with the educational advancement of their children, and an enormous change in the life chances and lifestyles of those people currently underserved by the education system. Communicating the intentions of the reform and signalling that the school is prepared to be accountable to the community are necessary steps in promoting effective relationships with the community. One way this is done in Te Kotahitanga is for the schools to hold annual staff induction workshops at local marae, hosted by local Māori families. At these events there are opportunities for the leaders, both formally and informally, to inform the local community, in a very convivial setting, of their intentions to develop and/or persist with the goal of raising the achievement of their children.

Communication of the outcomes of the reform in terms of raised student achievement is also important on a regular basis. Again we find that when students begin to achieve well at school, parents who have previously been absent from parent–teacher report meetings, for example, become only too visible. This visibility then begins to be seen in other activities of the school's life. Success attracts success. Principals and other teacher leaders can help the wider school community to understand the changes that are needed to strengthen teaching and learning. Research undertaken by Poutama Pounamu, detailed in Chapter Seven, illustrates how effective home and school relationships can further promote student learning.

Leaders need to spread the reform to others, within and outside the school, so as to align the new norms of the reform within the school, within the norms of supporting institutions and within communities in association with the school. Spreading the reform to include all staff can pose problems and is something that needs to be undertaken

---

1 See Chapter One for details of this process.

with care. Holloman et al. (2007) propose a "purpose-driven" leadership model, which requires an organisation to "define its purpose, maintain integrity … prevent burnout and sustain vitality" (p. 438). The model supposes a school culture in which there is constant reflection on why certain methodologies are favoured over others. Leithwood and Riehl (2003) suggest that educational improvement often means making personal changes to the way responses have been undertaken in the past, and in order to achieve this, effective principals must respect staff and show they are concerned for their feelings. Therefore, as Bolman and Deal (2003) note, effective leaders need to learn how to cope with power and conflict, and how to build coalitions, hone their political skills and deal with internal and external politics.

A questioning culture is one that will best support such developments. It is a way of challenging people more inclined to being negative about a reform to refocus their attention on constructive criticism that "could more clearly define the purpose of the school". In turn, refocusing resistance can foster "purposeful dialogue" (Holloman et al., 2007, p. 438). However, these ideas presuppose reform that is theoretically well informed and supported by valid empirical data. Robinson (2007) considers that "[p]eople cannot adapt descriptions of effective practice to their own contexts unless they understand the theoretical principles that explain why they work and under what conditions". Further, "[i]t is the combination of description, practical example and theoretical explanation that makes for powerful professional learning" (p. 5). To this end, leaders are reliant on robust evidence to support the direction of the reform initiative (see below). This means that any attempts to weaken the connection between research and practice can be expected to seriously compromise school leaders' capacity to support sustainable reform. Whatever the case, it is important that as many teachers as possible are included in the reform, because "effective professional development is likely to involve teachers investigating pedagogy and analysing data within their own settings" (Alton-Lee, 2004, p. 10), and because "quality of teaching is critical to … a shift" in student achievement (p. 4).

5. Effective leaders develop the capacity of people and systems to identify, gather and use evidence

"Effective leaders assess how well the school is performing, ask critical and constructive questions, emphasize the use of systematic evidence and encourage careful monitoring of pupils' progress" (Leithwood & Riehl, 2003, cited in Atkinson, 2006, p. 7). Fundamental to Collins's (2001) study of what moves an organisation from good to great is the understanding that effective leaders work continuously to select the right people, and to support and develop them. For example, Te Kotahitanga professional development facilitators as leaders of professional learning develop the capacity of teachers to identify and continually question their discursive positioning and theories of action by providing professional learning opportunities that use alternative theories, evidence and vicarious experiences. Leaders also provide the necessary resources and tools for teachers to be able to engage effectively with the reform goals and processes. Robinson et al. (2009) note that leaders of sustainable educational reform are able to reshape the situation in which they work so that others can learn to do their job strategically by selecting, developing and using tools that will assist their own learning and promote student learning. They found that these tools include physical qualities such as classroom furniture and smart whiteboards. However, of primary importance is what they termed "smart tools", which include software for student management systems to provide teachers with differentiated data about student attendance and achievement, formative assessment packages such as asTTle and PAT, schools' strategic plans, policy documents and the means of reporting student progress to the students, their families and the community.

Leaders also support the use of reform-specific smart tools such as those that enable teachers to critically reflect on their practice and theorise in such a way as to bring about changes in practice. One such example from Te Kotahitanga (elaborated in Chapter Two) is the PSIRPEG model, which, following the intervention elements of observations, feedback, co-construction and shadow coaching, affords teachers the opportunity to *plan* for their next learning activities, choose appropriate *strategies*, identify appropriate *interactions*, identify the *relationships* that are likely to develop the *positionings* that will be supported and the positive student *experiences* that will lead to reaching the *goals* of improved student achievement.

As Te Kotahitanga grows and develops in each school, systemic and institutional developments are necessary to support the changes taking place in the classroom. An area that needs to be developed is that of accurately measuring student attendance data, stand-downs, suspensions, early-leaving exemptions, retention rates and achievement data. There are two reasons for this. First, it allows teachers the opportunity to reflect collaboratively on these data to inform their ongoing practice. Second, they can use the same data for summative purposes to identify if there is a relationship between the implementation of the educational reform in question and positive changes in student participation and achievement. In order for these objectives to be met, it is important that the project schools be able to undertake the task of data gathering and processing in real time. To do so they will need to continue to develop the use of electronic student management systems so that the schools can use the data for formative purposes in collaborative settings, and then aggregate the data for summative purposes.

Probably more important than the systems for providing the evidence on the basis of which teachers can collaboratively make practice-changing decisions is the need for capacity building, in the sense of leaders of the reform providing professional learning opportunities for teachers to learn how to both identify and gather appropriate evidence for learning, and to be able to use evidence of student learning to ascertain where and how to modify their classroom practice through the ongoing provision of appropriate and responsive professional learning opportunities.

6. Leaders take ownership of the project

Effective leadership that aims to sustain an educational reform takes ownership of the reform. The first characteristic of ownership is a leader taking responsibility for the performance of students who are currently not benefiting from their school/system. This involves careful disaggregation of data to identify the learning outcomes of specific groups of students and the implementation of processes to ensure this information is disseminated and acted upon. To do so, leaders must work towards building a school culture that focuses on an ongoing reduction in educational disparities through the ongoing improvement of student learning and outcomes. To ensure *this* happens in an ongoing way, leaders must take responsibility for ensuring that the integrity of the means of producing increased achievement gains for the target students (such as the Cycle Plus and the facilitation teams in the Te Kotahitanga project) is not jeopardised by conflicting and competing interests and agendas.

Leaders also need to take responsibility for building capacity among students, staff and other leaders so that they are able to take responsibility for student outcomes, rather than focusing solely on accountability systems. This aspect of leadership is often at odds with national policies that limit the time available to develop support for the development of in-school capacity. Nevertheless, persistence in pursuit of the goals of reducing disparities is the hallmark of effective leadership. The unrelenting pursuit of goals that will also involve leaders in creating classrooms, a school culture and education systems where new situations are addressed from an in-depth understanding of the reform's aims and approaches rather than from past practice is crucial. Past practices have led us to a situation of educational disparities being based on ethnic lines. Effective leaders express their dissatisfaction with this situation and are prepared to own the consequences of promoting and sustaining educational reforms to reduce disparities through targeting and raising the achievement of students who are currently not well served by the education system.

Table 5.1 summarises the preceding discussion, which has been based on the GPILSEO model.

Table 5.1 GPILSEO: A summary of effective leadership

GPILSEO	Tasks associated with each GPILSEO element
*Leaders establish and develop specific measurable **goals** so that progress can be shown, monitored over time and acted upon.*	Leaders: • build from the dissonance that is created when the difference between the current reality and the desired state is highlighted • learn how to set smart goals for student participation and achievement in its widest sense • develop specific goals to ensure that all involved can judge their progress toward the goals and responsively adjust their practice or learning • have the capacity (self-belief) to meet goals from their current understanding, or be able to learn what is needed to meet the goals • communicate with others about performance in terms of goals

GPILSEO	Tasks associated with each GPILSEO element
*Leaders support the development and implementation of new **pedagogic** relationships and interactions in the classroom.*	• support the means of embedding the conceptual depth of the reform into the theorising and practice of the classroom teachers, principals and national administrators (teachers' conceptual depth is a major indicator of sustainability) • focus their relationships, their work and their learning on the core business of teaching and learning, which increases their influence on student outcomes • create learning contexts in which learners gain the capacity and self-belief that they will be able to meet goals from their current understandings, or will be able to learn what is needed to meet the goals • promote the cultural identity of learners as being fundamental to learning relations and interactions • engage in classroom observations and provide specific feedback and/ or co-construct with teachers ways to improve classroom practice • provide specific professional learning opportunities for the consolidation of content and strategy learning • create and sustain effective school-wide professional learning communities • build capacity for teachers to take collective responsibility for student outcomes and collective action for changing teaching practice based on student experiences and academic performance • ensure collective action for changing teaching practice is based on student experiences and academic performance
*Leaders change the **institutional** framework, its organisation and structure, to support the reform within the schools.*	• create opportunities for connections to, and collaboration with, other teachers (including teachers in other schools) engaged in similar reform • institutionalise the means for teacher collaborative decision making in a systematic manner • prioritise the establishment of new institutions so that they are seen to be supportive of the efforts of teachers and are aligned with school plans and policies, and which inform national policies • modify structural and organisational arrangements to accommodate new institutions (such as the Cycle Plus components of Te Kotahitanga) and staffing (re)allocations • (re)prioritise funding to support the ongoing implementation of the reform's professional learning processes beyond the initial project funding phase • ensure the reform is symbolically represented within the school
***Leaders** need to be knowledgeable about their role in the reform.*	• focus on improving the performance of those least well served by the system • have a sound understanding of the theoretical foundations of the reform and of what that theoretical basis means for classroom practice, school structure and culture • accept responsibility for student learning outcomes • demonstrate their understanding that: a) a focus on Māori has strong benefits for other students b) pedagogic leadership has powerful effects on student outcomes c) no one person can provide all leadership needs d) proactive, responsive and distributed leadership is essential for the sustainability of a reform in a school

GPILSEO	Tasks associated with each GPILSEO element
Leaders need to **spread** the reform to include all students, teachers and the community.	• spread the reform to others, within and outside the school, so as to align the new norms of the reform within the school and within the norms of supporting institutions, and within communities in association with the school • spread the reform so that parents, whānau and community are engaged in a manner that addresses their aspirations for the education of their children
Leaders develop the capacity of people and systems to produce and use **evidence** of student experiences and progress to inform change.	• develop the capacity of teachers to identify and continually question their own discursive positioning and theories of action • provide professional learning opportunities for teachers that use alternative theories, evidence and vicarious experiences • develop and grow systems in their schools that accurately measure student attendance data, stand-downs, suspensions, early-leaving exemptions, retention rates and achievement data for formative and summative purposes • develop the capacity of teachers to learn how to both create appropriate evidence for learning and use student evidence to modify their classroom practice
Leaders ensure that the **ownership** of and responsibility/ authority for the goals of the reform must shift to the school/system.	• identify and take responsibility for the performance of students who are currently not benefiting from their school/system • take responsibility for ensuring that the integrity of the means of producing increased achievement gains for the target students (the Cycle Plus and the facilitation teams) is not jeopardised by conflicting and competing interests and agendas • take responsibility for building capacity among students, staff and other leaders so that they are able to take responsibility for student outcomes • work towards building a school culture that focuses on an ongoing reduction of educational disparities through the raising of student learning and outcomes • work to create classrooms, a school culture and an education system in which new situations are addressed from an in-depth understanding of the reform's aims and approaches rather than from past practice.

Conclusion

On the one hand, leading school reform is difficult, basically because "[t]he complexity of interacting contextual variables ... is enormous" (Lindahl, 2007, p. 328). On the other hand, a great deal is known about the conditions that are necessary to support student learning, and this is a good starting point. Among the keys to sustainable reform is leadership that is cognisant of these conditions, and is willing to support the purpose of all school routines, procedures and practices and to shape a school culture centred on reform.

The fundamental changes that are needed in classroom relationships and interactions and in the culture of schools, through the institutionalisation of schools as professional learning communities focused on improving student learning, depend on leaders having a sound understanding of the theoretical underpinning of the reform while simultaneously being responsive and proactive about supporting and promoting reform processes and goals. To this end, principals' leadership is essential. However, principals' leadership to the exclusion of others is ineffective. Principals, therefore, in Kouzes and Posner's (2002) terms, need to inspire a shared vision, model the way forward, enable others to act and challenge the status quo.

Overall, a measure of the effectiveness of leadership will be seen in the actions and beliefs of teachers. Ineffectively led schools foster and support teachers who are likely "to attribute student achievement to global factors or student traits, such as experience and knowledge, socioeconomic conditions, inexperience with the English language, academic ability, lack of readiness and inadequate parental involvement" (McDougal et al., 2007, p. 74). Effectively led schools are characterised by teachers who attribute "student achievement toward specific, teacher-implemented, instructional actions and planning processes, and away from teacher and student traits, and non-instructional explanations" (p. 74). In other words, effective leaders support and foster committed, agentic educators.

In the next chapter we will focus on spreading the reform, and in particular, those aspects of spread that affect students' immediate schooling experiences.

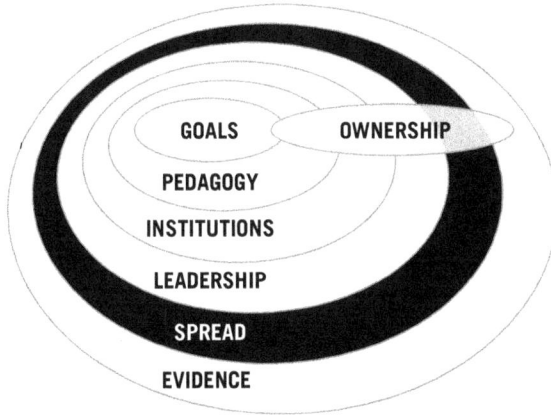

CHAPTER SIX

Spread

... spread not only involves increasing the number of schools that participate, but also the ways in which reform norms and principles influence district policies, procedures, and professional development.
(Coburn, 2003, p. 7)

Introduction

As we found very early on in our experiences with implementing Te Kotahitanga, attempts to improve Māori student achievement were severely limited when we only worked with a small number of teachers in a small number of schools. What we did find was that, together, we and the teachers were able to effect change in student participation, engagement with learning and achievement in classrooms where we were able to offer appropriate professional learning opportunities and in-class support for these teachers. However, we also found that the teachers in the project became isolated within their schools and distanced from their colleagues, and were tempted to leave the school looking for other settings where they felt their new practices would be appreciated. This situation also affected the behaviour and learning of the students, in that they were positive in the project teachers' classrooms but negative in their other classrooms.

This was obviously an unsatisfactory situation, and it rapidly became clear that we needed to increase the number of teachers involved in the project so that the improvements seen in the project teachers' classrooms could be replicated across schools. This quantitative *spread* in the number of teachers and schools involved in the reform is clearly crucial for bringing about the changes in classroom relationships and interactions that result in improvements in Māori student participation, engagement and achievement, because it provides students with a regular pattern from classroom to classroom. Coburn (2003) argues that the commonest approaches to scaling up education reforms in the research literature focus on replication: "increasing the number of teachers, schools or districts involved" (p. 3). She quotes Stringfield and Datnow (1998), who provide "an admirably concise formulation of the dominant view" (p. 4) when they define scaling up as "the deliberate expansion to many settings of an externally developed school restructuring design that previously has been used successfully in one or a small number of school settings" (p. 271, cited in Coburn, 2003, p. 4).

Just as we found with our own attempts to expand the project to more classrooms and schools in 2003, concern about the numbers involved is vital, because this is clearly how we will see the necessary changes in national statistics of disparity. However, there is also a qualitative shift that takes place, and this is, as Coburn (2003) notes, where the norms of the reform are spread beyond the initial classrooms to influence the depth of teachers' understanding of pedagogic interactions so that they can respond to new demands and changing contexts. There are also qualitative changes that take place in the institutional and organisational arrangements within the schools, leadership, the uses made of information gathered about student participation and progress and "the degree to which schools and teachers have the knowledge and authority to continue to grow the reform over time" (p. 4). This pattern of what Coburn (2003) terms "normative coherence" means that the fundamental practices and principles of the reform need to be present across the school: not only in classroom practices but also in the institutional and organisational frameworks, leadership practices, the use made of evidence of student activities, policy making and activities outside the classroom and the location of responsibility and authority for the goals of the reform.

In addition to the qualitative changes that take place at the classroom and school levels, the norms and underlying beliefs of the reform need to be spread to those people beyond the boundaries of schools, and these include parents and community members, project developers and policy makers. At the national policy level, which is considered in detail in Chapter Nine, spread involves increasing the number of schools involved in the reform as well as consideration of how the reform principles might become embedded in national policies.

In this chapter we will consider those aspects of spread that affect students' immediate schooling experiences, including classrooms, the school and the community, in order to identify what it means for reforms to become part of the total world of the students. It is our contention that unless there are changes in all aspects of the current status quo pertaining to educational inequalities, we cannot expect to see major changes taking place in the patterns of inequality in our schools and society.

Spread of the reform is a fundamental necessity for sustainability to ensure an alignment of the new norms of the reform within the schools, their supporting institutions and beyond. One major implication of this is that the conditions that pertain at one level of the reform—be it within the classroom, the school or the system—should pertain at all other levels of the reform. In other words, the mode of implementation, the relationships established and the interactions developed should be replicated at each level of the reform. For example, the relationships developed between classroom teachers and children should be of the same order as those between teachers and professional developers, between principal and staff, between teachers, parents and community members and between schools, policy makers and researchers.

Spread of the reform to include families and communities is also fundamental to its success, and again the guide to the types of relationships and interactions should be those that are developed as a central part of the reform. At a wider level, integration with existing and developing reform initiatives—such as national assessment packages, literature, video instructional materials and interactive use of information technology through the development of coherence between schools and national authorities—is also vital for sustainability and scalability. At this wider level, national policy initiatives should lead and be informed by reform developments.

Spread within schools

Within schools, the reform initiative must contain a means of spreading more than just classroom strategies, materials and activities. It must also contain a means of spreading the underlying beliefs, norms and principles of the reform to additional classrooms and schools; that is, both to the teachers involved in the reform and to nonproject teachers. In this sense, spread is not just a matter of quantitative expansion, but rather of identifying how the fundamental principles of the reform can influence teachers' other classrooms and draw in other teachers. Of immediate importance is that teachers be able to spread the use of the initiative beyond the specific classrooms in which they are receiving assistance and support to all of their teaching and decision-making processes.

Such a process will contribute to developing a normative coherence for students within the school, and will further increase the likelihood of the reform maintaining traction. However, just as it is unlikely that teachers will be able to implement new teaching practices on their own, one cannot expect teachers to spread their new knowledge about classroom practices to new and different settings without considerable and considered formal support in their other classrooms. Secondary school teachers, for example, often teach a number of different subjects across a range of age and ability levels, and it is unrealistic to expect them to spread their new practices, carefully nurtured in one setting, to others without considered review and support, both by professional support staff and through institutionalised support from their peers.

Spreading an educational reform to include all of the staff in a school is sometimes problematic because there is a danger that teachers will see reform as just another fashion, which, like all other fashions, will be short lived and soon replaced by another. Teachers, not surprisingly, are likely to see reforms in this way because:

> More so than any other profession, education seems fraught with innovation. Each year new programs are introduced in schools without any effort to show how they relate to the ones that came before or those that may come afterward. Furthermore, there is seldom any mention of how these various innovations contribute to a growing professional knowledge base. The result is an enormous overload of fragmented, uncoordinated, and ephemeral attempts at change. (Guskey, 1995, p. 124)

With this caution in mind, schools need to address the implementation of an innovation in their own ways. Nonetheless, there are a number of general principles that will help leaders' deliberations and decision making about spread. Hall and Hord (2006) argue that there are patterns to the adoption of an innovation—some people adopt an innovation quickly, while others take longer—and this pattern can be of great use to innovators keen to spread the reform to include as many staff as possible. They suggest the following pattern of adoption:

- *innovators:* These are the very first people to adopt an innovation. They often enjoy change, and because they are often very active in their profession they are attuned to the problem the reform is seeking to address.
- *early adopters:* This group of people adopt ideas very quickly, but only after reasoned consideration. They are well respected locally and tend to have been in the school for

some time. They are seen as solid, reliable and sensible decision makers. Once they adopt an innovation, others will tend to look more favourably on it.

- *early majority:* The members of this group are more deliberate and take time to weigh up the innovation. They are often well connected but with less likelihood of having positions of influence. This group, however, represents a large majority of the potential adopters of the reform.
- *late majority:* Members of this group are late to adopt and tend to do so only when there is some pressure from others or the need to adopt becomes very strong. They tend to want to avoid risk due to their concern about failure.
- *laggards:* Perhaps this could be seen as a pejorative term, but it describes the fact that members of this group are slow, and even resistant to adopting new ideas. They tend to be more conservative, professionally isolated, and overall resistant to change (Hall & Hord, 2006, pp. 71–72).

This kind of analysis is useful because it highlights the obvious fact that not all teachers are the same and that they will come to a reform with different backgrounds and experiences, and will adopt the innovation in different ways. What this means for innovators is, as Wheatley and Frieze (2006) suggest, "the world doesn't change one person at a time. It changes as networks of relationships form among people who discover they share a common cause and vision of what's possible" (p. 1).

For innovators, this means that rather than worry about it being their sole responsibility to spread the innovation, we need to foster critical connections with kindred spirits, and it is through these relationships that we will "develop the new knowledge, practices, courage and commitment that lead to broad-based changes" (Wheatley & Frieze, 2006, p. 1). In other words, as Hall and Hord (2006) note, the key is communication with, and among, as many of the adoption categories as possible through a variety of approaches, such as the following:

- Repeat messages often.
- Use existing communication channels.
- Identify opinion leaders and ensure they support the innovation.
- Initially focus on the first three categories of adopters—leave the others till later.
- Take time to socialise with opinion leaders—don't be all barriers.
- Be alert to interpersonal connections.
- Use a variety of media for communication.

Above all, the emphasis should be on creating networks through organising communication and implementation of the reform components. It is also vital for sustainability that when a school adopts an innovation, it signals that it is in for the long haul and that it is not just a trial. It is also essential that the components of the innovation be institutionalised as soon as possible so that the early adopters and early majority can begin to help spread the reform to others with the clear knowledge that this is the way the school will be organised in the future.

Once this security is provided, the innovation can proceed. Interestingly, change is not linear. Hall and Hord (2006) do not suggest that there is a progression through the five categories of adopters. Rather, adoption comes about through processes such as those identified by Wheatley and Frieze (2006) as "emergence", and what Gladwell (2000) calls the "tipping point". Emergence describes a process of change that begins as local actions that spring up simultaneously in many different areas. It is when these actions become connected that local actions can emerge as a powerful system with influence at a more comprehensive level. Hence the importance of creating interlocking networks of like-minded people, or people trying to address the learning needs of a common group of students via the development of professional learning communities. For example, from the simultaneous creation of shared experiences, and networked examples of the innovation in practice, a powerful system of influence will emerge suddenly, and what was once an innovation will rapidly become the accepted norm within the school.[1]

Gladwell (2000) describes the tipping point as that "magic moment when ideas, trends and social behaviours cross a threshold, tip and spread like wildfire" (p. xi)—the moment when adoption grows exponentially. Like the authors mentioned above, Gladwell argues that it is the early adoption by a few exceptional, committed people who have connections, networks, energy, enthusiasm and personality to communicate with others about the benefits of the innovation that makes the difference. This is Gladwell's "Law of the Few". He also suggests that there is "the stickiness" factor at work: innovators need to spend considerable time ensuring the "message makes an impact" (p. 25). And of course, as Schmoker (1999) insists, nothing succeeds like success, hence the need for results. The third consideration Gladwell identifies is "[t]he power of context" (p. 29), which means that innovators need to create contexts in which all participants are enabled to care personally and individually about the problem the innovation seeks to address. In this way, no individual can pass responsibility on to others in the group or school staff.

Although these considerations are concerned with increasing the number of teachers involved in the reform initiative, of equal importance is that spread at the school level not only involves more and more classrooms and teachers, but also "reform principles or norms of social interaction becoming embedded in school policy and routines" (Coburn, 2003, p. 7). To McLaughlin and Mitra (2001), this form of scaling means not only spreading reform practices across subject areas, but also applying reform principles to a selection of new materials, to reconstruct approaches to student assessment and evaluate discipline. This notion of scale not only means that the reform affects classroom practices: "it also means that the changed practices signify, emerge from, and reinforce layers of knowledge, norms, and activities that constitute a whole professional practice or the workings of a whole organization" (p. 315).

---

1   Emergence and tipping points are also important considerations when expanding the reform to other schools.

For example, the caring and learning relationships developed within Te Kotahitanga classrooms should inform the development of relationships outside the classroom. School-wide discipline policies and practices need to match those being developed in the project classrooms to provide consistency and coherence to students and teachers. In other words, school policies need to ensure that approaches to problem solving are familiar to staff and students and are informed by practices and principles developed elsewhere in the project.

One Phase 3 principal spoke to us about a problem that had been drawn to their attention following a recent visit to their school by the Education Review Office (ERO).[2] The ERO team had identified that although relationships were excellent in the classroom, these in-class relationships between teachers and Māori students were not as evident outside the classroom. One piece of evidence, apart from observations, that highlighted this situation was the greater number of incidents leading to stand-downs and suspensions that were originating from outside the classroom, compared to there being very few originating from within the classroom.

This caused the school's leaders to evaluate the external discipline policies of the school, which were based on the affirmative action discipline programme in relation to the discipline practices and principles of Te Kotahitanga. They identified that under the assertive discipline approach, too many Māori students were being caught up in punitive judgements, leading to stand-downs and suspensions. These outcomes were out of proportion to both their demographic representation as a group and also to their low representation in classroom incidents. They moved to investigate the potential efficacy of introducing restorative justice, which is an approach based on promoting quality, caring relationships. In line with Te Kotahitanga, the principal sought external expertise from a member of the Te Kotahitanga team to help teachers to work with the new policy and approach to discipline in a way that was consistent with Te Kotahitanga practices and principles. She explained that:

> We needed more skills—we grow them in the classroom with Te Kotahitanga … now we are going to grow these skills in regard to behaviour [outside the classroom]. Just as you co-construct learning relationships in your classrooms, with a restorative justice programme, you can co-construct behaviour in other settings.

Spreading the reform to more schools

As we have seen, the traditional view of expanding or spreading educational reforms tends to focus on the scale up of an externally developed reform in quantitative terms that talks of increasing the number of teachers, schools and regions. Most attempts at scaling up are seen in terms of this definition, other considerations being whether

---

2   The Education Review Office is a formal government agency that visits schools on a triannual rotation to identify how effectively the school is addressing government policy.

the expansion is by way of replication, mutual adaptation or including schools in a bounded geographic location. In short, to Coburn (2003), "the problem of scale tends to be framed, at least explicitly, as the problem of increasing the numbers of teachers, schools, or districts involved in a reform" (ibid.).

However, Coburn (2003) considers that this conceptualisation of scaling up reform— that is, expanding a reform to multiple settings—may be a necessary but not a sufficient condition for conceptualising scale. In other words, she considers that scaling up not only requires expansion of the reform to additional sites, but also giving consideration to "consequential changes in classrooms, endurance over time, and a shift such that knowledge and authority for the reform is transferred from external organisation to teachers, schools, and districts" (p. 4). In this way, the approach to scaling the reform will more properly address the complexity and multidimensionality of implementing educational reform.

In order to address this qualitative aspect of scaling up a reform, we have expanded on Coburn's (2003) original four elements and developed the GPILSEO model that is the subject of this book. It is our contention that reforms that have these seven elements built into them from their very inception will provide additional schools with an educational reform programme that is sustainable and effective in terms of addressing the goals of addressing educational disparities through raising targeted students' achievement.

The inclusion of families and communities

In 1997 the Ministry of Education and Te Puni Kōkiri (the Ministry of Māori Development) conducted widespread consultation with Māori communities on what could be done to improve education for Māori. A key message from that consultation was that Māori parents and whānau want the best for their children from the education system. Even though some parents said that they did not feel confident about approaching schools because of their own negative educational experiences, they did want to play a more active role in their children's education. Māori parents want to have a greater say in the education of their children, and they want schools to be more accountable and responsive to their concerns.

Where parents are incorporated into the education of their children on terms they can understand and approve of, then children do better at school (McNaughton & Glynn, 1998). This contention is well supported by research; for example, the Mangere Home and School project (McNaughton, Glynn, Robinson, & Quinn, 1981), which supported parents to effectively assist their children's reading at home, shows clearly that where parents are engaged and involved in the education of their children, children achieve better at school. This feature also has implications for better and less problematic home-to-school transitions. In other words, the closer the classroom experiences are to the home experiences for students, the more likely it will be that students will be able to participate in the educational experiences designed at the school. This helps to address the preference Māori people have for their problems to be dealt with in culturally familiar ways. Such understanding carries a major message for the way schools and teachers deal with people of all cultures.

Many teachers and Māori parents believe that young people do best when their families and whānau are actively involved in their schools, and that more Māori involvement in schools is likely to lead to enhanced Māori achievement. There are potentially many benefits for schools, Māori children and Māori communities if parents and whānau become involved in all aspects of school life, from management to classroom activities. Those benefits include higher student self-esteem and higher educational achievement (Ministry of Education, 1995).

In a set of guidelines for boards of trustees and schools for engaging with parents, whānau and communities (Ministry of Education, 2005a), a series of suggestions was offered based on the experiences of a number of schools. The schools contributing to these guidelines used a wide range of techniques to build relationships with Māori parents and whānau, and to develop a constructive environment in which to discuss and resolve problems. The most successful schools were guided by a set of underlying common characteristics:

- a strong leadership team
- a powerful school vision
- understanding and responding to the educational needs of Māori communities
- long-term strategies for change
- being prepared to change
- managing relationships proactively
- understanding how best to consult with Māori.

Collaboration between home and school

Home and school collaborations with Māori were prioritised as a central goal under National Education Goals 2000. Since then, collaborations between schools and their Māori communities have increased (Durie, 2006), and in 2004 ERO found that schools were increasingly focusing their collaborations on improving achievement. However, it remained true that only 56 percent of primary schools informed their communities of their policies, plans and targets for Māori achievement, while only 53 percent had reviewed the effectiveness of their communication with their Māori communities (Education Review Office, 2004).

Collaborative programmes should be based "on structured, specific suggestions rather than general advice, and on supportive group opportunities as well as opportunities for one-to-one contact, especially informal contact" (Biddulph, Biddulph, & Biddulph, 2003, p. vi). When home–school collaborations are effective, the impact "can be so substantial, compared to traditional institutionally-based educational interventions" (p. 143). Home–school collaborations are complex and can also be counterproductive, but it is the more structured collaborations that seem to be more successful.

Collaborations are supported by empowerment, or enhancement theory, which maintains that families' and children's strengths and expertise can be the basis for extension (Biddulph et al., 2003). These authors also explain that deficit, difference and empowerment theories "tend to reflect the differences between (i) 'experts' knowing what is best for families and children, and (ii) people with expertise working with families and communities in true collaboration to promote children's development and learning" (Biddulph et al., 2003, p. 10). They do, however, caution against the tendency of some studies to use the terms "empowerment" and "partnership" as "rhetoric to make efforts to control" (pp. 10–11). Control is unproductive because it arises from assumptions of family deficiencies, which simply produce a stand-off between home and the school (Durie, 2001, p. 6), especially where schools' understanding of how collaborative relationships should operate may "contain culturally-bound assumptions about good parenting" (Vincent, 1996, p. 47).

Culturally responsive relationships

The spread of the principles of the reform to include families can also ease the home-to-school transition by lessening the distance between home and school experiences, such that the schooling of, for example, Māori children is more likely to be located in a familiar cultural context (Bishop & Glynn, 1999). Scribner, Young, and Pedroza (1999) found that schools' understanding of home values characterised successful Hispanic schools in the USA. Teachers in these schools, who were largely not themselves Hispanic, took time to inform themselves of the cultural norms of the children they taught—their "funds of knowledge" (Moll, 1992). Successful Hispanic schools encouraged parents to "take part in their children's education within a cultural context that transcends home and school" (Scribner et al., 1999, p. 53). In this way, effective communication was fostered between the two. Successful Hispanic schools view this kind of communication as essential to their success.

Scribner et al. (1999) identified one example of different school and home cultural understanding in predominantly Hispanic schools in the USA, where teachers perceived parental involvement in schooling as being properly concerned with the educational process. Parents, however, were more concerned with participating in their children's schooling to support the "total well-being" of the child (Scribner et al., 1999, p. 37). The difference resulted in a contrasting emphasis on the valuable characteristics of parental involvement. Parents saw their participation as contributing to "enhancing the school environment, building and strengthening relationships, showing concern for the development of the child, providing role models for the child and accruing benefits for oneself" (Scribner et al., 1999, p. 41). School staff believed that participation should contribute to "increasing student achievement, building and strengthening relationships, creating a community environment, garnering support and assistance, and providing parent education" (ibid.).

To address such differences, Brooks and Kavanaugh (1999) make three recommendations concerning spread through school–community relations for teachers' professional development. Professional development should:

- consider the "cultural and economic characteristics of the communities"
- "recognise the dynamic changing nature of the communities themselves"
- "empower not only school staff, but the entire community if it is to move the schools away from dependency and toward leadership" (p. 91).

One New Zealand model for institutionalising school–community partnerships in a responsive manner is Te Pūtahitanga Mātauranga, a partnership between iwi in the Northland region and the Ministry of Education. The project involved 78 schools and was intended to improve the quality of education in these schools, improve access to and participation in the Māori language and improve the levels of Māori participation and influence in education. It was believed that these three goals were preconditions for the realisation of the project's ultimate purpose of sustainably raising Māori achievement in the region (Hohepa & Jenkins, 2004). By 2004 the partnership had seen the development of relationships "with schools and boards that have involved identifying areas of need and areas of development". These relationships included the development of eight specific initiatives or projects, three of which had been operating for at least one year (Hohepa & Jenkins, 2004).

Initially the partnership was met in some communities with a degree of cynicism and mistrust, but its kaupapa Māori approach, which involved gathering information about schooling from the community, helped to lessen that initial suspicion (Hohepa & Jenkins, 2004). The partnership established the expectation that communities would participate in the development of education plans to address educational needs identified by the communities themselves. Planning processes focused on whānau and community learning rather than on schools, given that raising Māori student achievement was being understood in relation to changing the attitudes and behaviours of parents to schooling, and addressing the parents' own learning needs (Hohepa & Jenkins, 2004).

Community and school collaboration

Research that describes the merging of roles and responsibilities of a community (whānau, immediate and extended family), a kura kaupapa Māori (Māori immersion school), its students and a researcher was reported as part of a community-initiated programme to improve students' transition from a Māori-language educational setting to a bilingual secondary school (Berryman, 2001; Berryman & Glynn, 2003). The researcher became a part of this community when she was invited to help in the development of a suitable programme to assist a group of fluent Māori immersion students to begin their bilingual secondary schooling (the only option available in their community). Prior to this programme few of these students had received any formal instruction in English. This situation had severely compromised the educational opportunities for previous graduates from this kura at their transition to secondary school. The community wanted their children to achieve at secondary school. They wanted their children to begin their secondary schooling with an improved competence in reading and writing in English, but without compromising their competence in Māori language.

After a 10-week intervention, devised and undertaken by this community and kura, with the researcher being responsive to their suggestions, it was found that tutors had efficiently implemented the literacy programmes and that all Year 8 students were able to read English journal stories and talk about them at age-appropriate reading levels. They also displayed greater confidence and improved rates of writing in English while maintaining their progress in reading and writing in Māori. The 10-week programme and results were replicated by this community and their kura over a further three terms with the Year 7 and again with the Year 6 students, with the researcher using a multiple baseline across-groups design.

The principal discussed the definite advantages arising from the relationship that had already been established in this community long before this project took place:

> the school had to become a vital cog in the community and we had to shift the community to the kura more so than it ever was. In fact we had to put the kura under their mantel, under their mana. Not above it, it had to be part, and that was my hope and aspiration, that the kura became part of and under the auspices or umbrella of ngā kaumātua, ngā kuia o Ngāti Ira. And that's where we were at that stage, we moved our karakia to the marae and whenever anything happened at the kura it became a total community thing inclusive of kaumātua, kuia, parents, whānau, hapū. It became more so in those years because I felt that was the answer. (Berryman, 2001, p. 65)

Respected community elders had for some years participated in the kura on a daily basis, carrying out their traditional cultural leadership roles and modelling these for teachers, students and others coming into the kura. This resulted in the Māori language and cultural practices in this kura being strong and affirming for Māori. The same strength and understanding of the Māori culture enabled this community to be receptive and discerning towards non-Māori things, especially if they were seen by the community to add extra value to what was already in place.

In all cultures, initial learning is acquired in responsive social contexts which reflect the cultural values and practices of the families in the community. Although sometimes there is a mismatch between the values and practices of the community and the school, in this project the interconnectedness that developed between the community, whānau and kura was much stronger than the more traditional relationships that exist between parents and teachers in many other schools. Within this responsive social context, the teaching, the curriculum and the school itself instigated and provided language contexts that were embedded in the experiences, skills and values of the community. The lives of the students were directly connected with the lives of the people from the community. Participation of elders in all phases of the project ensured that learning took place in appropriate cultural contexts. Reciprocal learning, or ako (Pere, 1982), meant that throughout the project people were learning from each other. New learning meant benefits could be passed on to others. A key factor in establishing the positive relationships was evidenced in the reciprocal sharing of knowledge and the balance of power. The community determined how they would participate in the school (Berryman, Glynn, & Glynn, 2001) so that benefits would be attributed to all.

It was the community that initiated the project and determined who would participate in it. They took ownership and control of the entire research process, including the selection of an appropriate researcher, and the particular research paradigms and methods of evaluation that would be employed. Many Western research methodologies were used (quantitative assessing, monitoring and measuring reading and writing gains), but the specific application of these measures was designed and implemented by whānau members themselves. Western concepts of reliability and validity were handled from a Māori perspective. This succeeded—despite some initial misgivings—in bringing everyone together for the common purpose of the improved achievement of students. Benefits to their students were seen and understood as being benefits to themselves.

Key people—in particular the elders, the principal and the home–school liaison teacher—remained actively involved throughout the entire research process, providing the programme and research with cultural validity (Glynn et al., 1996). This was shown through their affirmation of the appropriateness of people, processes and procedures undertaken to obtain knowledge (many trained and tutored themselves), and also through their providing guidance in understanding the research outcomes from within a Māori world view.

As mentioned above, not only were the tutors connected to their students through cultural and familial ties, but they had also formed very close and positive relationships with the students. Just as importantly—and this is further supported by the data from the process measures—tutors had learnt to use the tutoring procedures with a high level of expertise and were delivering them in a highly competent manner. A positive spiral of responsiveness between the school and the community had emerged. The community and school identified a need for their students to have specific support in their transition from Māori to English. The school put in place a training programme for community tutors, many of whom the school continued to employ in order to sustain the programme for transition. Mutual benefits were, and continued to be, clearly evident. School and community were able to share the credit for their successes rather than resorting to blaming each other for children's failure at secondary school.

Māori have always had their own cultural criteria for evaluating whether a process or outcome is valid. For this project, legitimation came from the people, and therefore from the world view in which the research was embedded. Having participants in both the role of researched and researcher enabled the outcomes of the project to be better understood from the participants' own world view. Indeed, by having three generations of participants in this project (kaumātua, rangatahi and tamariki mokopuna), the research findings could be triangulated and were agreed upon by all three groups.

Although issues of ownership and control over the research were more fundamental than issues of specific methodologies, it was the combination of kaupapa Māori and Western research methodologies and epistemologies that added to the richness of the ensuing outcomes. It is from these voices and from these outcomes that we are better able to understand the specific developments in this project and rationalise them as one effective approach for supporting students in their transition from Māori-immersion to English-language programmes.

Durie (2001) sets out three broad goals for Māori in education: to live as Māori; to participate successfully in the global community; and to enjoy a healthy lifestyle. These goals are certainly consistent with the goals and aspirations of the community in this project. This whānau demonstrated what can happen when a community and school with the same goals and aspirations collaborate in a shared cultural context. The Māori language and cultural practices, as maintained and modelled by these elders, provided the basis on which to build the link into the global community. These children were able to stand tall in their own language and culture, and from this strength they were able to move ahead to learn new skills with greater confidence, building in strength towards a more successful secondary school education—a successful education that will provide the skills and knowledge needed for employment and their future health and wellbeing. Culture drove the community and school collaboration, and in turn culture drove the success of this project.

Wylie, Thompson, and Lythe's surveys of 523 Wellington children found that children's achievement was positively associated with positive teacher–parent relationships (Wylie et al., 1999, 2001). They also found that children whose parents had little or no involvement in their child's schooling scored less than others on mathematics, most of the literacy measures, communication, perseverance and fine motor skills (Wylie et al., 2001). The authors reported the particularly important finding that "[t]he particular kind of parental involvement which seemed to make a difference for children was voluntary work at the school, but not being a school trustee, or taking part in the Parent–Teacher Association" (pp. 125–126). Indeed, Hattie (2003b) argues that in asking parents to help manage schools, their attention is diverted from their primary roles in the education of their children.

Cultural mismatches between families and schools can impede effective collaboration (Biddulph et al., 2003, p. ii). Schools need not copy the home culture—an impossible task in most classrooms anyway because of their multicultural nature. Rather, "the point of cultural compatibility is that the natal culture is used as a guide in the selection of educational program elements so that academically undesired behaviours are avoided" (Jordon, 1985, p. 110). Yet teachers, for example, believe that children are less competent where they perceive a dissonance in values between themselves and parents. This is particularly so among teachers who exhibit "curriculum-centred rather than student-centred practices" (Hauser-Cram, Sirin, & Stipek, 2003, p. 813).

St George (1983) found that teachers perceived that Polynesian parents had negative attitudes to schooling and education, spoke poor English, did not provide an intellectually stimulating home environment for their children and appeared to show less interest in the world around them than did Pākehā parents. From teachers' perspectives, this explained why "poorer reading skills, lower participation in class, a more negative reaction to new work and less independence (more need for teacher guidance) also tended to be associated with Polynesian students, as did a lower level of perseverance and concentration" (p. 52). Nevertheless, St George argued that it is factors other than ethnicity that influence teacher expectations, but when these factors are associated with an ethnic group, expectations have the effect of preserving the status quo in Polynesian underachievement. The consequence, she argues, is that teachers see little prospect of their teaching making a difference, and they come to attribute responsibility for school-related problems to the home "and little to themselves, while by contrast parents held teachers primarily responsible for their child's school problems" (p. 56).

Hill (2001) also identified an association between teachers' perceptions of parents and the achievement of their children. In particular, where teachers believed that the parents valued education, the children were inclined to achieve more highly in prereading. Notwithstanding the deficit assumptions in this view, there is some evidence that improving parental skill levels can have positive effects on children (Benjamin, 1993).

In a comparative study of African-American and Euro-American kindergarten children's readiness for school, Hill (2001) found that although different ethnic groups shared many similarities, "in relationships between parenting and school performance, family income moderated the relationship between parenting behaviours and pre-reading scores" (p. 686). The study also found that parenting was more strongly related to prereading performance among lower income families than among those earning higher incomes. The study argues that the only consistent predictors of achievement among African-American children, after controlling for demographic variables, are "parents' expectations for and satisfaction with the quality of their children's education" (Hill, 2001, p. 686). Hill also makes a distinction between parental involvement in schools that is teacher initiated and that which is parent initiated. It is the latter that is more positively associated with higher levels of achievement (Epstein, 1996).

Bishop and Berryman's (2006) assessment of structural barriers to Māori achievement is that although Māori parents want their children to succeed, they often feel alienated by the school's practices. Where parents feel excluded from the school, their children are likely to feel the same way (Edwards, 2001). Edwards also found that children's perceptions of themselves and their cultures are strongly influenced by how they are received by the school. Where parental involvement in schooling is largely for negative reasons, parents can become defensive and less inclined to engage with the school to support their child's learning (Durie, 2006, p. 10). However, positive collaboration can give children and whānau a "sense of ownership and control" of what is learnt, which "can help to transform 'schooling as an obligatory activity' to 'schooling as a sought after opportunity'" (p. 10).

Stoll and Fink (1996) argue that community partnerships are required to bring a sense of cohesion "to the fragmentation and mixed messages in the lives of many pupils, particularly those in lower socio-economic areas" (p. 132). Fragmentation and mixed messages are a function of the sociopolitical context of schooling and the school's need to mediate the competing agendas, priorities and self-interest of diverse participant groups: parents, teachers, policy makers and administrators, each of which "wants to have an impact on schools and through schools, on pupils" (Stoll & Fink, 1996, p. 132).

James Comer's School Development Program (SDP) was enhanced by its becoming an integral part of wider school/community culture. The SDP's focus is to promote an "academic and social climate that promotes students' development", which it does in part through the "frequency and quality of interactions among parents, teachers, students, principals, administrators, and adjunct staff", and through "the feelings of trust and respect that exist within the school community" (Comer, Norris Haynes, Joyner, & Ben-Avie, 1996, p. 43). Adult learning groups are also a central part of the Comer process. They are modelled by the project's trainers, and focus on learning and implementation strategies (McDonald et al., 1999, p. 34).

SDP began with two schools in 1968 and expanded to 70 in 1990. By 1995 the number had increased to 550 (Comer et al., 1996, p. 147). The approach is based on the assumption that school climate, rather than children's socioeconomic status and ethnicity, largely influences behaviour, attitude and achievement (p. 44). This assumption arises from the belief that:

> The child learns from the interactions that occur in the school setting, including interactions among the adults in the building and the connections between home and school. For example, the treatment of their parents by the school staff, of course, has an impact on how students perceive the school and education in general. The children's learning process involves environment in total, including both intentional, purposeful interactions and the offhand seemingly inconsequential remarkable gesture. Children learn by observing how their peers are disciplined, by overhearing how the adults in the building interact with one another, through contact with written and other cultural products, and especially, through significant adults who take an interest. (Comer et al., 1996, p. 45)

SDP maintains that relationships are the core of the learning community—not just between teacher and child, because teachers must be supported by strong relationships among adults: "Too often parents and teachers end up pitted against one another, and like two quarrelling parents, send double messages to their children" (Comer et al., 1996, p. 153). SDP begins from the view that good relationships are a prerequisite for effective schooling.

Conclusion

This chapter has considered the need to spread the reform in order to align the new norms of the reform within the schools and with the norms of supporting institutions at both the implementation and policy levels, and with the communities beyond the school. For example, spread of the reform means that the mode of implementation should be replicated at each level of the reform. Teachers (and this is especially so in secondary schools) should be able to extrapolate the use of the reform approaches in their other classrooms and be supported to do so. In addition, the new relationships between classroom teachers and children should be of the same order as those between teachers and professional developers, and so on.

Spread of the reform to include families and communities is fundamental to its ongoing success. The key to this appears to be the degree of responsiveness of the school to parent and community initiatives. Parents ought to be engaged in their children's learning as agents of their children. Yet schools are often inclined to collaborate to engage parents as agents of the school (Brown, 1993), or even to view parents as "pupils to be educated" (Walkerdine & Lucey, 1999, cited in Edwards & Warin, 1999, p. 332). This is problematic, because collaborations are only likely to enhance achievement if they are based on respect and add to, rather than undermine, family practices. Further, the most effective parental involvement relates to academic rather than behavioural matters (Biddulph et al., 2003). Relationships are the core of the learning community—not just between teacher and child, because teachers must be supported by strong relationships among adults. Good relationships are a prerequisite for effective schooling, and the quality of relationships is fundamental to achievement.

As will be discussed in Chapter Nine, integration of reform practices and principles with existing and developing reform initiatives through the development of coherence between schools and national authorities is essential to ensure sustainability and scale. National policy initiatives should lead, and be informed by, reform developments.

GOALS OWNERSHIP

PEDAGOGY

INSTITUTIONS

LEADERSHIP

SPREAD

EVIDENCE

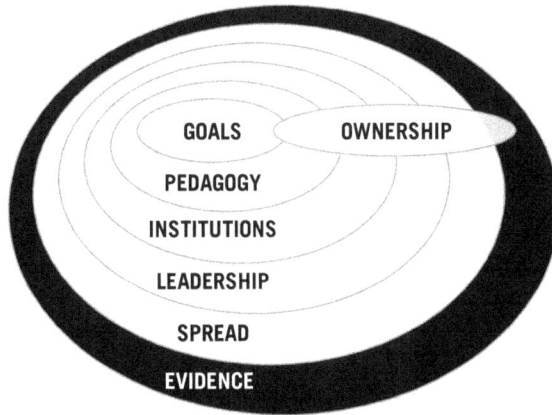

CHAPTER SEVEN

Evidence

Educational policy and practice must align to improve students' achievement. It must be informed by, and respond to information about what works. The increased use of evidence leads to clearer transparency and understanding of the critical influences that operate throughout the education system. The analysis of evidence to inform policy and practice creates a way to drive continuous improvement. (Ministry of Education, 2005b, p. 13)

Introduction

This chapter focuses on evidence and its role in sustaining a reform by helping educators to better understand what it is that works and under what conditions it works most effectively. In this context evidence has two important purposes: a summative purpose, by providing evidence of the impact of the reform; and a formative purpose, by building the capacity of participants in the project to use evidence as the basis for future planning. The formative purpose is based on the idea that the reform initiative must leave behind people with the systems and competence to continue the reform as business as usual. Together, both purposes (summative and formative) can contribute to the capacity of systems and the capability of people to produce and use evidence of students' progress and school change to effectively inform the reform effort and drive ongoing improvements.

A changing emphasis on evidence and assessment

Since the early 1990s many countries have begun a shift in emphasis from viewing assessment solely as a means of ascertaining achievement levels in individual learners and across whole cohorts, at particular points in time (summative purpose), to a focus on assessment as a tool for enhancing learning (formative purpose). *The New Zealand Curriculum Framework* (Ministry of Education, 1993) suggested at the time that:

> Assessment of individual students' progress is essentially diagnostic. Such assessment is integral to the teaching and learning programme. Its purpose is to improve teaching and learning by diagnosing learning strengths and weaknesses, measuring students' progress against the defined achievement objectives, and reviewing the effectiveness of teaching programmes. (p. 24)

In contrast to this diagnostic view, Black and Wiliam's (1998) synthesis of research on assessment and classroom learning clearly demonstrated how student achievement, particularly that of lower achievers, could be raised through initiatives designed to enhance the effectiveness of the way assessment is used in the classroom to promote learning. Black and Wiliam's research indicated that improving learning through assessment depends on the following five key factors:

- the provision of effective feedback
- the active involvement of pupils in their own learning
- adjusting teaching to take account of the results of assessment
- a recognition of the profound influence assessment has on the motivation and self-esteem of pupils, both of which are crucial influences on learning
- the need for pupils to be able to assess themselves and understand how to improve (Assessment Reform Group, 1999, p. 5).

This shift in emphasis in the aim of day-to-day assessment in classrooms has resulted in a focus on *assessment for learning*, or formative assessment, which means:

the ongoing day-to-day formative assessment that takes place to gather information on what a child or group of children understand or do not understand and how future teaching will be adapted to account for this. Effective ongoing day to day assessments would include effective questioning; observations of children during teaching and while they are working; holding discussions with children; analysing work and reporting to children; conducting tests and giving quick feedback and engaging children in the assessment process.[1]

Advice given on putting formative assessment into practice suggests that assessment of this kind should:
- be part of effective planning of teaching and learning
- focus on how pupils learn
- be recognised as central to classroom practice
- be regarded as a key professional skill for teachers
- be sensitive and constructive, because any assessment has an emotional impact
- take account of the importance of learner motivation
- promote commitment to learning goals and a shared understanding of the criteria by which pupils will be assessed
- provide constructive guidance for learners about how to improve
- develop learners' capacity for self-assessment and recognising their next steps and how to take them
- recognise the full range of achievement of all learners.[2]

Ongoing formative assessment can provide teachers with formal and informal opportunities to notice what is happening during learning activities, and to recognise where the learning of individuals and groups of students is going and how they, the teachers, can help to take that learning further. Using formative assessment can also enable teachers to ask themselves questions about what they should or can do differently. Thus they can use their professional knowledge, their knowledge of a range of pedagogical strategies and evidence about their students' current knowledge and understanding to connect to and respond to the thinking of each student. Such feedback to students is most effective when it:
- focuses on the tasks and the associated learning—not the student
- confirms for the student that he or she is on the right track
- includes suggestions that help the student (i.e., that scaffold their learning)
- is frequent and given when there is opportunity for the student to take action
- is in the context of a dialogue about the learning (Ministry of Education, 2004, p. 16).

It is when feedback connects directly to specific and challenging goals that relate to students' prior knowledge, experience and cultural understanding that students and

---

1 http://www.standards.dfes.gov.uk/primary/features/primary/1091819/1092063, accessed 28 July 2008
2 http://www.standards.dfes.gov.uk/primary/features/primary/1091819/1092063, accessed 28 July 2008

their teachers are better able to focus more productively on new goals and the next learning steps. In this situation, students are more likely to acknowledge their own skill levels and/or gaps and identify where they need and want to take their learning in the future. In Te Kotahitanga we have found that these exemplars can also be applied at the school level when working with teachers, and at the systems level when working with schools.

What counts as evidence?

In the wider educational context, due to the increased and ongoing emphasis on testing and assessment for both summative and formative purposes, and the developing technology to manage the influx of results, there is a wide range of opinion about what constitutes evidence and how it can be used most effectively in education. Alton-Lee (2004), Coe (1999) and others suggest that evidence that is used to develop findings about what is effective must be distinguished from evidence that is unsubstantiated, anecdotal or ideological. They suggest that the processes and criteria by which evidence is considered relevant need to be credible, justifiable and transparent. Increased pressure for accountability and effectiveness in the development of educational policies and systems clearly indicates that evidence rather than unfounded opinion is increasingly being sought and used as the basis for making informed decisions in education (Alton-Lee, 2004; Organisation for Economic Co-operation and Development, 2007; Slavin, 1986). Coe (1999), for example, has argued against policies imposed with inadequate evidence of their likely effects, suggesting that really worthwhile evidence comes from trying something out in an authentic learning situation and testing to see whether it has had the desired effect.

In this regard, teachers' experience and knowledge make their participation vital in the framing of questions, and in the gathering and interpretation of evidence in the context of education. Reid (2004) further argues that if 21st century educators are to teach their students to use evidence in order to become critical, flexible and creative, then they must model these qualities themselves. In concurrence with Darling-Hammond (2000), Reid (2004) contends that this requires the development of a culture of inquiry in which "educators are understood as people who learn *from* teaching rather than as people who have finished learning how to teach" (p. 3), which means "the notion of inquiry is not a project or the latest fad. It is a way of professional being" (ibid.). Reid posits "a process of systematic, rigorous and critical reflection about professional practice, and the contexts in which it occurs, in ways that question taken-for-granted assumptions" (p. 4) as being at the heart of a culture of inquiry. At the same time, he asserts that "[n]o education system or single institution should simply exhort people to engage in inquiry without an acknowledgement that inquiry skills need to be built thoughtfully and systematically" (p. 7).

This systematic approach implies that educational practitioners as well as those developing policies and reform require a similar culture of inquiry and skills to learn from the evidence of what works. This can be especially problematic when education systems are "overloaded and fragmented" (Fullan, 1999) or continue to service some groups of students inequitably (Bishop et al., 2003).

Hargreaves and Fullan (1998) propose *assessment literacy* as a solution. They suggest assessment literacy begins with the development of teachers' capacity, individually or with others, to examine student achievement (data or authentic classroom work) and make critical sense of it. On the basis of such critical examination, they propose the development and implementation of class and school improvement plans aimed at continuously improving results. Alongside this, assessment literacy involves the ability of educators to positively influence debates focused on the application of achievement data. Another solution proposed by the Ministry of Education (2004), in the field of special education, is *evidence-based inquiry*, requiring educators to incorporate and synthesise a range of evidence—from professional practitioners, from young people and their families and from national and international research—into planning for and understanding their work.

Evidence-based education calls for policy and practice decisions to be determined on the basis of reflecting on evidence and considering its relevance and likely effects from one authentic context to another. Across the OECD countries a number of brokerage agencies have begun to link research evidence to policy at the interface of educational stakeholders (Organisation for Economic Co-operation and Development, 2007). In New Zealand this has been led since 2002 by Alton-Lee (2004) with the development of an Iterative Best Evidence Synthesis (BES) programme. This programme provides a systematic approach to evaluating how different policies, contexts, systems, resources, approaches and practices from national and international research align with, influence and have an impact on the diverse range of learners. Each iterative BES has sought to identify and make accessible relevant evidence linked to a range of learner outcomes. This has been achieved by highlighting evidence of what works in education, how context is significant, what makes a bigger difference in optimising learner outcomes and what approaches are suggested by the evidence as being effective for educational development. An evidence-based approach such as this calls for researchers, policy makers and educators to collaborate in ways that can ultimately strengthen the capability of researchers and practitioners, while at the same time achieving policy that is more relevant and accessible for teachers and other educators.

Teachers' use of student evidence

Taking what we know about evidence informing the learning of students, Timperley et al. (2007) recently undertook a synthesis of international evidence on teaching and professional learning and development with the aim of developing a better understanding of how teachers could access professional development in ways that would have a more effective impact on the diverse range of students who are in their classrooms. In this synthesis, the authors identified and unpacked the particular professional learning opportunities received by teachers and the impact such opportunities have on their teaching practice and, in turn, on student outcomes. On this basis, Timperley et al. propose a cycle of teacher inquiry and knowledge building that is focused on the promotion of *valued* student outcomes. They propose a cycle of inquiry whereby teachers—individually and collectively—identify important issues relating to students' learning needs, and take responsibility for acquiring the knowledge required to respond to the issues, monitor the subsequent impact of their actions and adjust their practice accordingly.

A key assumption underpinning their cycle is that the inquiry occurs and is driven by evidence at three interdependent and parallel levels. Each level is driven by a series of critical questions that begin with a focus on the learning needs of students: "What do they already know? What sources of evidence have we used? What do they need to learn and do? How do we build on what they know?" (Timperley et al., 2007, p. xliii). In response to the evidence generated by these questions, the cycle continues with questions focused on the learning needs of teachers:

- "How have we contributed to existing student outcomes?
- What do we already know that we can use to promote valued outcomes?
- What do we need to learn to do to promote valued outcomes?
- What sources of evidence/knowledge can we utilise?" (p. xliii).

Evidence generated from these questions is responded to by teachers in the design and implementation of new tasks and learning experiences, which in turn are reflected upon by teachers in terms of their impact on students; that is, "[h]ow effective has what we have learned and done been in promoting our students' learning and well being?" (Timperley et al., 2007, p. xliii). Timperley et al. found that some of the most powerful outcomes emerged when teachers took responsibility for evidence that showed that what they had been doing had not optimised learning conditions for their students. On the basis of the evidence generated at this point, the cycle begins again with the identification of the learning needs of students as a result of the new educational initiatives.

A cycle such as this requires that teachers be informed about ongoing student evidence and receive opportunities to develop new understanding about how best to respond. Smylie (1995) suggests that "[w]e will fail … to improve schooling for children until we acknowledge the importance of schools not only as places for teachers to work but also as places for teachers to learn" (p. 92). This learning comes from teachers' use of student evidence as the basis for engaging, at a theoretical level, with pedagogical content and assessment knowledge before considering the implications and integrating new knowledge and understanding into their own practice. To do this, teachers need the support of their schools to provide an effective and accurate evidence base, the goals they collectively need to aim for and the circumstances that will continue to generate improvement. Schools therefore also have a major responsibility in terms of their expectations, use and final application of teacher and student evidence.

Schools' use of evidence

Earl and Katz (2006) support the argument that "data can and should be a compelling force in improving schools" (p. 1). Rather than being overwhelmed by data, school leaders should use data to inform planning and decisions, particularly as they relate to learning. In this way the school reform becomes a process of the evidence leading the learning and working to support the reform. However, the use of evidence, and indeed assessment, for purposes such as this in education is still a fairly recent phenomenon, and part of the reform may well be to assist schools to become *evidence ready*.

Although Herman and Gribbons (2001) contend that this does not mean teachers and school administrators need to become expert statisticians, Earl and Katz (2006) do suggest that if data are to become integral to school improvement, "leaders in schools must become active players in the data-rich environment that surrounds them" (p. 6). For some school leaders this will require new ways of understanding the nature, definition, collection, interpretation and presentation of data (Katz, Sutherland, & Earl, 2002). To this end, McNamara and Thompson (n.d.) identify the need for targeted professional development, which they suggest should:

- place the emphasis on applications and real-world data rather than mathematical theory
- use methods that allow practitioners to focus on discovery
- encourage a shift from calculation to interpretation
- make it easier to avoid the implication that statistical analysis is strictly a matter of finding the one "right" answer
- provide a dynamic process for experimenting and learning from actual data
- use data to uncover patterns and generate hypotheses
- endorse the need to use better graphical displays and verbal statements for communication (p. 383).

Earl and Katz (2006) outline three stages in a school becoming evidence driven: developing an inquiry habit of mind; becoming data literate; and creating a culture of inquiry. These themes are discussed briefly next.

Developing an inquiry habit of mind

Developing an inquiry habit of mind for organisational improvement means "developing a habit of using inquiry and reflections to think about where you are, where you are going, how you will get there, and then rethinking the whole process to see how well it is working and making adjustments" (Earl & Katz, 2006, p. 26). These writers contend that, historically, many professional decisions in schools were likely to be made on the basis of individual experiences, beliefs and values. Darling-Hammond and Sykes (1999) argue that choices and directions emerging from such a knowledge base all too often are resistant to change and perpetuate the status quo. In a time of rapid change and when schools are becoming increasingly complex, if more effective solutions are to be found, problem solving demands both inquiry and reflection that take a range of things into consideration.

Data literacy

Earl and Katz (2006) refer to data literacy as a thinking process that requires being able to objectively establish what you need or want to know and why, then being able to identify and gather the data required in order to make sense of, explain, support and perhaps challenge what it is you are seeking to establish. In so doing, they suggest that one should be aware of both the potential limitations of data and how data sources may be linked to reveal a richer and more compelling picture. Using evidence for school reform begins with understanding what it is you need or want to know and establishing what evidence will best provide the answers. In becoming data literate, a school actively "considers data in a range of different configurations; spends time trying to make sense of it through analysis, discussion, and interpretation; and transforms data into knowledge that they can use" (Earl & Katz, 2006, p. 28). As Hargreaves and Fullan (1998) suggest:

> In a changing world, a healthy school is one where teachers constantly revisit and renew their purposes; always looking for evidence and feedback about how well they are doing, and honestly examining whether they need to do things differently or better. (p. 30)

A culture of inquiry

When educators within schools consistently and systematically work together to reflect on evidence in order to share understanding and develop new knowledge, they are on their way to developing a *culture of inquiry*. Combining these practices with developing an inquiry habit of mind and becoming data literate can result in changes in practice that are consistent with professional learning communities (Earl & Katz, 2006). School leaders can help their school to develop a culture of inquiry by:

- focusing on the questions that will most effectively guide the school's strategic direction
- understanding what, in this context, will constitute good evidence
- knowing the fundamental principles of quantitative (descriptive, statistical) research
- appreciating the value of both qualitative and quantitative research to answer questions related to what happened, how it happened and what that resulted in
- being able to make interpretations that will transform the evidence into knowledge
- recognising the importance of disseminating evidence to various audiences
- creating a professional learning community or a culture of inquiry.

If schools use data in this way to discover the strengths and weaknesses of programmes, projects and innovations, make changes in accordance with their discoveries, evaluate the impact of the changes, make adjustments based on what is learnt from the evaluation and continue this cycle, then these schools will likely be data driven or data based (Earl & Katz, 2006).

This model for using data in schools is based on action research, first described in 1948 by Kurt Lewin. Action research is a process of progressive problem solving where individuals work in teams to critically reflect upon the way they identify and solve problems with an aim of improving their collective practice. Initially action research was brought into education by the Tavistock Institute in England and the Horace-Mann-Lincoln Institute at Teachers College, Columbia University, in the USA (Creswell, 2005). Although action research is not without its critics (see Stringer, 1999), today it is widely accepted and often used in educational research. The advantages in using this method in educational contexts are that it:

- encourages more purposeful change in schools
- fosters a participatory, more self-determining approach
- empowers people through collaboration
- positions educators as learners interested in working together to create a more successful future
- encourages reflective practice
- promotes the testing of new ideas (Mills, 2000).

According to Schmuck (1997), action research of this type is most appropriate for building the capability of teachers and school leaders to use data. Creswell (2005) contends that action research design should involve the study of local practices, involving either individual or group inquiry, and should focus on changes in teacher practices and improvement of student outcomes. Implementation of action plans such as this can build an evidence base and the capacity of teachers as researchers.

Stringer (1999) provides another model for conducting action research that fits well with the practical action research process. According to Stringer's model, the work of an educator acting as an action researcher is to:

- design the study and carefully refine the issue to be investigated
- plan a systematic process of inquiry that maintains ethical and valid standards
- gather data and other information from a variety of sources
- analyse the data to identify key features of the issue under investigation
- communicate the outcomes of the study to relevant audiences
- use the outcomes to improve future practice.

Mechanisms for gathering evidence

Increasingly, educators are using a wider range of tools designed to maximise teaching opportunities and take advantage of the positive benefits to be gained from their use in education. The variety of tools used to assist with the education of students ranges from whiteboards to sophisticated educational software packages used, for example, to gather and manage student evidence.

Some of the tools in the vast range currently used in education have been described by Robinson et al. (2009) as "smart tools", which we introduced in Chapter Three. These are tools that incorporate "a theory about how to achieve the purpose of the task in question" (p. 124), and that "are designed in ways that make them easy to understand and use" (p. 129). By this definition, a smart tool has "the qualities needed to help the users achieve the purpose of the activity in which the tools are used" and to support the process by which teachers learn "how to promote student learning" (p. 124). In an educational context, Robinson et al. have defined smart tools as tools that:

- have a theoretical base for how to achieve their purpose
- are designed so that they are easy to understand and can be used "smartly" by teachers and others concerned with education
- help the users achieve the purpose of the activity for which the tools are being used
- are linked to learning outcomes and support the processes by which teachers learn to reflect on and further promote students' learning.

To this end, researchers in Te Kotahitanga are using a range of smart tools focused on gathering evidence in order to provide specific feedback to those concerned and help them reflect on the implications of the evidence. In so doing, we have all been able to develop a better understanding of the reform in these schools. Some of these tools focus at the level of students and teachers, while others focus on teachers and school systems. Collectively these smart tools aim to provide schools with the evidence to support a systems-wide reform, with student and classroom evidence helping to inform change at the systems level, rather than the system continually setting and imposing the reform on students and classrooms from many other external influences.

Focus on students and teachers

As noted in Chapter One, we learnt from our experience in Te Kotahitanga Phase 2 that the development of specific contexts for learning does not necessarily result in evidence of changes in students' academic achievement. We have also learnt that there are two types of student evidence that can have a particular impact on and help to inform teachers' reflections, and therefore on work to reform their pedagogy and improve students' results: evidence of students' attendance from class to class and overall school attendance; and evidence of students' participation and achievement from the range of classes within which they are involved, and thus within all the curriculum areas. Teachers, and likewise school management, need to be able to gather and review evidence of this kind in a predetermined, consistent and ongoing manner in order to identify and reflect on patterns of attendance and curriculum participation for individuals and groups of students. This needs to occur in teachers' own classrooms and across yearly cohorts.

Teachers in the secondary schools in which we have undertaken our work have begun to benefit from a comparison of the patterns of evidence that emerge from the students they teach and from other teachers who teach the same groups of students. Together we have learnt that when particular groups of students (in the case of Te Kotahitanga the specific focus has been on Māori students) are consistently attending one teacher's class and showing consistent achievement, or consistently not attending other teachers' classes and/or showing poor or erratic achievement from class to class, there is a need for critical collegial reflection focused on the specific evidence that has been generated. We have also learnt that where no evidence has been generated or captured, there is a need to put systems in place that will ensure that future evidence can be systematically gathered and analysed.

As we discussed in Chapter One, co-construction meetings (where the focus is on improving learning and achievement through the ongoing interrogation of student evidence) provide term-by-term opportunities for professional reflection of this kind. Co-construction meetings are aimed at developing *professional learning conversations* such as Timperley et al. (2003a) describe. Students' participation and achievement results from class to class are used to provide valuable summative and formative information for reforming school systems and teachers' pedagogy and planning. The use of student evidence in this way also helps to avoid what Timperley et al. term *professional conversations*, where teachers focus more on the profession of teaching—that is, on themselves and their teaching—than on the achievement of their students and the role teachers have in supporting students to achieve.

In Te Kotahitanga, individual classroom evidence has been further supported by the overall gathering and analysis of evidence generated from national literacy and numeracy tools. We have found that the analysis and comparison of a range of individual, class and year-group evidence is particularly important when looking at the achievement of groups of students, such as Māori, who continue to miss out on the benefits of quality educational systems. The Assessment Tool for Teaching and Learning (asTTle) (Hattie, Brown, & Keegan, 2003; Hattie et al., 2004) and the Essential Skills Assessment (ESA) (Croft, Dunn, & Brown, 2001) have been important tools for providing evidence of student achievement in these areas.

ESA was originally conducted with Years 9 and 10 students in all 12 project schools. The ESA "Information Skills, Finding Information in Prose Text—Secondary" was used. This assessment tool consists of two sections: skimming and scanning for information and note taking; and organising information. This particular assessment was chosen for this project because it measures skills identified by the ESA designers as being important across a range of curriculum areas. The assessment was administered early in school years 2004 and 2005 as a pretest, and late in school years 2004 and 2005 as a post-test. The stanine and raw score results were then analysed for strength of differences between the pretest and the post-test by ethnicity (Māori and non-Māori students) using the criterion of effect sizes.

The asTTle tool has the added advantage that it enables teachers to create their own fit-for-purpose literacy and numeracy assessments, and in turn to collate, interpret and compare their students' results electronically. The reports generated show what students know, what gaps they have in their learning and what they need to learn next. Given its electronic capacity, the asTTle tool means that teachers can enter test results into the program then quickly analyse the performance of both individuals and groups of students (e.g., by class, gender or ethnicity). The results, which are able to be displayed graphically, can then be shared with students. Teachers can use them to identify subsequent learning steps for individuals, groups or classes by linking to an indexed online catalogue of classroom resources (What Next). AsTTle software also provides information on the strengths and weaknesses of individuals and groups, and can be used to identify what progress has been made. The results indicate how well students are learning in comparison to other students of the same year group, within the same class and school, as well as across national yearly cohorts. Teachers have found ESA and asTTle to be valuable tools for both formative and summative purposes.

Focus on teachers and schools

The Te Kotahitanga Observation Tool (Bishop et al., 2007), was developed as a framework for providing specific formative feedback to individual teachers on the extent to which they are incorporating the interactions and relationships described in the Effective Teaching Profile (see Box 1.1) into their everyday teaching. The first side of this Observation Tool is used to gather evidence of:

* the range of teaching interactions
* who the teacher is interacting with—whole class (W), individual student (I) or small group (G)
* where teachers locate themselves throughout the observation
* the lesson outline
* the degree of cognitive challenge of the lesson for the specific class of students being observed.

The first side is also used to gather information about the lesson from five Māori students, including their engagement with the lesson; work completion, in line with expectations observed to have been set by the teacher; and location throughout the observation. Finally, the first side is used to gather any other relevant information about the teacher's interactions with students, the lesson or the class in order to add richness to the observation information.

The second side of the Observation Tool is used to gather evidence about the:

* teacher's relationships with Māori students
* teacher's expectations of Māori students' learning and behaviour
* visible signs of culture in the classroom
* responsiveness of the teacher to Māori students and their culture
* strategies being used by the teacher.

Evidence from each of these elements can then be used to show the shifts in teachers' implementation of the Effective Teaching Profile. This Observation Tool was trialled and developed in Phases 1 and 2 of Te Kotahitanga and tested for reliability and validity in Phase 3 (aspects of the phases in Te Kotahitanga are discussed in Chapter One).

Important information is obtained from the direct observation of teachers and students in authentic responsive social settings such as are encouraged through the implementation of the Effective Teaching Profile in classrooms. In these settings it is possible for the teacher to implement strategies that will promote a responsive and interactive role, where students have opportunities to exercise a measure of autonomy in their learning and where teachers assume a facilitative interactive role in the construction of knowledge, rather than the traditional mainly directive transmission role. Accurate use of the Te Kotahitanga Observation Tool by facilitators trained in the observation administration conventions enables teachers to share in the process of monitoring and reflecting on their own practice through the term-by-term facilitated cycle of classroom observation followed by individual feedback and goal setting. These processes apply the implementation and evaluation process (Figure 1.1) of GEPRISP and PSIRPEG at an individual level, which are central to the evidence and feedback cycle shown in Figure 1.2.

Evidence from the Observation Tool can also be used for summative purposes at the school level. Once observers analyse individual teachers' observations, and this is shared with them in private for individual formative purposes, their data are entered anonymously into an electronic database. This is done using an electronic tool that has been both informed by this process of individual observation/feedback and designed specifically for making these processes more efficient. Facilitators are able to combine teachers' observational data, then average it to provide a picture of the shifts in traditional to discursive teaching practices across all Te Kotahitanga teachers in the school. Observational data can then be compared with other evidence from the reform and used by schools over time for both summative and formative purposes.

In each Te Kotahitanga school, school-based facilitators learn how to use this tool to observe and gather evidence of teachers' relationships and interactions with Māori students. This specific evidence is then fed back to teachers by the observer/facilitator and discussed as the basis for their ongoing professional learning and goal setting. Used in this manner, the Te Kotahitanga Observation Tool enables teachers to examine their own evidence and reflect on this with a skilled observer. Such critical reflection, within collaborative professional learning conversations, is being developed as the basis for promoting a range of effective and meaningful solutions to address Māori students' participation and achievement. The Te Kotahitanga Observation Tool is a smart tool in that it provides the framework for monitoring and reflecting on the degree to which participating teachers are incorporating the relationships and interactions from the Effective Teaching Profile into their everyday teaching.

Evidence from the use of the Observation Tool across the school is used for project-wide summative purposes to inform the progress of the reform. Results from the data analysis of the Phase 3 schools (Bishop et al., 2007) showed a reduction in the teaching and learning patterns that have been described as traditional, whereby teachers are actively engaged in transmission teaching while the students are expected to be passive and in receptive mode (Young, 1991). Problematically for Māori students, the pedagogy evident in baseline observations was exactly the pattern of interactions that the narratives of experienced participants identified as having little positive impact on their learning (Bishop & Berryman, 2006). Rather, this traditional pedagogy left them learning little, being expected to copy a lot of teacher notes and becoming increasingly frustrated in the process. This situation was then manifested in poor behaviour in the classroom by some (nonengaged Māori students), or in a sense of having to give up their cultural identity in order to succeed at school by others (engaged Māori students). In such classrooms the evidence gathered using the Observation Tool at baseline indicated that a high proportion of time was spent by teachers in telling students what to do, checking that they have followed instructions and disciplining them for a range of minor misdemeanours. This evidence indicated that teachers were spending more time trying to control and manage students' behaviour rather than working to manage the classroom and curriculum pedagogy and thus more effectively supporting students' learning.

Evidence of the overall pattern of in-class interactions from baseline for teachers in Te Kotahitanga Phase 3 also illustrated that teachers need time and ongoing support to incorporate the new learning into their thinking and classroom practice. It also demonstrated the benefits of providing intensive ongoing professional development support, which provides teachers with feedback and feedforward in the form of observations, individual feedback and group co-construction sessions applying GEPRISP and PSIRPEG, and the setting of evidence-based goals, followed by in-class shadow coaching.

The analysis of observational data gathered since the baseline measures were taken indicates that within Te Kotahitanga classrooms there has been a shift away from the dominant traditional/transmission pattern of pedagogy within the classrooms of the observed Te Kotahitanga teachers to a more interactive approach, including a wider range of more discursive teacher–student interactions. This shift is indicated by a decrease in interactions such as formal instruction, monitoring of and feedback on behaviour and an increase in the type of interactions where teachers seek to engage with their students' own prior experiences, respond to student-initiated interactions by giving feedback and feedforward on their learning and increase opportunities to co-construct learning contexts with students.

Ongoing observational data analysis has revealed that as teachers participate in the cycle of professional development described in Chapter One and move towards facilitating more discursive classrooms, they change the way they relate to the students at the level of academic interactions, spending less time interacting with the whole class and becoming more available to interact with individuals and groups of students. Interestingly, this change was also reflected in teachers changing their proximity to Māori students in their classrooms. Previously teachers had spent much of their time distanced from Māori students. After teachers began to participate in the cycle of professional development, teachers and Māori students were more likely to be communicating one to one or in small groups.

This trend towards more open, interactive classrooms is one that was strongly supported by Māori students when the original narratives of experience were gathered and constructed (Bishop & Berryman, 2006). These Māori students spoke of their reluctance at having to interact with the teacher in front of the whole class, and this was supported by their teachers. Māori students' self-removal to the periphery of the classroom, beyond the usual zone of interaction, kept them away from these perceived "embarrassing" interactions, but it also kept them out of the learning conversations.

Evidence from observations has also indicated that Māori student engagement and work completion increased when teachers changed the way they related to and interacted with Māori students. By being responsive to Māori students and encouraging contexts where their collective experiences were used as the basis for defining and constructing new knowledge, teachers created learning contexts that were responsive to learning, rather than remaining overly dependent on contexts where knowledge was merely being transmitted by teachers to some of the learners. Te Kotahitanga teachers achieved this by changing the way they related to Māori students, and on the basis of these new relationships they have been able to introduce new teaching and learning strategies into their classrooms that change the way they interact with these students. From these new relationships, more effective ways of engaging and interacting have begun to emerge.

Overall, the analysis of observational data demonstrated that a number of key shifts in teacher and student outcomes had occurred in the classrooms of teachers participating in the ongoing Te Kotahitanga research and development. As teachers developed relationships of care with Māori students and raised the learning expectations of these students, and teachers moved from traditional, transmission-type interactions to more interactive, discursive interactions, Māori students showed higher levels of engagement with learning and also completed more work that was of greater cognitive challenge. Important new learning outcomes achieved by these students in association with these pedagogical changes were reported in the Phase 3 report to the Ministry of Education (Bishop et al., 2007).

Focus on school reform efforts at a system level

Earl and Katz (2006) assert that "accountability and data are at the heart of contemporary reform efforts worldwide" (p. 2). In this regard, schools in some countries are increasingly required to focus on high standards for all students and provide evidence conceived explicitly in the language of data (Fullan, 1999). This requires these schools to implement large-scale assessment programmes, establish indicators of effectiveness, review and inspect programmes and provide rewards and sanctions in line with these outcomes (Leithwood, Edge, & Jantzi, 1999). In these schools, the main purpose of assessment has begun to move into the public domain of accountability, where schools are required to demonstrate and report on their progress, and away from being used mainly to make decisions about students' learning (Earl & Katz, 2006). The competitive climate encouraged currently by some governments, intent on target setting and narrowly conceived achievement, often creates tensions for those schools that are focused on creating inclusive classroom environments and/or responding more effectively to educational disparity (Wearmouth & Berryman, 2009).

The emphasis on school improvement, target setting and inter school comparisons has had its difficulties. In England, for example, permanent exclusions rose from 3,000 in 1990 to over 12,000 in 1997/98 (Department for Education and Skills, 2002). This rise coincided with the implementation of the national curriculum, the publication of league tables of school examination and test results and the local management of schools in which individual school budgets were largely determined by the number of students on the roll. In this regard Tomlinson (2001) contends that:

> creating competitive markets in education based on parental 'choice' of schools and fuelled by league tables and competition for resources, is totally incompatible with developing an inclusive education system. In England there is now a divided and divisive school system, with middle-class and aspirant parents avoiding schools catering for children with special educational needs, and some schools finding ways of rejecting socially and educationally vulnerable children. (Tomlinson, 2001, p. 192)

Currently, in England, all students in state schools are tested in English, science and mathematics at the ages of 7, 11 and 14 through the Standard Attainment Tests and Standard Assessment Tasks (SATs). Attainment is then recorded in terms of attainment levels from 1 to 8 and reported to parents. The data collected from the assessments at key stages 1–3, and from examinations set by external examination boards, are then published through the print media and the Internet as schools' league tables. With some degree of parental choice of school in England, publishing raw school-level results places schools in a marketplace environment and tends to "reinforce local schooling hierarchies and increase differences in the mean pupils' academic attainment between schools" (Adnett & Davies, 2001, p. 1).

Similarly, in the USA, the No Child Left Behind legislation requires schools, districts and states to assess and report annually on student achievement data. Among other things, there is an expectation that gender, race, migrant status, English competency, disability and income will be regularly reported on (Earl & Katz, 2006). Schools are being judged not only by the data they produce, but many reforms also require schools and school leaders to have the capacity to use data internally in order to understand the progress of their students and thus be able to prioritise the changes that are required, establish plans for improvement and monitor for outcomes (Herman & Gribbons, 2001).

In countries such as England and the USA, where there are very high stakes attached to external summative test results, these assessments serve to classify people and schools according to specific, often narrow, criteria and with a narrow operational definition of education. Research evidence (Black & Wiliam, 1998) suggests that particular assessment practices of this sort inhibit rather than support students' learning. These findings suggest:

- a tendency for teachers to assess quantity of work and presentation rather than quality of learning
- greater attention is given to marking and grading, much of it tending to lower the self-esteem of pupils rather than provide advice for improvement
- a strong emphasis on comparing pupils with each other, which demoralises the less successful learners
- teachers' feedback to pupils often serves managerial and social purposes rather than helping them to learn more effectively (Assessment Reform Group, 1999, p. 5).

In Chapter Two we discussed Schmoker's (1999) contentions in terms of the sustainability of school reform being predicated on establishing measurable goals, monitoring the outcomes of the innovation in reference to these goals, followed by adjustment of the reform to suit the particular circumstances of the schools and the students. In Te Kotahitanga we have found that this is most effective when evidence is used to show how and in what ways the reform initiative needs to develop, and is developing, and also when evidence is used to guide, develop and evaluate the initiative in an ongoing, iterative manner.

We concur with Fullan (2005), who notes that "there is no chance that large-scale reform will happen, let alone stick, unless capacity building is a central component of the strategy for improvement" (pp. 10–11). Fullan is critical of large-scale reform such as No Child Left Behind, which requires that all states in the USA have an achievement-driven system in which annual progress in student achievement is documented and reported publicly, and with a sequence of consequences for those schools not demonstrating improvement. Fullan states that because there is little investment in capacity building, "it places people in a high-alert dependency mode jumping from one solution to another in a desperate attempt to comply" (p. 11). Earl and Katz (2002) highlight the importance of engaging in, and seeking to sustain, continuous learning across teachers and schools in order to develop capacity that is focused on enhancing student learning.

In Te Kotahitanga we have found that this capacity building needs to include some professional development support in the areas of collecting relevant evidence, and then in its analysis, interpretation and dissemination. We have found that evidence is central to capacity building, and thus fundamental to growing and/or sustaining a change initiative. Fullan and Sharratt (2007) define capacity building as "any strategy that develops the collective efficacy of a group to raise the bar and close the gap of student achievement through (1) new knowledge, competencies and skills; (2) enhanced resources; and (3) greater motivation" (p. 3). An essential component of a reform might be to convince teachers, through demonstrable evidence, that their collective efficacy is higher than they themselves believe.

However, looking at collective teacher efficacy alone is not enough to evaluate capacity building within a school. Educators need to talk about developing a culture of evaluation in schools focusing on an "assessment for learning" (Fullan, Cuttress, & Kilcher, 2005). We believe it is important for schools and teachers to develop their capacity in four areas:

• collecting and analysing student achievement data
• breaking down the data for detailed understanding
• creating action plans based on the results of data analysis
• communicating with parents and the community by teachers and students about student outcomes.

Further, educators and those interested in education need to look at how the different sectors in New Zealand education (teachers, administrators and the Ministry of Education) might use evidence. Coburn and Talbert (2006) argue that using data to guide decision making is the most important strategy when it comes to improving student achievement. However, they caution that "a coherent systemic strategy for evidence-based practice may require a system of evidence use that allows for and supports access to different kinds of evidence for different purposes at different levels of the system" (p. 491).

A further caution, particularly to school management, is made with regard to using data for monitoring rather than improvement (Earl & Katz, 2006). Darling-Hammond (2004) offers further insights into this debate. One view seeks to induce change through extrinsic rewards and sanctions for both schools and students, on the assumption that the fundamental problem is a lack of will among the educators to change. The other view seeks to bring about change by building knowledge among school practitioners on alternative methods, and by stimulating organisational rethinking through opportunities to work together on the design of teaching and schooling, and then to experiment with new approaches. Based on the idea of accountability for improvement or formative purposes, rather than monitoring, educators can create learning communities where they can work interdependently to develop their capacity to collectively grow the reform (Senge et al., 1999).

Principals, and perhaps also their senior management teams, play a critical mediating role between the Ministry of Education and teachers in determining what constitutes evidence and research. The tension emerges largely on the basis of teachers being more likely to have a formative focus and the Ministry of Education a more summative focus with regard to the role of research and evidence (Coburn & Talbert, 2006). The Ministry of Education is interested in knowing if a project is making a difference and how important that difference is. To determine this, it relies strongly on effect size evidence, usually of student achievement results. Once pretest and post-test data are collected for an intervention, data are analysed for inferential statistical significance. If statistical significance is found, then effect sizes are calculated to determine if the significance is of practical importance to educators and others interested in education, and to compare the results of one initiative with other similar initiatives.

In Te Kotahitanga, our work as educational researchers is to build the capacity of educators in schools (teachers, principals and senior management teams), and at the same time contribute to the Ministry of Education's knowledge base and capacity to make informed decisions. In order to do this, we work with schools to review research literature, plan research studies, gather evidence from schools, analyse and interpret their evidence and present the results to various audiences. In our experience, because schools have traditionally relied heavily on anecdotal information and intuition to support teacher practices (Coburn & Talbert, 2006), the educational-support aspect of capacity building takes time. St John (2002) suggests an infrastructure that includes permanent positions for professional developers (and coaches), who can work with outside experts (intermediary organisations), administrators and teachers in the respective schools. He suggests these professional development positions be recognised as a distinct and permanent part of the school. This is often very challenging given that the current Ministry of Education funding model provides temporary, short-term funding for outside expertise to catalyse and initiate the process of change, but seldom provides funds to sustain the process of change. Nor are funds provided for building an improvement infrastructure. Funding is needed to provide people, resources and processes to support administrators and teachers in ways that allow improvement in classroom teaching and learning.

Conclusion

We have learnt the importance of developing and using appropriate tools that will provide evidence of the progress students are making towards specific goals as a means of modifying classroom and school practices and policies, and that will in turn establish and grow school reform. This means teachers and students are able to gather, examine and understand a range of formal and informal assessment measures. They are also able to use the evidence formatively and summatively to make more informed and effective changes in instructional practice. Teachers can benefit from school-based facilitators and researchers to help them develop the capacity to work in this manner. Schools can also benefit from their ability to use appropriate smart tools to monitor the implementation of the reform in order to provide data for formative and summative purposes.

Finally, national-level support for the production of appropriate tools and resources, and the development of supportive policies regarding standards and assessments, is also needed. With a mix of accountability and capacity building to enable collaborative formative problem solving and decision making that is ongoing and interactive, evidence will support teachers, schools and systems to become agentic; that is, to focus on what they are responsible for in terms of students' learning. In this way, evidence can become an important basis upon which school reform can be determined and grow.

In the next chapter we move on to look at an important aspect of sustaining a reform: developing staff and school *ownership* so that a reform is maintained in the face of competing and changing priorities.

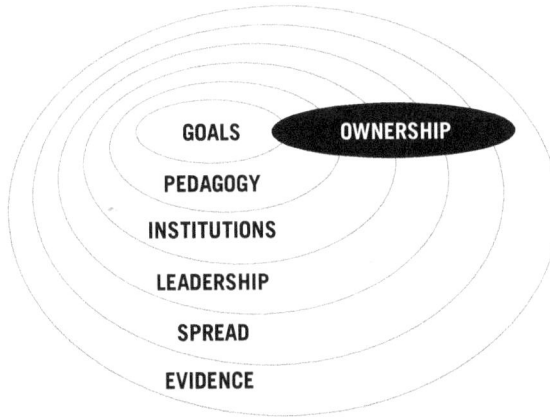

GOALS **OWNERSHIP**
PEDAGOGY
INSTITUTIONS
LEADERSHIP
SPREAD
EVIDENCE

CHAPTER EIGHT

Shift in Reform Ownership

Scale, in the instance of theory-based change, is affected by the degree of
consistency between the value basis and the beliefs underlying a reform,
and those of its organizational and institutional setting. A reform can be
said to be an accepted practice when it is no longer seen as an interruption
or exception to organizational life. 'Going to scale' has as much, if not
more, to do with the normative structures of the organizational setting
as it does with the procedural structures ... The problem of scale alters
the reform founder's relationship to the reform itself. Internalizing reform
involves reconceptualization of proprietorship, moving from reformer as sole
proprietor (or limited partnerships with practitioner co-creators) to reformer
as one of many sources of wisdom—and authority—about the reform.
(McLaughlin & Mitra, 2001, p. 314)

Introduction

Coburn (2003) argues that one of the key considerations for a reform to become sustainable and extendable, in both the initial and subsequent schools, is that authority and responsibility for the reform and its goals must shift from the external originators to teachers, schools and policy makers. This shift in ownership will ensure that the reform becomes self-generative in that teachers, school leaders and policy makers will have the knowledge and skills to deepen, spread and sustain the reform principles, while continuing to meet the agreed aims of the reform. In short, they will *own* the reform. McLaughlin and Mitra (2001) insist that allowing for this transfer of ownership needs to be part of the reform from its very inception.

This condition of sustainability—that is, developing staff and school ownership so that the reform is maintained in the face of competing and changing priorities—stands in contrast to those reforms concerned with creating conditions that promote staff "buy-in", or how the professional developers might continue to provide professional development. Coburn (2003) argues that there is little on this topic in the literature, yet it raises some of the most important strategic issues to do with sustaining a reform in the initial sites and when taking reform to scale in the long and medium term. For example, what strategies are effective for attaining this goal? Are they different at different levels in the system? How is such a procedure located within the reform initiative, and how is the integrity of the project maintained once the reform is "handed over"; indeed, is "handing over" an appropriate metaphor? Are there more appropriate metaphors to conceptualise such a process?

One appropriate metaphor is koha. A koha is literally a gift. However, when it is embedded within Māori cultural practices and understanding, for example, during the proceedings of a hui (a ritualised Māori meeting), the koha is the contribution that visitors make towards the cost of the meeting. In the past this koha was often a gift of food to contribute to the running of the hui; nowadays it is usually money, which is laid down on the ground by the last speaker of the visitors' side, between the two groups of people—the hosts and the visitors—who are coming together at the welcoming ceremony. The koha remains an important ritualised part of a ceremony that generally proceeds without too much trouble. What must not be forgotten, however, is that the reception of the koha is up to the hosts: it is up to them to pick it up. The koha, as a gift or an offering of assistance towards the cost of running the hui, goes with the full mana (status, power) of the group offering it. It is placed in a position, such as on the ground between the two groups coming together, that enables it to be considered by the hosts. It is not often given into the hands of the hosts, but whatever the specific details of the protocol, the process of " laying down" is a very powerful recognition of the right of others to self-determination; that is, to choose whether to pick it up or not.

The koha generally precedes the final coming together of the two sides. The placing of the koha comes at a crucial stage in the ceremony, where the hosts can refuse to accept the mana of the visitors, and thus display their ultimate control over events. This means that the hosts can choose whether they want to become one with the manuhiri (visitors) by the process of the hongi and haruru (pressing noses and shaking hands). Symbolically, by picking up the koha, the hosts are taking on the kaupapa (agenda) of the guests by accepting that which the manuhiri are bringing to the hui. It is important to understand that the koha—that is, the metaphorical kaupapa the guests laid down at the hui—once picked up is now the "property" of the whole whānau (literally the extended family, but more generally all the people involved). It is now the task of the whole whānau to deliberate the issues and to *own* the problems, concerns and ideas in a way that is real and meaningful; the way of whakakotahitanga (developing unity), where all will work for the betterment of the idea.

Just as the koha is literally picked up by the host side, so too the schools need to figuratively pick up that which is offered by the developers of the reform. The schools have self-determination over whether they pick it up at all. However, once it is taken up, the koha goes with all the commitments and responsibilities associated with the picking up of a gift.

The first action in taking ownership of the reform is therefore "picking up" the koha: taking on the challenge of implementing the reform and all that means for the school. This chapter examines a number of indications of a school having committed to taking up the reform—having taken ownership of the reform. These indications include a school asking hard questions of itself, changing the culture of the school, building capacity among teachers, confronting resistance, reallocating and reprioritising resource allocations and celebrating achievements and gains. By these actions, a school demonstrates that it has an unwavering focus on the goals of reducing disparities through raising achievement.

Asking the hard questions

Taking ownership of the reform initiative involves schools asking hard questions about the progress they are making towards the goals they have set. This implies that a number of conditions are satisfied. The first is that schools will be seen to be asking hard questions of themselves rather than of others. They will be ensuring they have the capacity among their staff to generate data that will answer the questions in an appropriate manner. They will demonstrate that they are prepared to organise the institutional framework of the school in ways that will enable all involved to be able to use the data purposefully and to spread the practices and principles of the reform to the school's policy and routines to support these activities across the school. They will also demonstrate that they are prepared to critically question funding prioritisation and allocation. In Collins's (2001) terms, this approach is characterised by "disciplined thought and action [in] confronting the brutal facts" (p. 13).

Schools accepting student failure as an identifiable part of the system, such as in the 50 percent pass rates for School Certificate,[1] is no longer acceptable. The demands of our emerging "knowledge economy" and the increasing demands for social justice for all mean that schools must now provide a high-quality academic education for all students. In other words, our schooling system, originally designed to produce an élite, must now educate the masses. This "massification", as Meade (1996) terms it, is creating challenges for all levels of the education sector. It is no longer acceptable for schools to ask questions such as, "How can we improve the behaviour of the students?" or "Why don't parents take advantage of the opportunities we offer, and engage with us?" Similarly, it is not useful for tertiary professional development providers or researchers to ask, "Why don't schools take more notice of our research?" Such questions perpetuate the notion of blaming others, because the questioner is refusing to acknowledge and accept responsibility for their part in the educational relationship. Such questions are also not going to create learning relationships where all students can reach their potential, because in asking such questions schools continue to abrogate their professional responsibility and the commitment that is necessary to bring about sustained change in educational disparities through raising educational achievement.

Asking hard questions of oneself is a characteristic of those organisations that Collins (2001) identifies as shifting from being good to being great organisations. The main characteristic of this shift is that those organisations that could well be satisfied with their overall student achievement averages are not satisfied to rest there but want to improve the education of all students. The principal of one of the Phase 3 schools described to us how their school could have continued along the path they were travelling, but they were not satisfied that they were addressing the needs of all of their students:

> Twenty percent of our students are Māori. We had some key issues with Māori achievement. We were in that absolutely luxurious position where we could have sat back and said, 'This isn't about us. We are doing OK as a school. We have no problems.' We have a significant number of Māori students, and their future was in our hands and we have not been meeting their needs. We had been looking for the way to make a difference and had tried several things but we just weren't making the breakthrough that we wanted. So when the programme came along, what we liked about it was the depth of thinking that had gone into it. (Principal, School 1)

Asking the hard question requires of schools that they have the systems to prepare high-quality, robust and reliable data. The preparation of data for formative purposes in professional learning communities, such as those described by Timperley (2003b) and others, is an exacting task and requires an agreed technology, people with the capacity to manage the technology and a commitment by all staff to participate in the gathering and production of quality data. For example, attendance is a vital element of

---

1   School Certificate was the first level of national examination for school students until it was replaced by a standards-based assessment system in 2001.

student achievement: one of the most constant indicators of achievement is time spent at school (Hattie, 2003b). However, currently many schools do not have robust means of generating reliable data on student attendance. This problem is very pertinent in secondary schools, with their segmented timetables and multiple opportunities for students to miss lessons. Unless there is a robust student management system—apart from individual teachers keeping a record of attendance—it is rarely possible for teachers or leaders to gain a satisfactory overview of period-by-period attendance patterns that could indicate specific subject-related or teacher-related attendance issues. Of course, where such data are available, and they are robust and reliable, then schools, when questioning patterns shown in the data, need to check the type of questions they are asking of the data and whether these questions are of themselves or of others. For example, is selective absenteeism a matter of student misbehaviour, or is it students "voting with their feet"?

When asking hard questions of themselves, schools must also question whether they are prepared to reorganise their institutional framework so that teachers are able to ask problem-solving questions of data in a purposeful way. Is it simply passed out to them by the leaders for them to "think about"? As we saw earlier, the establishment of the school as a professional learning community requires institutional reorganisation. This is necessary so that teachers can collaboratively reflect on robust and reliable data in settings that will support them to ask hard questions of themselves about the ways they can be self-determining in their relations with others involved in these new institutions.

Finally, schools must ask themselves hard questions about the (re)prioritisation and (re)allocation of funds. At the school level consideration needs to be given to the issue of how the school's resources can be creatively reprioritised and reallocated to ensure the sustainability of the reform. Is there sufficient commitment to cut some programmes and reallocate current staffing to allow for those who will support the implementation and realisation of the goals of the reform?

Changing the culture of the school

McLaughlin and Mitra (2001) emphasise the importance of the reform having a means of cultivating reform-centred knowledge among key leaders in such a way that these leaders can interrogate the new initiatives they are offered. Leaders with an in-depth understanding of the reform principles are better able to interrogate new policy initiatives to ascertain their degree of coherence and potential for support for the central reform initiative. As Hargreaves and Fink (2000) note, there is no external answer that will substitute for the complex work of changing one's own situation.

In this way, leaders can be discerning when evaluating new projects so that they select those with coherence to ensure that the benefits of the reform remain within the school. Effective school leaders are expected to be able to weave new initiatives and priorities into the framework provided by the reform model, selecting those that support the overall goal of the school reform and rejecting all others. One example from Te Kotahitanga is that where schools are able to weave together other content and strategy-based initiatives, like the current literacy and numeracy initiatives within the more context-changing initiative that is Te Kotahitanga, then students do even better than in schools where the projects are kept as discrete entities. Indeed, many of the schools from Phase 3 experiment with how they can reduce the number of externally generated initiatives by pulling them together within the framework provided by Te Kotahitanga. Metaphors used vary from Te Kotahitanga being the "roots" on which they grow other initiatives and developments, to it being an "umbrella" for all that happens within the school. Whatever the case, it is clear that the schools' leaders have become critically selective consumers of educational initiatives. This is based on the contribution new initiatives might make to the schools' overall goal of raising Māori students' achievement through improving the professional capacity of teachers, whereas once they would probably have accepted initiatives based on different criteria, such as funding or the benefits to staff alone.

One large school, prior to the implementation of Te Kotahitanga, had a large number of different initiatives being implemented. Three years after implementation of Te Kotahitanga the senior management team of this school were working to reduce these to four. In addition, these four had to fit in with the strategic goals set by the school for the reduction of educational disparities within the school through the improvement of Māori students' educational achievement. As their principal explained to us, one of the main tasks she faced was "sticking to the knitting". By this she meant, in Fullan's (2008) terms, the Ministry of Education has "initiative-itis"—the "tendency to launch an endless stream of disconnected innovations that no one could possibly manage" (p. 1). Her concern with the plethora of new projects promulgated by the Ministry is that they need to be worthy:

> A lot of time is spent evaluating new initiatives. Staff are very busy so we can't afford to just get involved into any new initiative. We are to look carefully at any new initiative to see how it fits into our school's philosophy and goals. Something new has to rate. We have a ruler now as [to] what is an effective programme and we use that … Any new initiative has to match up to Te Kotahitanga. (Principal, School 1)

Hall and Hord (2006), however, argue that "initiator"-type leaders have always been able to act in this manner. This is because they already have decisive long-range policies and goals that include but transcend any innovation. These actions stand in contrast to "manager"- and "responder"-type leaders, who are more likely to make decisions in reference to short-term, more immediate needs. Leaders who exhibit these two latter styles tend to take on an initiative on its merits, or the money it brings, rather than its coherence with school goals. Hall and Hord (2006) show that effective leaders and teachers weave innovations into pre-existing goals and understanding.

However, just as there are teachers who are currently effectively addressing educational disparities in their classrooms, there are leaders whose planning transcends and incorporates such practices into previously determined, morally based social justice objectives. The problem is there are just not enough of these teachers/leaders to bring about effective change on their own. Nor are there enough that can spread such innovations across their institutions in a way that provides coherence and continuity across the organisation without assistance, hence the importance of a systematic means of providing professional learning opportunities for teachers and leaders.

This approach is necessary in order to develop a systematic means of identifying and spreading the number of leaders who are both more certain of where the school needs to go and also more selective when considering offers of support from external agencies. As one principal explained to us, they now focus their decision making on how they can support classroom activities and address the other issues as they come up. One outcome of this approach permeating the school is that staff are happy to accept responsibility for the learning of all students because they have the capacity to do so. Indeed, staff now see all students as people they have caring and learning relationships with, and this understanding extends to those students with the most severe needs (Berryman, 2008). So what began as a project to benefit Māori students has done so, but it has also been extended to benefit other students as a result of the cultural shift undergone by the school.

One of the 12 Phase 3 school principals explained to us how the fundamental principles of the reform were beginning to permeate the whole culture of the school and how they see the future. The principal described how, as a result of their five-year participation in the reform, their school has developed an ongoing problem-solving culture where staff members now seek to examine and seek solutions to problems in relational terms rather than trying to find singular or blaming causes. The outcome of this culture change is that solutions necessarily involve co-construction between partners rather than decisions being handed down from the more powerful to the less powerful. In addition, the indicators of these problems are now evidence based rather than based on assumptions or majority opinions.

In many ways this process is an indication of the understanding that all cultures are socially constructed and are based on differing ideological foundations. What is different in the new culture of the school is a critical evaluation and rejection of a culture that was taken for granted, sometimes not even acknowledged or understood, yet quietly dominant. Now there is a purposeful acknowledgement and understanding of those ideologies, beliefs and values that are fundamental to the new discourse that drives the school. The principal described the school as now having a culture that is relationship and evidence based, wherein problem solving is through co-construction.

They had also managed to shift the culture of the school from one where teachers held all the knowledge (and hence the power) and transmitted this knowledge in privatised spaces. These spaces were separate from one another, with limited collective responsibility and accountability to one another beyond their classrooms. The new culture that had developed over the five years was one where they had built learning communities in which knowledge was located in what Datnow, Hubbard, and Mehan (2002) term "situated activities". In these contexts, students learn from one another as well as from teachers. Teachers are part of the learning culture of the school and demonstrate this quality on a daily basis. The emphasis is now on leaders at all levels creating responsive contexts for learners and learning at all levels of the school. In this way, these schools are examining the school's culture and power relations, the discursive positioning people occupy, whose voices are legitimate, who will benefit from the school's activities and to whom their schools are accountable (Bishop, 2005). How these issues of power relations are addressed will strongly determine the overall culture of the school.

Creating a new school culture by examining how power relations are played out in the school's policies, procedures, rules, relationships and interactions at all levels (students, teachers, senior management, parents, community and policy makers) is a crucial step to restructuring the school. Fullan (1993) suggests that reculturing leads to restructuring more effectively than the reverse. He, along with Elmore (2004), suggests that most experiences of restructuring reforms show that new structures are expected to result in new behaviours and cultures, but mostly fail to do so. It is problematic when teachers and administrators begin working in ways that suit the reform only to discover that school structures are ill suited to the orientation and cannot be altered (Fullan, 1993, p. 68). In other words, structural changes, such as those that support the implementation of new institutions, need to be undertaken in response to the cultural and relational changes that are taking place in discursive positioning, relationships and interactions in classrooms and within the wider school. As Elmore (2004) found in his 1996 study, referred to earlier, "changing structures did not change practice, it only relabeled existing practice with new names" (p. 4).

Confronting resistance

Ownership by a school of a reform initiative means a common acceptance of the mission and goals of the organisation by all those who are employed within it. As we have seen, collaborative efforts among staff members generate the most productive outcomes, so it is vital that all staff are encouraged to participate. However, as DuFour and Eaker (1998) insist, if the mission and goals of the school are to be communicated, "those who violate the vision and values must be confronted" (p. 112). They suggest that in an ideal world, every member of staff should be engaged in this process, but in reality it is most likely to fall to the principal to address resistance. It is critical that "principals fulfil this leadership function if vision and values are to be reinforced" (p. 112).

This means that if the reform process is one that promotes collaboration between teachers, and the school wishes to take ownership of this process, then it is essential that all staff are offered the opportunity to participate. Where it is agreed by the majority that this is worthwhile, "the principal must be willing to insist that a teacher who works in isolation change his or her behaviour" (p. 112). To not do so is to put the reform initiative at risk, and consequently continue to perpetuate the status quo. The reform will not progress satisfactorily when individuals act in their own best interests in the face of the collectively determined interests of the students, their families and the school. Indeed, as DuFour and Eaker (1998) argue, all those involved suffer: the principal, the resistant teacher, the other staff, the targeted students and the wider school community. The principal can lose credibility and can be viewed as prioritising the avoidance of conflict in preference to promoting the goals of the reform. The resistant teacher can lose the opportunity for professional growth and learning. The proactive staff miss the opportunity for the gains that nonconfrontational, co-operative activities can produce for themselves and their students' achievement. Target students and their families can miss out on the opportunities being offered by the full implementation of the reform initiative across the school.

To place all these gains at risk for the sake of an individual's self-determination is to misunderstand the meaning of self-determination, because it ignores the point that self-determination is only able to be realised in relation to other people. Self-determination is not a call for isolation, but rather for the promotion and protection of an individual's mana (status/power), and this only occurs in relation to others. Therefore, it is vital that when principals identify resistance and move to address it, they do so within this understanding of self-determination; one that promotes and addresses the mana of individuals involved in a respectful manner, but in relation to others. Of course how principals and schools address resistance will vary from setting to setting, but above all the evidence is clear that "change efforts stall when leaders do not address violations of vision and values" (DuFour & Eaker, 1998, p. 113).

The issue of compromise is something that will probably arise during conversations between the principal and the resistant teacher or teachers. However, before agreeing to a compromise, it would be better for the principal to use the approach promoted by narrative therapists, who suggest externalising a problem by saying, "There is a problem. How might we together address this issue?" This approach is preferred to personalising the problem to the resistance or to the resistant teacher. Whatever the case, it is important that the principal has the opportunity to re-emphasise the school goal and the agreed-to processes for addressing that goal, and talking through how the resistant person can be assisted to support the goal.

Resource allocation and prioritisation

Time and money are two resources that are always scarce in schools, yet the prioritisation of these two resources is a very clear indicator of a school's ownership of the reform. As was identified in Chapter Four, in order to bring about sustainable educational reform it is necessary to develop new *institutions*. As Elmore (2004) has argued, unless there are new institutions developed to support the classroom changes, these developments in the classroom will not flourish. However, it is very clear that new institutions such as classroom observations and feedback sessions, or the development of small-scale professional learning communities such as the co-construction meetings promoted in the Te Kotahitanga project, all take up teachers' time. If this is added to an already busy schedule without a reduction in demands on teachers' time in other ways, then the reform is destined to fail.

The introduction of new institutions requires that the school re-evaluate the priority of some other time-using institutions that teachers are expected to take part in. The allocation of time, and consequent behaviours, is one of the best indications of what is really important and valued by the school. Just as there needs to be a quantitative evaluation of time allocation, there also needs to be a qualitative evaluation. For example, if the school promotes the movement from individual traditional transmission teaching approaches towards more collaborative, interactive, facilitative and discursive learning approaches, yet maintains the dominance of meetings where better ways of transmitting subject knowledge are discussed, then the reform initiative will founder in confusion and conflict between traditional institutions and the newer ones.

A further indication of the value placed on transformative practice will be seen in the roles and function of staff. If the power structures remain the same as those developed under traditional approaches to teaching, then the incumbents will come into conflict with newly influential and powerful staff who are charged with promoting the new approaches to learning. Responsive restructuring, therefore, does not only mean developing new institutions that are only pertinent to the reform initiative; it also means re-examining the power relations within the staff. In this way, power relations that promote the new vision and goals will be developed.

One example from Te Kotahitanga is where the traditional power of middle managers (heads of subject departments, heads of faculties) is being challenged by the rise in importance of professional development leaders within the schools. Where the traditional role of these middle managers remains unchanged, there arises considerable conflict with the innovation, and in some schools traditional power holders who have been unwittingly bypassed have become resistant. In other schools, middle managers have been expected to become leaders or at least significant participants in the new order. Whatever the case, it is vital that participants understand from the outset that involvement in theory-based reforms that seek to change the very core of classroom practice will involve critical reflection on all aspects of the school culture, including power relationships.

The second resource that will need to be reprioritised is funding. As Elmore (2004) notes, implementing educational reform (e.g., involving teachers' time, in-school professional developers, outside experts and supporting principals, and creating time for observations and feedback sessions) is very expensive. The classic response from most administrators who have financial responsibility is that they are happy to try the new approach as long as someone else is prepared to pay for it. Generally that someone else means someone in the "next level of government above the one in which they are working" (p. 123). However, Elmore questions whether schools are currently actually spending the money they allocate for professional development effectively. In other words, is all the money that is spent directly aimed at improving student learning? If not, then maybe it should not continue to be spent, and the funds should be reallocated to activities that directly promote student learning and achievement.

There are other ways of gathering funds from within schools, and Elmore (2004) identifies from Miles (1995) and Miles and Darling-Hammond (1998) such activities as:

> reducing the staffing demands of specialised programmes for teachers and students, carefully tracking differential staff patterns across schools and grade levels, scheduling longer blocks of interactional time, refocusing categorical and special purpose funding for instructional purposes, reallocating non-instructional administrative funds to service instructional purposes, and most importantly, reallocating and focusing existing expenditures on professional development. (p. 124)

Celebrating achievement and gains

Ownership of the reform will be seen in the ways that schools recognise and celebrate the progress that is being made towards the goals by students. This will also be seen in how schools include families and the wider community in the reform. Celebrating achievement and gains is also important for those staff members who were perhaps less enthusiastic participants and who had to be encouraged to participate, because they will be keen to hear about gains that are being made. On this matter it is vital to appreciate Guskey's (1995) suggestion that outcomes can be seen in a variety of variables, not just in student test achievement. Ownership of the reform will be seen in the means schools have to identify gains across a range of indicators, from student experiences, to participation, to engagement with learning, to achievement. Also worth rewarding is the energy that is extended to build up skills and capacity among the staff to gather and process evidence of student gains across a range of indicators. Where they are unable to do so, appropriate external assistance should be sought to meet these needs.

In addition, schools and districts need to fully understand the value and impact of the reform so that they are able to allocate funding appropriately, or creatively seek new funding sources once external research-generated funding is no longer available.

Conclusion

The seventh consideration for sustaining a reform—both within the original schools and when extending a sustainable reform to other sites—is that there needs to be a means, built into the reform from the very outset, whereby ownership of the reform shifts from the external originators to those within the school. One of the key considerations is the creation of conditions within the project itself that will ensure that knowledge of and authority for the project shift from external actors to teachers, schools and districts. This shift in ownership ensures the reforms become self-generative while being of sufficient depth to maintain the integrity of the reform. Above all, the model must contain a way for schools to take responsibility for the ongoing success of the initiative in terms of ensuring that the aims of increasing student achievement and reducing disparities continue to be met.

Shifts in the ownership of the reform mean that within the reform there needs to be a means of developing the capacity of in-school teachers, professional developers and other leaders, including the school's principals and national and regional education leaders, so that they can maintain the integrity and progress of the reform within the school/s, and generate funding and ongoing supportive professional development and research associated with the reform. Such a process should be designed to overcome the problems created by ongoing staff and administrator turnover, and to provide ongoing support for the new institutions that have been developed within the schools as part of the reform.

Perhaps the best test of whether a school has taken ownership of the reform, which is a major test of the sustainability of any reform initiative, would be to imagine what we would see in a school in five to 10 years from the time the external innovators left. There is no simple answer to this question, as Timperley et al. (2007) note. To them, a surface answer would be that after a number of years we would expect to see "the programme or pedagogical approaches that were promoted through the professional learning/development experience" (p. 218). However, they point out that this may actually lead to a static interpretation of what the reform set out to achieve, because what remains could be just surface manifestations of the deeper underlying principles of the reform. McLaughlin and Mitra (2001) agree. They acknowledge that sustaining theory-based reform means more than continuing the level of implementation that was achieved at the point of departure of the external initiators, resources and support. Both sets of authors argue that a more useful definition of sustainability should include those conditions that are an integral part of the reform and have been so from its very inception; that is, in this case, the GPILSEO criteria.

The first criterion is whether the process of measurable goal setting and measurement for the reduction of educational disparities through improvements in student outcomes can still be identified. The second criterion is whether there remains an opportunity for teachers to continually interact with the principles of the new pedagogies. This would need to exist in such a way that it has become part of the thinking and practice of teachers to the extent that they are able to continue to demonstrate their understanding of "how their adaptations fitted with the fundamental principles of the change agenda and their practice context" (Timperley et al., 2007, p. 219). As McLaughlin and Mitra

(2001) suggest, the reform needs to include the means to deepen changes in teaching practice and theorising in ways that will keep practice vital and responsive to changes in curriculum, student demographics and the context of the school and the classroom.

In addition, as Robinson et al. (2009) argue, the reform needs a means whereby teachers' theories of action are engaged in an ongoing manner so that teachers' theories—those filters through which change messages are interpreted—are engaged and challenged on an ongoing basis. This is to "help teachers to make their beliefs explicit, and to evaluate their worth in relation to the proposed alternative theory of action" (p. xiii). In other words, as Coburn (2003) suggests, whether a reform moves from being "external" to "internal" hinges on whether teachers, schools and policy makers have the capacity to "sustain, spread, and deepen reform principles themselves" (p. 7). Indeed, this is a major test not only of the schools but also of the reform itself. For while it becomes the ultimate responsibility of policy makers, schools and teachers to implement and sustain the reform in such a way as to reduce educational disparities by improving the achievement of those students currently not benefiting from education, it is also a major test of the reform itself as to whether it creates those conditions that are necessary to shift the authority and knowledge of the reform's principles and practices from external designers to those who will put it all into practice on an ongoing basis.

The third criterion is that leadership should have created wider policy, institutional and organisational arrangements that support "the sustainability of principled practice and improved student outcomes" (Timperley et al., 2007, p. 219). Of particular importance to this condition is that there remains evidence of the maintenance of ongoing opportunities for teachers to continue to critically reflect on their own discursive positioning and their theories of action, and to problem solve collaboratively with colleagues about the impact of their practice on student learning and associated outcomes.

The fourth criterion is that leadership will be distributed in such a manner as to be seen to be supporting the reform. By this we mean that in-school facilitation team members will be part of the organisational structure of the school, with permanent positions as professional developers. In addition, principals and boards of trustees will be seen to be acting as pedagogic/instructional leaders in that their actions will closely support what is happening in the classrooms.

The fifth criterion is that the core classroom practices will be spread to all the classrooms and subjects of all the teachers in the school. While the principles and practices of the reform will be adopted to varying degrees, there will be systems and processes in place to support teachers to continue their adoption through critical investigation of the ongoing usefulness of the reform. There will also be a significant and measurable increase in family and community participation in the education of their children, and the relationships between the families and the schools will be based on those promoted by the reform.

The sixth criterion is that there will be an institutionalised means of engaging teachers in individual and collaborative evidence-based problem solving. Leaders and teachers will have the individual and collective capability to gather and critically reflect on appropriate evidence of student performance to inform their ongoing practice and to evaluate the effects of their efforts. Accurate measures of student attendance, stand-downs, suspensions, early-leaving exemptions, retention rates and achievement data will have been developed and will be in use in real time. Electronic student management systems will be being used effectively to provide data for formative purposes in collaborative settings and for summative purposes.

Finally, there will be evidence of ownership having shifted from the originators of the reform to the school itself. Evidence of this will be seen in schools asking hard questions of themselves in terms of target students' achievement; the school will be a comprehensive responsive organisation; capacity building among teachers will be an easily identifiable feature; resistance will be regularly confronted; resources will be reallocated and reprioritised in relation to the specific goals of the school; and achievements and gains will be acknowledged and celebrated. Above all, schools will demonstrate that they have an unwavering focus on the goals of reducing disparities through raising the achievement of those students the system has failed to serve well in the past.

CHAPTER NINE

System-wide Support for Sustainability

Governments can push accountabilty, provide incentives (pressure
and supports), and/or foster capacity building ... If they do all three,
they have a chance of going the distance. (Fullan, 2007, p. 237)
... teachers and schools are more likely to be able to sustain and
deepen reform over time when school and district policy and
priorities are compatible or aligned with reform. Spreading reform
norms, beliefs, and principles within schools and districts may be
a key mechanism for developing this normative coherence.
(Coburn, 2003, p. 7)

Introduction

Although this book primarily focuses on sustaining and expanding large-scale
educational reforms at the school level, we would not have completed the picture if we
did not look at the important role and responsibilities that governments, their policy
development and implementation agencies and associated groups at the system level
play in sustaining and extending educational reform. As Fullan (2003) says, "only
small-scale, non-lasting improvement can occur if the system is not helping" (p. 219).
Governments, as the primary policy-making arm of the wider education sector, must

lead and support educational reforms by creating appropriate and responsive policy frameworks within which reform can flourish. Other agencies, such as researchers, professional developers, evaluators (e.g., the Education Review Office), teachers' professional bodies and schools, must also play their part in informing and working within these policy frameworks.

Although it is clear that classrooms are the most effective sites in which to commence educational reform (Alton-Lee, 2003; Hattie, 2003a), it is vital to remember that classrooms are situated in, and inextricably linked to, the school and the wider education system. This suggests the need for reform to include the systemic level, because, as Coburn (2003) suggests, teachers are better able to implement and sustain change when there are "mechanisms in place at multiple levels of the system to support their efforts" (p. 6). In other words, teachers are further strengthened in their ability to sustain change if it is supported by a broader systemic focus on reform at school, and when this is reflected at the national level.

In this book, as identified in Figure 1.3, we suggest the need for an expansive view of who is involved in developing and implementing educational reform. This is achieved by providing a framework that will enable all those involved to participate in the reform. This will be achieved by everyone critically reflecting on the part they themselves can play within an interdependent relationship, which includes changing classroom practice alongside school-level and system-wide policy-level reforms.

GPILSEO at the system level

In this chapter we will again use the GPILSEO model as an aid to identifying the necessary elements at the system level. We will focus on actions the individuals at this level need to undertake in order to develop, implement, sustain and extend theory-based reforms. In Figure 1.3, the GPILSEO model identifies that at the system level there need to be:

- *goals:* national policy goals to realise the potential of those least well served by the system by raising their overall achievement, thereby reducing historical disparities
- *pedagogy:* a means whereby inservice professional learning opportunities and professional development for teachers is onsite, ongoing and dialogic, and where preservice teacher education is aligned with inservice professional development so that each supports the other in implementing culturally responsive pedagogies of relations
- *institutions:* the development of supportive policies and infrastructure that provide incentives for teachers, and support for schools that is ongoing, interactive and consistent
- *leadership:* national-level support and professional development for leaders to promote distributed instructional/pedagogical leadership models

- *spread:* collaboration between policy funders, researchers and practitioners that is responsive to community needs and aspirations, in an iterative process of interaction, feedback and adaptation
- *evidence:* national-level support for the production of appropriate evidence that will enable collaborative, formative problem solving and decision making that is ongoing and interactive, and from which grow supportive policies regarding standards, assessments and the mix of accountability and capacity building
- *ownership:* national ownership of the problem and the provision of sufficient funding and resources to see solutions within a defined period of time, and in an ongoing, embedded manner.

Goals: Revisiting the current policy context

The current system-wide response to educational disparities in terms of policy is to "continue New Zealand's transformation to a dynamic, knowledge-based economy and society, underpinned by the values of fairness, opportunity and security" (Ministry of Education, 2006, p. 9). To attain this objective, the Government has set two goals for the New Zealand education system: "to build an education system that equips New Zealanders with 21st century skills and to reduce systemic underachievement in education" (p. 11). To reach these goals, the Ministry of Education has as its mission "to raise achievement and reduce disparities" (p. 17). This dual approach is seen as necessary because, although by international standards average student achievement is high, "we still have one of the widest gaps between our highest and lowest achievers" (p. 17), and this situation exists within schools rather than between schools (Alton-Lee, 2003). In addition, according to Hattie (2003a) and Ballard (2008), it exists despite, rather than because of, the socioeconomic status of the school.

The Ministry of Education has identified three areas that will receive special support and attention over the decade 2004–14 in order to address these aims of raising achievement and reducing disparity. The first is quality teaching. "The research is unambiguous—effective teaching is the single biggest influence over a student's learning and success. Good teaching is powerful and can offset many factors that can exert a negative influence in a student's life" (Ministry of Education, 2004, p. 5). The second is to support families and communities to play a greater part in the education of their children: "Supportive families and communities are also powerful influences on learning outcomes. The better the formal learning environment respects and affirms the learner's home environment and community, and incorporates this into the learning process, the higher the level of likely achievement" (p. 5). The third means of improving learning outcomes is to support quality providers that are first and foremost focused on student achievement: "We need to help create a culture of professional debate and provide professional support that helps make a real difference for students" (p. 5).

The Ministry of Education's Statement of Intent (2006) states that to ensure achievement levels are maintained and improved we need an education system that:

- has a broad view of quality and relentlessly strives to increase the achievement and learning of all learners throughout their lives
- recognises the importance of rapid increases in new knowledge
- emphasises new technologies and the ability to use and apply that knowledge and technology
- encompasses growing global influences
- better prepares people to keep investing in their own learning and personal development in a society that will change and become more diverse.

These points are further elaborated in policy released in 2008; namely, that reducing disparity[1] is about every individual being given the encouragement, support and opportunity to realise their educational potential, regardless of their social or cultural background, their location or their individual needs (Ministry of Education, 2008).

One problem that has been identified in these Ministry of Education documents (2004, 2006, 2008) is that there is too heavy an emphasis on the power of quality teaching to bring about change in historical educational disparities. Thrupp (2008) suggests that "overemphasising the power of quality teaching has the effect of scapegoating teachers for wider problems" (p. 2). In other words, such an approach to policy has the potential to underplay the part the Government and other agencies at this level can and need to play in addressing contextual issues that have an impact on schooling. The net effect is that an overemphasis on quality teaching has the potential to be divisive and can lead to everyone involved "constantly sniping at one another" (Fullan, 2007, p. 249) rather than playing a collegial part in solving what after all is a collective problem. It is vital to remember that classrooms are situated in and inextricably linked to the broader school and its systems, and also reflect the wider society. Patterns of discrimination and inequality that exist in the wider society may well be reflected in the arrangements of the education system, schools and classrooms. Although this need not be a limitation on teachers' or schools' potential for change, it does signal that policies that address the wider context are necessary.

The education debt

Reducing disparities and raising achievement have long been conflated with addressing the achievement "gap", but recently in New Zealand the policy focus has shifted to one

---

1 The disparities between our highest and lowest achieving students are evident in truancy, suspension and participation rates, which identify groups that are disengaged from the education system. Young children missing out on the opportunity to participate in quality early childhood education, too many people leaving schools and tertiary education without qualifications, Māori and Pasifika people and those from low socioeconomic backgrounds receiving less value from education and being overrepresented among students who underachieve, learners with special education needs and people for whom English is a second language are other groups which evidence suggests are achieving at a lower level than they ought to be.

of "realising Māori potential" (Ministry of Education, 2008), the gaps metaphor having been seen as too negative. However, as identified above, these policy frameworks have as their fundamental basis the concept that increasing Māori student achievement can primarily be attended to in the nation's classrooms. Yet the problem is not likely to be addressed there in any sustainable manner unless there is long-term, system-level attention given to what Ladson-Billings (2006) identifies as the accumulation of achievement disparities, which she terms the "education debt".

Using the notion of the national debt as a metaphor, Ladson-Billings (2006) suggests that it is the *annual accumulation* of achievement gaps, as has been seen in New Zealand since educational disparities were first identified in the Hunn report in 1960, that needs to be addressed rather than any one gap. By this she means that just as the accumulation of annual fiscal deficits produces an economic debt, so the accumulation of achievement gaps over time has produced an education debt; a debt the education system owes to Māori children who have been short changed by the education system for generations. In other words, it is the long-term intergenerational effects of the legacies of an education system that is oriented to the interests of the dominant group that has created this education debt. She quotes Robert Haverman, an eminent economist, who suggests that the education debt is:

> the foregone schooling resources that we could have (should have) been investing in (primarily) low income kids, which deficit leads to a variety of social problems (e.g., crime, low productivity, low wages, low labor force participation) that require on-going public investment. This required investment sucks away resources that could go to reducing the achievement gap. (p. 5)

However, it is not just a matter of more funding. Ladson-Billings (2006) argues that the "historical, economic, socio-political, and moral decisions and policies that characterize our society have created the education debt" (p. 5). Christine Sleeter (2005) agrees:

> Like the US, New Zealand has spent over a century building an educational system, infrastructure, and set of beliefs around the education of students of European descent. The severe underachievement of Māori students reflects this history. Although it is not clear that conventional teaching processes that emphasize transmitting knowledge didactically promote the most optimal learning among students of European descent, it is clear that this system has been abysmal for Māori students. Conventional classroom processes and their supporting beliefs have a very strong weight of tradition and on-going institutional support, which makes them extraordinarily difficult to change. (p. 4)

After visiting seven Te Kotahitanga schools in 2005, Sleeter (2005) went on to warn of the danger of shifting the direct focus of the Te Kotahitanga project from Māori student achievement toward a focus on all students. Should this happen, the traditional ways of developing relationships and interactions will reassert themselves, to the detriment of Māori students. She then suggested that policy makers need to be very courageous and continue "to intentionally and explicitly maintain its primary focus on Māori student achievement, evaluating the potential benefit of any proposed action in relationship to its impact on Māori students" (p. 5). Sleeter continues by suggesting a way forward:

> Ultimately, the only way to reconfigure the schooling process so that it works for *both* Māori and Pākehā students is to reconfigure schooling around Māori ways of knowing, using a focus on Māori student achievement as the touchstone for evaluating changes to the processes and systems of education. What will emerge from a sustained focus on reconstructing classroom processes for Māori student achievement will be schooling that works better for both Māori and Pākehā students. (p.6)

Ranginui Walker (1990) has long maintained that Māori educational failure is a product of an unjust social order that has arisen out of the colonial experience. Through the process of colonisation, Māori history, knowledge and ways of being have been devalued and replaced with those of the coloniser, with educators often ignoring or denying Māori a voice or a place within the education system, and education itself serving to reproduce the cultural practices and values of the dominant group (Tuuta, Bradnum, Hynds, & Higgins, 2004). Such a situation means that schools allow for the transmission and reproduction of validated and socially approved knowledge and cultural practices, typically of the dominant social group, while excluding or negating knowledge and cultural practices of minority, indigenous or diverse groups (Bertanees & Thornley, 2004; Bishop & Glynn, 1999). Durie (2005) suggests that:

> it is illusory to develop policies, programmes and practices that purport to be 'blind' to race and ethnicity when for an increasingly large number of people an ethnic orientation underlies both personal and collective identity, provides pathways to participation in society, and largely influences the ways in which societal institutions respond to their needs. (p. 1)

Denying Māori culture and ethnicity a significant place in New Zealand educational theorising and policy making has long been the norm and has played a major part in developing the education debt. As G. H. Smith (1997) has argued, the marginalisation of Māori cultural aspirations, preferences and practices in education has occurred alongside the economic and political subordination of Māori. Denial of the lived realities of Māori people and the role education has played has also been a common feature of educational theorising. G. H. Smith (1997) and L. Smith (1999) see the consistent underachievement of Māori as a struggle between Māori rejecting a schooling system that does not fit them and the persistence of educators' attempts to convert Māori to the mainstream way. This struggle is represented as that between educational institutions as agents of social reproduction while also being seen as places that can achieve social change, and policy makers not attending to this tension.

The centrality of culture to learning has been identified by a number of authors (Bishop & Glynn, 1999; Gay 2000; Ladson-Billings, 1995, 2006) when they identified how the dominant culture plays a major role in supporting the learning of children of their culture. These authors suggest that a necessary part of the policy shift that is needed in education is a means whereby the previously marginalised cultures can be allowed a place in contemporary classrooms. In the USA, for example, there are several studies suggesting that "African-centred" education intertwines cultural competence with academic achievement (Asante, 1991; Hilliard, 1992; Lee, 1994; Murrell, 1993; Ratteray-Davies, 1994). Cultural dissonance, in contrast, occurs in classrooms because traditional power structures are inherently unequal, and because knowledge and communication styles are often culturally rooted. If, therefore, Māori are to benefit from schooling, the system cannot set out to invalidate Māori knowledge.

Systemic support for pedagogic reform to depth

The provision of effective learning opportunities for teachers

Given the caveats identified above, there have been a number of improvements in a positive direction in New Zealand in recent years (Wylie, 2007). It has been recognised at a policy level that providing effective professional learning opportunities for teachers so that they understand the basis of their core business is probably the most effective school-based change initiative that any policy maker and funding agency can undertake. Building the capability of those currently working within the education system will increase the capacity of the whole system to bring about effective educational reform (Elmore, 2004). However, realising this aspiration is not simple, because current assumptions and practices continually need to be assessed and challenged where they are found to be wanting. For example, currently professional developers are mainly external to the schools, and they tend to provide professional development opportunities externally or on a limited in-school basis. However, as Timperley et al. (2007) state, in a detailed investigation of the provision of professional learning opportunities for teachers:

> it is generally accepted that listening to inspiring speakers or attending one-off workshops rarely changes teacher practice sufficiently to impact on student outcomes. Yet, at least in the United States, this type of activity is the predominant model of professional development. The popularity of conferences and one-day workshops in New Zealand indicates that it is not too different in this country. (p. xxv)

Timperley et al. (2007) also warn of a number of other common assumptions about the efficacy of providing professional learning opportunities for teachers. They discovered a number of extended opportunities for teacher learning that were having an impact on student outcomes, but they found that these are not necessarily more effective than one-off opportunities because it is more the quality of the interaction than the time involved. Indeed, they found no evidence that the provision of sufficient time and money for teachers would see them engage in effective professional learning that would have a positive impact on student outcomes—a common assumption made by many associated with New Zealand schooling. Nor did they find evidence that the opposite extreme was effective; that is, where outside experts develop strictly prescribed practices for teaching "with an underpinning rationale and monitor their implementation carefully to ensure integrity" (p. xxvi).

The professional development model for Te Kotahitanga began with ideas from a professional development model that we had identified in the stocktake of diagnostic tools used in Māori-language learning settings (Bishop et al., 2001b) and the evaluation of Aro Matawai Urunga-ā-Kura (AKA) (Bishop, Berryman, Richardson, & Glynn, 2001c). In both of these studies, teachers had identified from their own experiences the type of professional development that was most effective for them. To them, professional development should create power-sharing contexts in which self-determining individuals and groups/communities work together to set goals and outcomes as part of their ongoing professional activities. The successful design and implementation of professional development, according to these teachers, is not a matter of one-off sessions provided by outside experts transmitting knowledge. They understand that this latter type of professional development results in minimal teacher uptake of skills and knowledge with very little flow-on implementation, whereas the former engages them in meaningful developments in their classrooms. These teachers also noted that procedures are learnt and implemented with greater reliability when they go from professional development (instruction, demonstration and practice) to immediate implementation and practice in their own classroom setting, with in-class support and ongoing reflection and feedback.

For them, this model was far more beneficial than if professional development is distributed to the school using the outside expert model only. These teachers felt that an interactive approach to professional development that treats teachers as capable, reflective professionals leads to greater opportunities for ako (reciprocal teaching and learning) to occur. They thought that teachers and trainers themselves stand to learn much from the ongoing interactions and patterns of practice that occur between teachers and students after their participation in the professional development.

The period between professional development and applying the procedure in an authentic classroom context is also crucial to the successful uptake of the skills and knowledge required to use the newly acquired procedures reliably. Indeed, as identified by Hall and Ramsay (1994), these two studies (Bishop et al., 2001b; Bishop et al., 2001c) also found that the most effective professional development is onsite, ongoing and collaboratively reflective. The teachers in the two studies suggested that effective professional development requires a model of dynamic interactions that are the result of power-sharing relationships being established between the professional developers and the professional development participants. This dynamic model of professional development suggests a spiralling approach that initially involves collaborative reflection on the experiences, and then the ongoing development of relationships among the participants.

On a broader front, the more extensive study by Timperley et al. (2007) supported this approach to professional development. This investigation of 97 core studies (along with other supplementary studies) of teacher professional learning and development that had substantive student outcomes—including personal, social and academic attributes—found that there are seven elements in the professional learning context that have positive impacts on student outcomes:

- providing sufficient time for extended opportunities to learn, and using the time effectively (i.e., the quality of the use of time is as important as the amount of time)
- engaging external expertise, which requires funding
- focusing on engaging teachers in the learning process, which is more important than being concerned about whether they volunteered or not
- challenging problematic discourses, which involves iterative cycles of teachers considering alternatives and the impact on student outcomes of a range of discursive positions
- providing opportunities to interact in a community of professionals that focus on analysing the impact of teaching on student learning in an iterative, ongoing manner
- ensuring content is consistent with wider policy trends
- in school-based initiatives, having leaders actively leading the professional learning opportunities (p. xxvi).

These findings were published in 2007 as part of the Best Evidence Synthesis programme of the New Zealand Ministry of Education, which was developed in response to the need for policy development to be based on evidence rather than rhetoric. This movement to policy that sees the Ministry of Education "strengthening its approach to use evidence to make decisions" (Ministry of Education, 2008, p. 37) has seen the publication of seven best evidence syntheses since June 2003, all aimed at providing the Government, its agencies and schools with an evidential base from which to develop policy, introduce new practices through its service providers and support schools to assess and modify their own practices. Alongside this new focus on evidence is the policy of focusing research, development and evaluation on student achievement rather than the implementation of programmes.

This focus has been supported by the development of a number of initiatives that are evidence based and where the focus on enhancing student achievement is central. These include the National Education Monitoring Project (NEMP), which has been examining what achievement looks like across the curriculum and across the schooling sector since 1995 (see http://nemp.otago.ac.nz). The researchers and developers of this project use teacher experiences at all levels, including the development of test items, marking and evaluation. Teachers also undertake the testing, providing them with valuable professional learning opportunities they can take back into their own classrooms and schools. Along with NEMP, national education exemplars have been developed, which provide examples of authentic pieces of evidence of student achievement at each level across the curriculum for teachers to match their students' progress and to inform the next learning steps. These exemplars have been developed for both English- and Māori-medium schooling. Finally, asTTle (Assessment Tools for Teaching and Learning) is a large, flexible, electronic bank of test items that teachers can draw on for formative and summative use in English and Māori, again developed and trialled by teachers in conjunction with researchers.

The development of these national smart tools helps teachers to implement the policy of teaching as achievement focused and evidence based. These tools are being implemented with professional development support at a national level by programmes such as AtoL (Assess to Learn), a professional development programme that works with schools to gather and analyse student data and to introduce more effective learning programmes based on the analysis of student performance. These approaches and understandings, along with the appropriate smart tools, have been used and applied in other research and development programmes such as Te Kotahitanga. The professional development programmes both inform and implement the findings of the Best Evidence Synthesis programme in an iterative way. In other words, alongside the shifts in policy has been the development of the smart tools and the professional development programmes that inform, support and implement the policies that seek to make education for Māori and other marginalised students more effective.[2]

There have been some promising gains made as a result of the changes in policy by the Ministry of Education. Wylie (2007) argued that:

> It is only recently, after the Ministry of Education took the lead in providing research-based professional development, new assessment tools that could quickly identify gaps in student learning, and resources that teachers could use to meet those identified needs, that New Zealand saw gains at the primary level, particularly for low-performing students. Māori student achievement has shared in these gains: but 53 percent of Māori boys still left school with no qualifications in 2005.[3] (p. 2)

Alignment between preservice and inservice teacher education

In a recent international study, Cochran-Smith and Zeichner (2005) identified the lack of links between preservice teacher education and inservice practice and the perceived

---

2   However, currently there are no structured ways of introducing the best evidence synthesis documents themselves into schools other than simply posting them out and providing lectures on their content. Part of the irony of this approach is that it is these documents that have synthesised what we know about the approaches that best support teacher learning. There is a need to use this knowledge to effectively introduce these publications to schools in ways that best reflect this learning.
3   This figure was reduced to 37 percent by 2007 (Hood, 2008).

hierarchies within the education sector as major impediments to comprehensive educational reform. In New Zealand there is need for a policy-driven rectification at a systemic level of this misalignment between preservice teacher education and inservice professional development so that each can support the other in implementing the benefits of large-scale, theory-based educational reforms. Such alignment would also create ongoing systems to support teachers as lifelong learners; as Smylie (1995) notes, "[w]e will fail … to improve schooling for children until we acknowledge the importance of schools not only as places for teachers to work but also as places for teachers to learn" (p. 92).

One example of this misalignment was seen recently when 422 teachers in the Te Kotahitanga project (Bishop et al., 2007), 60 percent of whom had been to teacher education institutions in the previous five years, were surveyed. They stated that they were keen to implement a wide and effective range of classroom interaction types. That is, they aspired to actively engage their students in the lessons, use the prior knowledge of students, use group learning processes, provide academic feedback, involve students in planning lessons, demonstrate their high expectations, stimulate critical questioning and recognise and include the culture of students in their lessons. However, detailed measured observations of their classrooms showed that 86 percent of their interactions were of a traditional nature, where they were engaged in the transmission of predetermined knowledge, monitoring to see if this knowledge had been passed on, and providing behavioural feedback in order to control the class. Only 14 percent of their classroom interactions allowed them an opportunity to create the sorts of learning relationships to which they themselves aspired. In short, despite these teachers' aspirations, the dominant classroom interactions remained active teacher and passive students, the very learning environment that Māori students identified as limiting their opportunities to engage with learning (Bishop & Berryman, 2006).

Explanations for this phenomenon vary. One theory is that this is a measure of the pervasiveness of transmission education and the schools' insistence on transmitting preset curricula. However, it has also been suggested that this situation might indicate that preservice teachers are not being provided with the appropriate knowledge and skills by their teacher education institutions, and that they rely on the school for practical training. For whatever reason, the graduates of preservice education institutions appear to be facing problems with implementing interactive approaches in their classrooms— despite aspiring to do so.

Elmore and Burney (1996) and Bishop (2007) suggest that preservice teacher education programmes need to emulate those practices outlined for the implementation of theory-based educational reforms in schools. For example, preservice teachers should be organised into professional learning communities so that they are able to become familiar with modes of assessment that will allow them to collaboratively analyse the multitude of data that are routinely collected about children to inform and modify their practice. These findings signal the need for preservice educators to integrate the theory and practice of teaching and learning (using evidence of student-teachers' instructional practice and student achievement for formative purposes) in a systematic manner so that they can practise what they learn. It also signals that schools that are receiving the new teachers need to provide preservice teachers with opportunities to receive similar classroom support to inservice teachers. They need to do this by providing ongoing objective analysis and feedback on their classroom interactions, which they critically reflect on in a collaborative problem-solving setting. In other words, because "teaching consists of a repertoire of behaviours or teaching methods and … student learning follows more or less directly from the frequency with which teachers use specific behaviours or apply a specific method" (Nuthall, 2004, p. 286), there is a need to "translate … outcomes-linked evidence into policy and into teacher education in ways that fairly represent what is actually known from the research and attends to the needs of teachers and policy-makers" (Alton-Lee, 2006, p. 623).

Preservice programmes that are conducted at universities are well placed to support ongoing teacher learning by developing a programme and culture of teacher research, because teacher research "is a way of organising professional development in such a way that it remains closely related to what teachers acknowledge as their domain of professional autonomy" (Tillema & Imants, 1995, p. 142). Introducing such practices at both the preservice and inservice levels would allow the reform and its associated paradigm shift to become self-monitoring on a day-to-day basis. The research may also enhance the status of the reform because it would be "closely related to meaningful school development in which there is a close connection among development, reflection, professionalization, and school renewal" (Tillema & Imants, 1995, p. 146).

Institutionalisation

Systemic-level support is necessary for those structural and organisational changes that schools will need to undertake in order to support the sustainability of the educational reform. That is, policy makers will need to look at the way in which reform projects and schools are funded so that changes in personnel, resourcing for in-school professional developers and the overall structure of the school can be made by the school's governance and management. Fullan (2007) points to the example of the Ontario Literacy and Numeracy Strategy, which sought to substantially improve literacy and numeracy within one election period for all 72 school districts and all 4,000 or so elementary schools in the province (p. 246). One of the eight interlocking strategies that was developed to implement the policy was that the budget for education for the province of Ontario be increased by 22 percent (12 percent accounting for inflation) in the first three years of the initiative. "Much of the new money is devoted to capacity building, with all those in challenging circumstances receiving additional earmarked resources. All this as the government is working to reduce an overall budget deficit" (p. 255).

This example shows the level of commitment that is needed at the funding level to support large-scale educational reform. It is not sufficient to promulgate policies that are responsive to identified needs, such as the plight of Māori students, and then not provide sufficient funding to make the reform a reality. The danger of embarking on a reform and its foundering due to lack of funding is too great. As we have seen, many teachers are wary of what Fullan (2007) calls "initiative-itis", where more and more programmes are promulgated, many without sufficient long-term funding support. Similarly, schools will be loath to reprioritise their own funding until they have firm evidence that the professional learning programme they are engaged in is going to be productive in terms of enhanced student outcomes. Hence the Government needs to provide substantial upfront *and* long-term monies to get the whole process going in such a way that the reform will be able to be successfully embedded. The Government needs to see this initial and long-term funding as an investment rather than a cost—an investment that will be financially beneficial for society in the long run in terms of the reduction in costs for downstream services such as welfare, health and crime prevention and incarceration needed by the students currently not well served by education.

Where the funding is to come from is a major debating point. Elmore (2004) suggests there is substantial evidence that there is considerable money available in most system-level budgets that could be used to finance large-scale improvements that use professional development effectively. He is in no doubt that the money is there. That, he says, is the good news. The bad news is that "[i]t's already been spent on something else" (p. 123) and the money has most probably been allocated to programmes that do not focus on improving student achievement. He maintains that the question is not one of funding, but of the will to reallocate funding to programmes that have a demonstrated track record of success.

The question of the wise allocation of funding and resources within schools has been addressed by Cathie Wylie (2007) in a comparison of school management structures between New Zealand and Edmonton, Canada. In this paper she identified that while both systems are of the "self-managing" type, the New Zealand approach to self-management is at the "extreme end of the continuum" (p. 2). The impact of this situation has been that it has been "harder to tackle systemic issues such as disparities in educational achievement, disparities in school capacity and capability, and the demands of school administration that frustrated principals' desire to focus on educational leadership" (pp. 2–3). Wylie explains that although schools in New Zealand act within a framework of government regulations, accountability is enacted through a three-yearly cycle of review undertaken by an entity separate from the Ministry of Education, the Education Review Office. As a result, the Ministry may work through a school's annual plans, reports and support documentation, but "it has no formal authority to work with principals in a formative way" (p. 1). This situation limits the supportive feedback it can provide to schools in ways that can enhance student learning through capability building among staff, such as supporting principals to allocate the power and resources the system has devolved for their care and use.

Although much of the funding allocated to schools is tied to specific areas such as staff salaries, there remain significant resources and funding whose allocation is at the discretion of the principals and their boards of trustees (the schools' governing body elected by parents and largely made up of parents). Although many schools do not receive sufficient operational funding to support running the school at a number of levels, there are other resources, including the use of Resource Teachers: Learning and Behaviour (RTLBs) and other support services, Special Education Grant funding and decile-weighted funding for low-decile schools, which are often not used to their best advantage. Wylie (2007) suggests a model of increased accountabilty for principals is needed that would see advances in schools as learning organisations. This model would assist principals and boards of trustees to reprioritise funding to support improvements in learning through embedding educational reforms within their schools. In this model, accountability would occur "within regular discussions of progress, that is largely formative" (p. 23). Wylie's suggestion would provide an extra feedback loop in the educational reform model (see Figure 1.2), where progress is made at each level through the provision of feedback for the learner by an educated other working from a more knowledgeable level—in this case a more experienced principal—to support the learning of the learner through collaborative examination of the performance of the learner.

Supporting schools to reform their organisational structures

The recent evaluation (Hindle, Marshall, Higgins, & Tait-McCutcheon, 2007) of the role of in-school facilitators in effectively implementing professional development found that these skilled and knowledgeable people are essential to support the implementation and sustainability of educational reform programmes. Drawing on two case study projects, Te Kauhua and Te Kotahitanga, Hindle et al. found that at the school level it is essential that a permanent position of professional development facilitator becomes confirmed within project schools so as to sustain the gains made. Hindle et al., drawing on Fullan (2005), Hall and Hord (2006) and Hargreaves (2006), suggest that policy makers should identify effective reform initiatives through robust qualitative and quantitative means and then continue to support these initiatives on an ongoing basis so that they become normal and embedded into the system and culture of the schools. Just as schools are funded for maths teachers and guidance counsellors, so too there needs to be an allocated fund for professional development facilitators so that teacher capacity building remains ongoing.

Hall and Hord (2006) and McLaughlin and Mitra (2001) go further and suggest that removal of the funding and materials from those responsible for educational reform within the schools (e.g., from the in-school professional development facilitators) will mean the end of the project and the waste of all the money expended on the project.

McLaughlin and Mitra suggest that "[m]aking provision for the resources necessary to sustain a reform effort is a 'bottom line' reformers need to negotiate at the outset with the implementing site or with funders" (p. 305).

These findings indicate that the development of a cadre of professional developers within schools—rather than at present, where they are external—will become a necessary feature of schools' staffing entitlement in the near future. Just as classroom teachers have been joined by, among others, guidance counsellors, social workers, RTLBs and teacher aides, professional staff developers will be among the next group of support staff that will need to be added to the staffing entitlements of schools because, as Elmore (2004) and Guskey (2005) explain, change in teaching practice is incremental and teachers need ongoing support to work through the steps in implementing reform practices in line with reform principles.

The necessity for ongoing in-school professional development support is illustrated by Elmore (2004). He observed a guided reading programme in which, although the intervention itself was being implemented successfully, there was little coherence with the work the target students were doing when they were not in the programme. In other words, the intervention was not successful in a cumulative sense, and despite initial student gains the results soon went flat. Clearly the next step was to "increase the level of intensity, cognitive demand, and coherence for all students" (p. 239). However, expecting teachers to consistently identify and rectify this problem on their own is problematic, for as Elmore noted, it often takes another pair of eyes to see what the teacher or principal just cannot see because they are busy solving the current problem rather than identifying the next one. Just as with students in classrooms, all learners become more powerful in their learning when a barrier or problem is identified for them and knowledge and/or skills about how they might address the problem are either provided or co-constructed with them. Hence the need for the initial intervention to morph into something that will allow teachers to continue to grow. To do so requires ongoing professional development support, and this support needs to be staffed adequately.

Other policy considerations at a national level, suggested by the Consortium for Policy Research in Education (1995), are that successful implementation, sustainability and going to scale require using all policy levers available to the state to promote and give incentives for participation in the professional development initiative. It could, for example, be connected to teacher remuneration, promotion, registration and re-registration and formal higher qualifications. There is a need for a range of initiatives to "recruit and retain talented teachers, increase teachers' knowledge and skills, and motivate greater effort, more learning, or different practices on the part of teachers" (Darling-Hammond, Cobb, & Bullmaster, 1998, p. 150). Smylie et al. (2003), in Chicago, support this analysis by suggesting that sustainable school development is more likely where there is a "coordinated focus on multiple essential supports"; for example "school leadership, teacher professional community, parent and community involvement, student-centred learning climate, high-quality instruction, social trust, and instructional program coherence" (p. 146).

Whatever the case, the message for national policy makers is that once a reform project is proven to be successful in addressing the goals that were established in the first place, then it is important to see it as an integral part of schooling and no longer as an adjunct. In effect, system-level support is needed for the development, at both national and school levels, of what St John (2002) terms the "improvement infrastructure". In this way, the *project* becomes a *programme*—a normal part of what schools are funded to provide to their communities. The message is clear: unless this essential step takes place, unless the project becomes funded as part of the normal part of schools' ongoing core business, then the project and its goals will always remain peripheral to schools' business, and the national goals of addressing educational disparities—let alone the education debt—will always remain as goals and will never be realised.

Leadership: Accountability and capacity building

According to Fullan (2007), governments can support the development of systemic leadership by promoting *accountability*, providing *incentives* (such as pressure and supports) and/or fostering *capacity building*, and it is getting the right balance between these three approaches to policy development that is crucial to supporting large-scale reform. He, along with Elmore (2004) and Guskey (2005), argue that systems that promote accountability and/or provide incentives at the expense of capacity building are systems that do not see successful educational reform.

In the USA, No Child Left Behind, an accountability-heavy policy, was legislated for in 2002. As part of No Child Left Behind all states were required to establish a series of annual standardised reading and mathematics tests for Grades 3 through to 8, and reading and mathematics tests in Grades 10, 11 or 12. Tests are to be administered to at least 95 percent of all students enrolled in each grade level. The legislation requires that each school demonstrates annually adequate progress according to a set of targets that are predetermined by the policy. If a school fails to meet these targets, there is a sequence of consequences, culminating in their being placed in a "restructuring" category after year 5, when they may be closed down or merged with a more successful school.

There are a number of problems with such approaches to national testing. Fullan (2007) reports that so much time is taken at the school and classroom level complying with assessments for students to measure their proficiency in terms of the goals set by No Child Left Behind that there is "little time left for doing the actual work of improvement" (p. 241). However, more problematic is the situation where an external accountability scheme does not allow for building the capacity of the staff to learn how to undertake the "work of improvement". As Elmore (2004) argues, no external accountability scheme can succeed in the absence of internal (school-level) accountability, which he defines as "the capacity (knowledge, skills, resources) of the entity for individual and collective responsibility to engage in daily improvement practices" (p. 241). In other words, an overemphasis on accountability systems seriously underestimates the importance of the need for school-based capacity building. Indeed, capacity building needs to precede accountability, or at least be part of a dialogue, with a realistic time frame so that both can be present. As one Te Kotahitanga principal told us after being in the project for five years, as a result of the capacity-building focus of the project, their staff were no longer concerned about being accountable for the achievement of all students, including Māori, because they now have the capacity to be accountable.

Elmore (2004) and Fullan (2007) are both very critical of policies that promote accountability-focused systems, the latter author reporting that in the USA "the gap between high and low performance has widened since 2000, precisely the opposite of what [No Child Left Behind] so forcefully intended" (p. 242). What is essential in New Zealand is that we learn from these experiences and do not introduce policies of national testing for students that are not supported by appropriate capacity-building programmes. Fullan (2007) also warns of the tendency over the past decades of governments to implement centralised high-stakes accountability systems without providing for appropriate supportive capacity building linked to results. Such scenarios have not produced ownership. Capacity building as a means of guiding and directing people's work "is carried out in a highly interactive professional learning setting. All else is clutter. Policies need to be aligned to minimize distractions and mobilize resources for continuous improvement" (p. 263).

Spread

From their detailed examination of a number of large-scale reform projects in North America, Glennan et al. (2004) distil some general lessons that can be learnt about producing widespread, deep and lasting educational reform. The first point they make is that "No matter the target of reforms or the design construct, the scale-up process is necessarily iterative and complex and requires the support of multiple actors. This is likely to remain so for the foreseeable future" (p. 647). Secondly, from an examination of the core tasks for scaling up the respective reforms in their study, they identified that "If the scale-up is to succeed, the actors involved—including developers, district officials, school leaders, and teachers—must jointly address a set of known, interconnected tasks, especially aligning policies and infrastructure in coherent ways to sustain practice" (p. 648).

In other words, as Datnow and Stringfield (2000) also identified, collaboration between policy funders, researchers and practitioners in an iterative process of interaction, feedback and adaptation is part of the wider picture that supports the sustainability of theory-based educational reforms. Timperley et al. (2007) illustrate this relationship:

The pedagogical approaches promoted in mathematics and science professional development in particular were consistent with policy emphases and recommendations by national subject associations and/or were based on generally accepted research findings. They did not occur in isolation of a wider research/policy environment. Some studies of interventions that had low or no impact were also justified on the basis of 'research', but this research was typically not of the kind that had survived the rigours of adoption by a policy or professional body or was part of a wider programme of research. The research was usually used for the purposes of prescribing particular teaching behaviours. (p. xxxi)

Communities of practice

These authors are describing what Wenger (1998) terms a "community of practice", which is a community of practitioners who share practice and understanding in order to be effective in certain specified domains. Surrounding community practices are boundaries across which "brokers" may transfer understanding and procedures. In this light, the education system may itself be conceptualised as comprising a "constellation" of communities bound together by the overall institutional enterprise(s), and in this way achieve transfer between the various groups in ways that foster a collective response to Māori and national aspirations for effective educational reform for Māori students at all levels of the system. As cited in Wearmouth and Berryman (2009), Wenger, McDermott and Snyder define "communities of practice" as:

> groups of people who share a concern, a set of problems, or a passion about a topic, and who deepen their knowledge and expertise in this area by interacting on an ongoing basis … These people … meet because they find value in their interactions. As they spend time together, they typically share information, insight and advice … They discuss their situations, their aspirations and their needs. They ponder common issues, explore ideas … They may create tools … manuals and other documents—or they may simply develop a tacit understanding that they share … However they accumulate knowledge, they become informally bound by the value that they find in learning together. This value … accrues in the personal satisfaction of knowing colleagues who understand each other's perspectives … Over time, they develop a unique perspective on their topic as well as a body of common knowledge, practices, and approaches. They also develop personal relationships and established ways of interacting. They may even develop a common sense of identity. (pp. 4–5)

Communities of practice are "important places of negotiation, learning, meaning and identity" (Wenger, 1998, p. 133). Successful communities support their own members to address the wider aims of the community. For individuals, community membership can offer access to expertise in the core function and purpose of that community, confidence in approach to problems and challenges, and a sense of purpose and belonging to both the community and the institution. Schools cannot thrive where students are not clear about the way in which they as individuals will benefit, because they will make no personal investment. Similarly, at a system level, unless all are involved in a reciprocal, iterative manner then ownership of the reform is unlikely.

Schools as institutions can do a lot to create the kind of context in which communities of practice can thrive: overtly valuing their knowledge production and learning, giving them resources (including time), encouraging participation in community work, integrating such communities into the institution and enabling their voices to be heard in decision making at the top level. Combining the needs of students (and staff and the local community) and schools is crucial in the knowledge that institutions succeed if they engage the creativity and strengths of their own stakeholders. System-wide communities of practice are those that gather round a common agenda, share understanding and practices that go towards the effective application of the reform in question and also go beyond the specific project to both co-construct new policies and practices in other areas. It is through the actions of such communities that Coburn's (2003) normative coherence (i.e., spreading the reform norms, beliefs and principles within schools and beyond) may be achieved.

Evidence to enable collaborative formative problem solving and decision making

As we saw in Chapter Seven, different forms of assessment of learning and behaviour in schools produce evidence that can reinforce or undermine the motivation of students to strive for future achievement. Assessment practices can affect students' sense of themselves as having the potential to be effective, and so student achievement may be constructed and/or constrained by the forms of assessment used (Murphy, 2002). Assessments should therefore acknowledge the importance of students being able to develop positive learning identities. There is a strong argument for assessment whose prime purpose is formative and designed to offer constructive support towards achieving competence. There is also a need to acknowledge that learning takes place in multiple localities (Gee, 2000; Street, 1993), which means that processes that seek to assess the learning and behaviour of students need to take into account students' real-life experiences. This emphasis implies a broader conceptualisation of what needs to be assessed beyond simply the characteristics of the individual learner and what has been achieved over a particular period of time. If evidence is to effectively inform educational reform, assessments need to be responsive to the different knowledge, experiences and cultural understanding within the diverse communities in which students live and are educated.

Therefore, we need to question whether some government-supported assessment policies and practices serve to keep students in a marginalised position. Some of the assumptions associated with the identification of individual difficulties in learning through norm-referenced testing intrinsically contradict notions of inclusion. For example, statistical, norm-referenced tests often lead to deterministic views of ability and a resulting restriction in expectations of achievement for some student groups. This identification of a few *problem* students results in the reproduction of underprivileged groups in society. Furthermore, poor scores on normative tests are often associated with *blaming* student attributes rather than opening up discussion about amending pedagogy to support learning and behaviour. Access to available resources and the need to determine eligibility for additional services (special educational provision) are typically argued as the need for norm-referenced assessments. Such assessments are designed to compare individual students' achievement against that of their peers (Cline, 1992). Standardised tests such as these reflect a view of intelligence as an innate capacity, which is assumed to be randomly distributed throughout populations. Norm-referenced tests of ability and attainment can "determine selectively the way in which issues are discussed and solutions proposed" (Broadfoot, 1996, p. x). However, the underlying assumption discounts a view of students as having the potential to achieve very highly given the right learning opportunities. The influence of psychometric approaches to measuring human achievement can therefore lend support to deterministic views of ability and achievement.

Goldberg and Morrison (2003) warn of the harmful effects of using standardised tests if these are not well managed and if teachers do not have an in-depth understanding of their uses and pitfalls. They warn that teachers must understand the statistical concepts necessary to interpret test results, must be able to interpret results within the context of other data and must work in an environment in which such results are taken seriously. They argue that the judicious use of standardised testing is more likely to occur where there is a strong professional community which examines data "with a good mix of curiosity and scepticism" (Goldberg & Morrison, 2003, p. 73).

Unless teachers are provided with appropriate learning opportunities to understand how these mechanisms work, such views can limit teachers' expectations of what to expect of certain students, which in turn restricts the future contributions of these students. In this regard, Tomlinson (1988) argues that, for some students from poor or disadvantaged backgrounds, lowered expectations can lead to a reproduction of underprivileged groups in schools and society. The function that such assessment practices serve in maintaining the power of the privileged and dominant groups in society may be interpreted as a powerful determining factor in explaining their continued use.

A similar problem is that of measuring Māori students against progress made by non-Māori students, especially those in the same class. Durie (1995) warns that to measure Māori progress against non-Māori is to perpetuate non-Māori being seen as the norm, the standard against which all others are to be measured, ignoring the advantage that non-Māori students have had over Māori during their entire education. He suggests that Māori student progress should be seen against their peer group. However, this continues to beg the question of how we are to address disparities if we do not make wider comparisons.

In Bourdieu and Passeron's (1973) terms, such practices are the means by which schools help to reproduce the patterns of control and subordination within society which are linked to the economic context. The rhetoric of education to promote equality is not supported by the reality that the system of education functions to maintain the children of underprivileged groups in powerless positions in society. Seen from this perspective, "success" and "failure" are social categories whose labels serve the vested interests of dominant, powerful groups in society. However, they are not simply givens; rather, some students' lack of achievement in the education system may be understood as a function of the societal, economic and political status quo which requires some children to fail in the education system.

Learning is "a fundamentally social phenomenon, reflecting our own deeply social nature as human beings capable of knowing" (Wenger, 1998, p. 3). However, the competitive climate encouraged currently by some governments, intent on target setting and narrowly conceived achievement, is in tension with policies that seek to create an inclusive classroom environment where all students have the potential to achieve. Ironically, such conflicting aspirations can be seen in the same policy documents. Assessment can be a powerful contributor to the promotion of effective learning if used in the right way. However, there is little evidence that increasing the amount of testing will enhance learning. Rather, the focus needs to be on helping teachers to use assessment and to promote teaching and learning in ways that will raise the achievement of students. To be successful, learners need to be able to take ownership of their learning, and to understand the goals they are aiming for and the motivation and skills to achieve success. Ongoing formative assessment can provide teachers with formal and informal opportunities to notice what is happening during learning activities, and to recognise where the learning of individuals and groups of students is going and how they can help to take that learning further. Formative assessment can generate evidence to enable teachers to ask questions about what they should or can do differently, thus placing teachers in a better position to use their professional knowledge, their knowledge of a range of pedagogical strategies and evidence about their students' current knowledge and understanding to be responsive to and connect to students.

The focus and process of assessment of students in minority cultures needs to include pedagogical strategies that are culturally safe, responsive and effective. Assessment that does not take cultural sense-making factors into account may lead to inappropriate classifications and, therefore, faulty understanding or interpretation of the problem. It may also lead to educators looking for solutions that try to remedy perceived deficits in individuals and families, rather than solutions that try to remedy deficits in the classroom and school-learning contexts and practices. This in turn can lead to placing individual students in inappropriate and culturally unsafe programmes, with long-term adverse consequences (Wearmouth & Berryman, 2009).

Ladson-Billings (1995) points out that attempts by Western European educational professionals to educate children from minority cultures are shaped by theorising about principles such as cultural appropriateness, cultural congruence and cultural compatibility. However, these approaches aim to fit the child (and their communities) into the preconceived educational programme by selecting those cultural aspects of the children's culture that seem most useful to the educator. Ladson-Billings seeks instead to operate from the principle of cultural responsiveness, a concept that reflects the need to respond to minority culture values, needs and preferences, acknowledges the legitimacy of practices in the child's background and adapts the programme to the child.

Ownership

There are two major implications for government policy from this analysis. The first is that in order for our country to address the current educational crisis that is afflicting Māori and that is also affecting the potential of our whole country to realise the aspirations to become a "knowledge" society, there needs to be national ownership of the problem. This would be seen when policy makers intentionally and explicitly maintain the primary focus of educational policy on Māori student achievement in ways that make sense to Māori. Policies that promote the whole range covered by the GPILSEO model—goals, pedagogies, institutions, leadership, spread and evidence—need to demonstrate national-level ownership. Evaluation and support of the potential benefit of any proposed action should be undertaken with reference to its impact on Māori students.

The second implication is that policies regarding funding need to be specific. To address the economic marginalisation of Māori associated with the education debt, current government policies such as that outlined in *Ka Hikitia* (Ministry of Education, 2008), to "realise Māori potential", need to be amended to set specific government funding targets for outcomes for Māori. The Government has been able to set specific dates and has allocated specific resources (albeit limited) to see an end to the process of addressing historical grievances under the Treaty of Waitangi. In a similar vein, the Government needs to set specific dates and allocate specific resources in association with its education policy documents to see an end to educational disparities within a set period of time.

Current approaches to professional development by the New Zealand Ministry of Education generally run to a short-term funding timetable, where initial funding is provided for a limited period of time, reduced, then withdrawn. The expectation is that the schools will reprioritise funding to support the long-term implementation and maintenance of the reform from their own resources. The reality is that this rarely happens. Sarason (1990) identifies this as one of the main causes of what he terms "the predictable failure of school reform"; that is, the failure to provide schools with sufficient ongoing funding to support effective reforms in the face of competing claims for limited funding.

A number of common outcomes result from this type of policy. The first is that schools shift from reform to reform as the funding becomes available from the central government agency, not one of which is ever embedded to depth in the school. The second is that there is never enough money invested in schools to develop the necessary infrastructure that will allow the reforms to flourish. The third is that there is a lack of opportunities to provide responsive support for schools in a climate that promotes curriculum content reforms such as those that focus on literacy and numeracy. Current government policies that seek to reduce educational disparities through raising the educational achievement of those students who are not currently well served by the education system is a necessary, but far from sufficient, condition for addressing the long-term education debt, as seen in the long-term educational statistics of educational disparities in this country. What is needed is a long-term policy that is not subject to the electoral cycle, one that in Fullan's (2001) terms provides an expansive rather than a contracting resource base for individual schools, and that seeks to reallocate to Māori people their fair share of the benefits that our society has to offer.

Such a vision needs to be taken on board by the nation as a whole in an approach that goes beyond party politics and the three-year electoral cycle, to acknowledge that beyond the calls of justice, our society and economy cannot survive with an increasing demographic of nonparticipating young people. In many ways, Māori people's future is New Zealand's future.

The questions that stand out for our political leaders are: Who has the courage to take on this challenge? Who has the courage to address the education debt that is owed to Māori and the nation as a whole? We as a nation have addressed similar "debts" in the past, through the enfranchisement of women in the late 19th century, the establishment of the welfare state in the early 20th century and affirmative action policies for women in the 1980s. In these areas our nation has been a world leader. We have also had the courage to stand up for our nuclear-free position, we have ceased whaling and we join peace-keeping forces rather than armed incursions into the territories of others.

We as a nation have the courage to undertake these actions. We now need to call on that courage again to address this long-term debt that will otherwise cripple us as a people and a country unless we attend to it with haste and determination.

References

Ackerman-Anderson, L., & Anderson, D. (2001). *The change leader's roadmap: How to navigate your organization's transformation.* San Francisco, CA: Pfeiffer.

Adnett, N., & Davies, P. (2001, September). *Schooling reforms in England: From quasi-markets to competition?* Paper presented at the Quasi-Markets and Social Services workshop, Louvain-la-Neuve UCL.

Alton-Lee, A. (2003). *Quality teaching for diverse students in schooling: Best evidence synthesis.* Wellington: Ministry of Education.

Alton-Lee, A. (2004). *Using best evidence syntheses to assist in making a bigger difference for diverse learners.* Wellington: Ministry of Education.

Alton-Lee, A. (2006). How teaching influences learning: Implications for educational researchers, teachers, teacher educators and policy makers. *Teaching and Teacher Education, 22,* 612–626.

Alton-Lee, A. (2008, November). *Te Kotahitanga using research and development (R & D) to make a much bigger difference for our children and our society.* Keynote address presented at the inaugural Te Kotahitanga conference, University of Waikato, Hamilton.

Anyon, J. (1997). *Ghetto schooling: A political economy of urban education reform.* New York: Teachers College Press.

Applebee, A. (1996). *Curriculum, as conversation.* Chicago and London: University of Chicago Press.

Asante, M. K. (1991). The Afrocentric idea in education. In W. L. Deburg (Ed.), *Modern black nationalism: From Marcus Garvey to Louis Farrakhan* pp. 289–294). New York and London: University Press.

Assessment Reform Group. (1999). *Assessment for learning: Beyond the black box.* Cambridge: University of Cambridge School of Education.

Atkinson, L. (2006). *How do exemplary principals manage and sustain change in order to enhance student learning outcomes?* Primary principal's sabbatical leave report. Wellington: Ministry of Education.

Ballard, K. (2007, December). *Education and imagination: Strategies for social justice.* The Herbison Lecture presented to the national conference of the New Zealand Association for Research in Education, University of Canterbury, Christchurch.

Ballard, K. (2008, November). *Teaching in context: Some implications of a racialised social order.* Keynote address presented at the inaugural Te Kotahitanga conference, University of Waikato, Hamilton.

Benjamin, L. (1993). *Interpersonal diagnosis and treatment of personality disorders.* New York: Guilford Press.

Berends M., Bodily, S., & Kirby, S. (2003). New American schools: District and school leadership for whole-school reform. In J. Murphy & A. Datnow (Eds.), *Leadership lessons from comprehensive school reforms* (pp. 109–131). Thousand Oaks, CA: Corwin Press.

Berends M., Bodily, S., & Nataraj Kirby, S. (2004). *Facing the challenges of whole-school reform.* Santa Monica, CA: RAND Education.

Berryman, M. (2001). *Toitū te whānau, toitū te iwi: A community approach to English transition.* Unpublished Master of Education thesis, University of Waikato, Hamilton.

Berryman, M. (2008). *Repositioning within indigenous discourses of transformation and self-determination.* Unpublished Doctor of Philosophy thesis, University of Waikato, Hamilton.

Berryman, M., & Glynn, T. (2003). *Transition from Māori to English: A community approach.* Wellington: New Zealand Council for Educational Research.

Berryman, M., Glynn, T., & Glynn, V. (2001). *Me hoki whakamuri, kia haere whakamua: Building culturally competent home and school partnerships* [video]. William and Associates for Specialist Education Services.

Bertanees, C., & Thornley, C. (2004). Negotiating colonial structures: Challenging the views of Pakeha student teachers. *Asia-Pacific Journal of Teacher Education, 32*(2), 81–93.

Biddulph, F., Biddulph, J., & Biddulph, C. (2003). *The complexity of community and family influences on children's achievement in Aotearoa/New Zealand: Best evidence synthesis.* Wellington: Ministry of Education.

Bishop, R. (1994). Initiating empowering research. *New Zealand Journal of Educational Studies, 29*(1), 1–14.

Bishop, R. (1996). *Collaborative research stories: Whakawhanaungatanga.* Palmerston North: Dunmore Press.

Bishop, R. (2003). Changing power relations in education: Kaupapa Maori messages for "mainstream" education in Aotearoa-New Zealand. *Comparative Education, 39*(2), 221–238.

Bishop, R. (2005). Freeing ourselves from neocolonial domination in research: A kaupapa Māori approach to creating knowledge. In N. Denzin & Y. Lincoln (Eds.), *The Sage handbook of qualitative research* (3rd ed., pp. 109–138). Thousand Oaks, CA: Sage.

Bishop, R. (2007). Lessons from Te Kotahitanga for teacher education. In L. F. Detretchin & C. J. Craig (Eds.), *International research on the impact of accountability systems* (pp. 225–239). Lanham, MD: Rowman & Littlefield Education.

Bishop, R., & Berryman, M. (2006). *Culture speaks: Cultural relationships and classroom learning.* Wellington: Huia Publishers.

Bishop, R., Berryman, M., Cavanagh, T., & Teddy, L. (2007). *Te Kotahitanga Phase 3 whanaungatanga: Establishing a culturally responsive pedagogy of relations in mainstream secondary school classrooms.* Wellington: Ministry of Education.

Bishop, R., Berryman, M., Cavanagh, L., Teddy, L., Clapham, S., Lamont, R. et al. (2008). *Te Kotahitanga: Towards sustainability and replicability in 2006 and 2007.* Wellington: Ministry of Education.

Bishop, R., Berryman, M., Glynn, T., McKinley, E., Devine, N., & Richardson, C. (2001a). *The experiences of Māori children in the year 9 and 10 classroom: Part 1: The scoping exercise.* Report to the Research Division of the Ministry of Education. Wellington: Ministry of Education.

Bishop, R., Berryman, M., & Richardson, C. (2001b). *Te Toi Huarewa: Effective teaching and learning strategies, and effective teaching materials for improving the reading and writing in te reo Māori of students aged five to nine in Māori medium education.* Wellington: Ministry of Education.

Bishop, R., Berryman, M., Richardson, C., & Glynn, T. (2001c*). Teachers' perceptions and use of Aro Matawai Urunga-ā-kura (AKA). Final report.* Wellington: Ministry of Education.

Bishop, R., Berryman, M., Tiakiwai, S., & Richardson, C. (2003). *Te Kotahitanga: The experiences of year 9 and 10 Māori students in mainstream classrooms.* Wellington: Ministry of Education.

Bishop, R., & Glynn, T. (1999). *Culture counts: Changing power relations in education.* Palmerston North: Dunmore Press.

Bishop, R., & O'Sullivan, D. (2005). *Taking a reform project to scale: Considering the conditions that promote sustainability and spread of reform.* A monograph prepared with the support of Ngā Pae o te Māramatanga, The National Institute for Research Excellence in Māori Development and Advancement. Unpublished manuscript.

Black, P., & Wiliam, D. (1998). Assessment and classroom learning. *Assessment in Education, 5*(1), 7–74.

Bolam, R., McMahon, A., Stoll, L., Thomas, S., & Wallace, M. (2005). *Creating and sustaining professional learning communities.* Research report number 637. London: General Teaching Council for England, Department for Education and Skills.

Bolman, L. G., & Deal, T. E. (2003). *Reframing organizations' artistry, choice and leadership* (3rd ed.). San Francisco: Jossey-Bass.

Bolman, L. G., & Deal, T. E. (2006). *The wizard and the warrior: Leading with passion and power.* San Francisco: Jossey-Bass.

Bond, L., Smith, T., Baker, W., & Hattie, J. (2000). *The certification system of the National Board for Professional Teaching Standards.* Greensboro, NC: Center for Educational Research and Evaluation, The University of North Carolina at Greensboro.

Bosker, R., & Witziers, B. (1995, January). *School effects, problems, solutions and a meta-analysis.* Paper presented at the international congress for School Effectiveness and School Improvement, Leeuwarden, The Netherlands.

Bourdieu, P., & Passeron, J. C. (1973). *Reproduction in education, society and culture.* London: Sage.

Bourke, R., Holden, B., & Curzon, J. (2005). *Using evidence to challenge practice.* A discussion paper. Wellington: Ministry of Education.

Broadfoot, P. (1996). *Education, assessment and society.* Buckingham, PA: Open University Press.

Brooks, A., & Kavanaugh, C. (1999). Empowering the surrounding community. In P. Reyes, J. Scribner, & A. Paredes Scribner (Eds.), *Lessons from high-performing Hispanic schools: Creating learning communities* (pp. 61–93). New York: Teachers College Press.

Brown, A. (1993). Participation, dialogue and the reproduction of social equalities. In R. Merttens & J. Vass (Eds.), *Partnership in maths: Parents and schools* (pp. 190–213). London: Routledge Falmer.

Bruner, J. (1996). *The culture of education.* Cambridge, MA: Harvard University Press.

Bryk, A., & Schneider, B. (2002). *Trust in schools: A core resource for improvement.* New York: Russell Sage Foundation.

Burr, V. (1995). *An introduction to social constructionism.* London: Routledge.

Chapple, S., Jefferies, R., & Walker, R. (1997). *Maori participation and performance in education: A literature review and research programme.* Wellington: Ministry of Education.

Clark, J. A. (2006). The gap between the highest and lowest school achievers: Philosophical arguments for downplaying teacher expectation theory. *New Zealand Journal of Educational Studies, 41*(2), 367–382.

Cline, T. (Ed.). (1992). *The assessment of special educational needs.* London: Routledge.

Coburn, C. (2003). Rethinking scale: Moving beyond numbers to deep and lasting change. *Educational Researcher, 32*(6), 3–12.

Coburn, C. E., & Talbert, J. E. (2006). Conceptions of evidence-based practice in school districts: Mapping the terrain. *American Journal of Education, 112*(4), 469–495.

Cochran-Smith, M. (2004). Multicultural teacher education: Research, practice and policy. In J. A. Banks & C. M. Banks (Eds.), *Handbook of research in multicultural education* (2nd ed., pp. 931–975). San Francisco: Jossey-Bass.

Cochran-Smith, M., & Zeichner, K. (2005). *Studying teacher education: The report of the AERA panel on research and teacher education.* Hillsdale, NJ: Lawrence Erlbaum Associates.

Coe, R. (1999). *A manifesto for evidence-based education.* Retrieved 12 March 2007, from http://www.cemcentre.org/RenderPage.asp?LinkID=30317000/

Cohen, D. S. (2005). *The heart of change field guide: Tools and tactics for leading change in your organization.* Boston: Harvard Business School Press.

Collins, J. (2001). *Good to great: Why some companies make the leap and others don't.* New York: Harper Business.

Comer, J., Norris Haynes, M., Joyner, M., & Ben-Avie, M. (1996). *Rallying the whole village: The Comer process for reforming education.* New York: Teachers College Press.

Consortium for Policy Research in Education. (1995). *CPRE policy brief: Helping teachers teach well: Transforming professional development—June 1995.* Retrieved 30 August 2005, from http://www.ed.gov/pubs/CPRE/t61/t61b.html/

Cook-Sather, A. (2002). Authorizing students' perspectives: Towards trust, dialogue, and change in education. *Education Researcher, 31*(4), 314.

Copas, S. (2007). *Te Kotahitanga: Organisational development and sustainability.* A discussion paper based on the 2006/2007 training hui for project leaders and staff from the 12 Phase 3 schools. Unpublished manuscript.

Creswell, J. W. (2005). *Educational research: Planning, conducting and evaluating quantitative and qualitative research* (2nd ed.). Upper Saddle River, NJ: Pearson.

Croft, C., Dunn, K., & Brown, G. T. L. (2001). *Essential skills assessment: Information skills manual.* Wellington: New Zealand Council for Educational Research.

Crooks, T., Hamilton, K., & Caygill, R. (2000). *New Zealand's national education monitoring project: Maori student achievement, 1995–2000* [Electronic version]. Retrieved 9 May 2007, from http://nemp.otago.ac.nz/i_probe.htm/

Cummins, J. (1989). A theoretical framework for bilingual special education. *Exceptional Children, 56*(2), 111–120.

Cummins, J. (1995). Power and pedagogy in the education of culturally-diverse students. In J. Fredericskon &. A. Ada (Eds.), *Reclaiming our voices: Bilingual education, critical pedagogy, and praxis* (pp. 139–162). Ontario, CA: California Association for Bilingual Education.

Cuttance, P. (1998). Quality assurance reviews as a catalyst for school improvement in Australia. In A. Hargreaves, A. Lieberman, M. Fullan, & D. Hopkins (Eds.), *International handbook of educational change (Part Two)* (pp. 1135–1162). Dordrecht: Kluwer.

Cuttance, P. (2001). The impact of teaching on student learning. In K. J. Kennedy (Ed.), *Beyond the rhetoric: Building a teachers profession to support quality teaching. College yearbook 2001* (pp. 35–55). The Australian College of Education.

Danaher, G., Schirato, T., & Webb, J. (2000). Understanding Foucault. Sydney: Allen & Unwin.

Darling-Hammond, L. (2000). Teacher quality and student achievement: A review of state policy evidence. *Educational Policy Analysis Archives, 8*(1). Retrieved from http://epaa.asu.edu/epaa/v8n1/

Darling-Hammond, L. (2004). Standards, accountability and school reform. *Teachers College Record, 106*, 1047–1085.

Darling-Hammond, L., Cobb, V., & Bullmaster, M. (1998). Professional development schools as contexts for teacher learning and leadership. In K. Leithwood & K. Louis (Eds.), *Organizational learning in schools* (pp. 149–175). Lisse, The Netherlands: Swets and Zeitlinger.

Darling-Hammond, L., & Sykes, G. (1999). *A handbook of policy and practice.* Stanford: Jossey-Bass.

Datnow, A., Hubbard, L., & Mehan, H. (2002). *Extending educational reform: From one school to many.* London and New York: Routledge Falmer.

Datnow, A., & Stringfield, S. (2000). Working together for reliable school reform. *Journal of Education for Students Placed at Risk, 5*(1), 183–204.

Davies, B. (2007). Developing sustainable leadership. *Management in Education, 21*(3), 4–9. London: Paul Chapman.

Davies, B., & Harre, R. (1997). Positioning the discursive production of selves. *Journal of the Theory of Social Behaviour, 20*, 43–65. Reprinted in M. Wetherall, S. Taylor, & S. Yates (Eds.). (2001). *Discourse theory and practice: A reader* (pp. 261–271). London: Sage.

Department for Education and Skills. (2002). *Statistics of education: Permanent exclusions from maintained schools in England.* Issue 09/02. London: Author.

DuFour, R. (1998). *Professional learning communities at work.* Alexandria, VA: Association for Supervision and Curriculum Development.

DuFour, R., & Eaker, R. (1998). *Professional learning communities at work: Best practices for enhancing student achievement.* Bloomington, IA: National Education Service.

Durie, M. (1995, March). *Principles for the development of Maori policy.* Paper presented at the Maori Policy Development AIC conference, Wellington.

Durie, M. (1998). *Te mana, te kawanatanga: The politics of Maori self-determination.* Auckland: Oxford University Press.

Durie, M. (2001, February). *A framework for considering Māori educational advancement.* Opening address, Hui Taumata Mātauranga, Turangi and Taupo.

Durie, M. (2005). Race and ethnicity in public policy: Does it work? *Social Policy Journal of New Zealand, 24*, 1–11.

Durie, M. (2006, October). *Whānau, education and Māori potential.* Paper presented at the Hui Taumata Mātauranga V, Taupo.

Earl, L., & Katz, S. (2002). Leading schools in a data-rich world. In K. Leithwood, P. Hallinger, G. Furman, P. Gronn, J. MacBeath, B. Mulford et al. (Eds.), *The second international handbook of international leadership and administration* (pp. 1003–1024). Dordrecht: Kluwer.

Earl, L. M., & Katz, S. (2006). *Leading schools in a data-rich world: Harnessing data for school improvement.* Thousand Oaks, CA: Corwin Press.

Education Review Office. (2002). *Māori students: Schools making a difference.* Wellington: Author.

Education Review Office. (2004). *Māori student achievement in mainstream schools.* Wellington: Author.

Education and Science Committee. (2008). *Inquiry into making the schooling system work for every child.* (I.2A). Retrieved 23 December 2008, from http://www.parliament.nz/en-NZ/SC/Reports/7/f/3/48DBSCH_SCR3979_1-Inquiry-into-making-the-schooling-system-work-for.htm/

Edwards, A. (2001). Researching pedagogy: A sociocultural agenda. *Pedagogy, Culture and Society, 9*(2), 161–186.

Edwards, A., & Warin, J. (1999). Parental involvement in raising pupils' achievement in primary schools: Why bother? *Oxford Review of Education, 25*(3), 325–341.

Elbaz, F. (1981). The teachers' "practical knowledge": Report of a case study. *Curriculum Inquiry, 11*, 43–71.

Elbaz, F. (1983). *Teacher thinking: A study of practical knowledge.* New York: Nicholas.

Elmore, R. (1996). Getting to scale with good educational practice. *Harvard Educational Review, 66*(1), 1–26.

Elmore, R. (2000). *Building a new structure for school leadership.* Washington, DC: The Albert Shanker Institute.

Elmore, R. (2002). Unwarranted intrusion. *Education Next, 2*(1), 30–35.

Elmore, R. (2004). *School reform from the inside out: Policy, practice and performance.* Cambridge, MA: Harvard Education Press.

Elmore, R., Peterson, P., & McCarthey, S. (1996). *Restructuring in the classroom: Teaching, learning, and school organization.* San Francisco: Jossey-Bass.

Elmore, R. F., & Burney, D. (1996). *Staff development and instructional improvement: Community District 2, New York City.* Philadelphia: Consortium for Policy Research in Education.

Epstein, J. L. (1996). Perspectives and previews on research and policy for school, family, and community partnerships. In A. Booth & J. F. Dunn (Eds.), *Family-school links: How do they affect educational outcomes?* (pp. 209–246). Mahwah, NJ: Lawrence Erlbaum.

Farrell, G. (2003). Expeditionary learning schools: Tenacity, leadership and school reform. In J. Murphy & A. Datnow (Eds.), *Leadership lessons from comprehensive school reforms* (pp. 21–36). Thousand Oaks, CA: Corwin Press.

Foucault, M. (1972). *The archaeology of knowledge.* New York: Pantheon.

Freire, P. (1970) *Pedagogy of the oppressed.* London: Penguin Books.

Freire, P. (1997). *Pedagogy of the heart.* New York: Continuum.

Fullan, M. (1993). *Change forces: Probing the depths of educational reform.* Bristol: Falmer Press.

Fullan, M. (1999). *Change forces: The sequel.* London: Falmer Press.

Fullan, M. (2001). *The new meaning of educational change* (3rd ed.). New York: Teachers College Press.

Fullan, M. (2003). *The moral imperative of school leadership.* Thousand Oaks, CA: Corwin Press.

Fullan, M. (2005). *Leadership & sustainability: Systems thinkers in action.* Thousand Oaks, CA: Corwin Press.

Fullan, M. (2007). *The new meaning of educational change* (4th ed.). New York: Teachers College Press.

Fullan, M. (2008). *The six secrets of change: How leaders survive and thrive.* San Francisco: Jossey-Bass.

Fullan, M., Cuttress, C., & Kilcher, A. (2005). Eight forces for leaders of change. *Journal of Staff Development*, 26(4), 54–64.

Fullan, M., & Sharratt, L. (2007). Sustaining leadership in complex times: An individual and system solution. In B. Davies (Ed.), *Developing sustainable leadership* (pp. 116–136). London: Sage.

Gallos, J. V. (2006). Reframing complexity: A four-dimensional approach to organizational diagnosis, development and change. In J. V. Gallos (Ed.), *Organization development* (pp. 344–362). San Francisco: Jossey-Bass.

Gay, G. (2000). *Culturally responsive teaching: Theory, research and practice.* New York and London: Teachers College Press.

Gee, J. (2000). New people in new worlds: Networks, the new capitalism and schools. In B. Cope & M. Kalantzis (Eds.), *Multiliteracies: Literacy learning and the design of social futures* (pp. 43–68). London: Routledge.

Gladwell, M. (2000). *The tipping point: How little things can make a big difference.* London: Abacus.

Glennan, T. K., Bodilly, S. J., Galegher, J. R., & Kerr, K. A. (2004). *Expanding the reach of education reforms: Perspectives from leaders in scale-up of educational interventions.* Santa Monica, CA: RAND Research.

Glynn, T., Berryman, M., Bidois, P., Furlong, M., Thatcher, J., Walker, R. et al. (1996). Bilingual reading gains for tutors and tutees in a Māori reading programme. In *He paepae kōrero: Research perspectives in Māori education* (pp. 35–58). Wellington: New Zealand Council for Educational Research.

Goldberg, B., & Morrison, D. (2003). Co-Nect: Purpose, accountability, and school leadership. In J. Murphy & A. Datnow (Eds.), *Leadership lessons from comprehensive school reforms* (pp. 14–31). Thousand Oaks, CA: Corwin Press.

Goldsmith, M., & Reiter, M. (2007). *What got you here won't get you there: How successful people become even more successful.* New York: Hyperion.

Guskey, T. (1995). Professional development in education: In search of the optimal mix. In T. Guskey (Ed.), *Professional development in education: New paradigms and practices* **(page nos)**. New York: Teachers College Press.

Guskey, T. (2005). Taking a second look at accountability. *National Staff Development Council, 26,* 10–18.

Guskey, T., & Sparks, D. (1996). Exploring the relationship between staff development and improvements in student learning. *Journal of Staff Development, 17*(4), 34–38.

Hall, A., & Ramsay, P. (1994). Effective schools and effective teachers. In C. McGee & D. Fraser (Eds.), *The professional practice of teaching* (1st ed., pp. 196–227). Palmerston North: Dunmore Press.

Hall, G., & Hord, S. (2006). *Implementing change: Patterns, principles, and potholes.* Boston, MA: Pearson Education.

Hargreaves, A. (2005). Educational change takes ages: Life, career, and generational factors in teachers' emotional responses to educational change. *Teaching and Teacher Education, 21,* 967–983.

Hargreaves, A. (2006). From recovery to sustainability. *Journal of Reading Recovery, 5*(2), 39–44.

Hargreaves, A., & Fink, D. (2000). Three dimensions of educational reform. *Educational Leadership, 57*(7), 30–34.

Hargreaves, A., & Fink, D. (2006). *Sustainable leadership.* San Francisco: Jossey-Bass.

Hargreaves, A., & Fullan, M. (1998). *What's worth fighting for out there.* Buckingham: Open University Press.

Hargreaves, A., & Goodson, I. (2006). Educational change over time? The sustainability and non-sustainability of three decades of secondary school change and continuity. *Educational Administration Quarterly, 42*(1), 3–41.

Harker, R. (2007). *Ethnicity and school achievement in New Zealand: Some data to supplement the Biddulph et al. (2003) Best Evidence Synthesis: Secondary analysis of the Progress at School and Smithfield datasets for the iterative Best Evidence Synthesis Programme.* Wellington: Ministry of Education.

Hattie, J. (1999, August). *Influences on student learning.* Professorial inaugural lecture, University of Auckland, Auckland.

Hattie, J. (2003a, February). *New Zealand education snapshot: With specific reference to the years 1–13.* Paper presented at the Knowledge Wave 2003, leadership forum, Auckland.

Hattie, J. (2003b, October). *Teachers make a difference: What is the research evidence?* Paper presented to the Australian Council for Educational Research conference, Melbourne.

Hattie, J. A. (1997). *Influences on achievement.* Retrieved from http://www.arts.auckland.ac.nz/edu/staff/jhattie/

Hattie, J. A., Brown, G. T. L., & Keegan, P. J. (2003). A national teacher-managed curriculum-based assessment system: Assessment tools for teaching & learning (asTTle). *International Journal of Learning, 10,* 771–778.

Hattie, J. A. C., Brown, G. T. L., Keegan, P. J., MacKay, A. J., Irving, S. E., Cutforth, S. et al. (2004). *Assessment Tools for Teaching and Learning (asTTle) manual (Version 4, 2005).* Wellington: University of Auckland, Ministry of Education and Learning Media.

Hauser-Cram, P., Sirin, S., & Stipek, D. (2003). When teachers' and parents' values differ: Teachers' ratings of academic competence in children from low-income families. *Journal of Educational Psychology, 95*(4), 813–820.

Hawk, K., & Hill, J. (2000). *Towards making achieving cool: Achievement in multi-cultural high schools.* Wellington: Ministry of Education.

Herman, J., & Gribbons, B. (2001). *Lessons learned in using data to support school inquiry and continuous improvement: Final report to the Stuart Foundation.* Los Angeles: University of California Center for the Study of Evaluation (CSE).

Hill, N. (2001). Parenting and academic socialization as they relate to school readiness: The roles of ethnicity and family income. *Journal of Educational Psychology, 93*(4), 686–697.

Hilliard, A. G. (1992). Behavioural style, culture and teaching and learning. *Journal of Negro Education, 61,* 370–377.

Hindle, R., Marshall, M., Higgins, J., & Tait-McCutcheon, S. (2007). *A study of in-school facilitation in two teacher professional development programmes.* Wellington: Ministry of Education.

Hohepa, M., & Jenkins, K. (2004). *The evaluation of Te Pūtahitanga Mātauranga: Final report.* Wellington: Ministry of Education. Retrieved 23 December 2008, from http://www.educationcounts.govt.nz/publications/maori_education/5299/

Holloman, H., Rouse, W., & Farrington, V. (2007). Purpose-driven leadership: Defining, defending and sustaining a school's purpose. *International Journal of Leadership in Education: Theory and Practice, 10*(4), 437–443.

Holmes, J. (1982). *Language for learning: Education in the multicultural school.* Wellington: Department of Education.

Hood, D. (2008). *Statistical analysis of Māori students' participation and achievement data.* Unpublished paper.

Hunn, J. (1960). *Report on Department of Maori Affairs.* Wellington: Department of Maori Affairs.

Irwin, K. (1992, November). *Maori research methods and processes: An exploration and discussion.* Paper presented to the joint New Zealand Association for Research in Education / Australian Association for Research in Education conference, Geelong, Victoria.

James, C. (2008, 1 July). Nation's duty to protect vulnerable. *New Zealand Herald.* Retrieved 23 December 2008, from http://www.nzherald.co.nz/colin-james/news/article.cfm?a_ id=338&objectid=10519201/

Johnston, M. (2007). *Unpublished research note: The effect of Te Kotahitanga on success rates in NCEA level 1.* Wellington: Research and Knowledge Services, New Zealand Qualifications Authority.

Jordon, C. (1985). Translating culture: From ethnographic information to educational program. *Anthropology & Education Quarterly, 16*(2), 105–123.

Katz, S., Sutherland, S., & Earl, L. (2002). Developing an evaluation habit of mind. *Canadian Journal of Program Evaluation, 17*(2), 103–119.

Kincheloe, J., & Steinberg, S. (1997). *Changing multiculturalism.* Buckingham, PA: Open University Press.

Kouzes, M., & Posner, B. (2002). *The leadership challenge.* San Francisco: Jossey-Bass.

Ladson-Billings, G. (1995). Toward a theory of culturally relevant pedagogy. *American Education Research Journal, 32*(3), 465–491.

Ladson-Billings, G. (2006). From the achievement gap to the education debt: Understanding achievement in US schools. *Educational Researcher, 35*(7), 3–12.

Latham, G. P., & Locke, E. A. (2006). Enhancing the benefits and overcoming the pitfalls of goal setting. *Organizational Dynamics, 35*(4), 332–340.

Lee, C. D. (1994). The complexities of African centered pedagogy. In M. Shujaa (Ed.), *Too much schooling, too little education: A paradox of Black life in white societies* (pp. 295–318). Trenton, NJ: Africa World Press.

Leithwood, K., Edge, K., & Jantzi, D. (1999). *Educational accountability: The state of the art.* Gutersloh, Germany: Berelsmann Foundation Publishers.

Leithwood, K., & Jantzi, D. (2006). Transformational school leadership for large-scale reform: Effects on students, teachers and their classroom practices. *School Effectiveness and School Improvement, 17*(2), 201–227.

Leithwood, K., Jantzi, D., & Fernandez, A. (1994). Transformational leadership and teachers' commitment to change. In J. Murphy & K. Louis (Eds.), *Reshaping the principalship: Insights from transformational reform efforts* (pp. 77–98). Thousand Oaks, CA: Corwin Press.

Leithwood, K., Seashore Louis, K., Anderson, S., & Wahlstrom, K. (2004). *How leadership influences student learning.* New York: Wallace Foundation. Retrieved 14 September 2005, from http://www.wallacefoundation.org/

Leithwood, K. A., & Riehl, C. (2003, April). *What do we already know about successful school leadership?* Paper presented at the annual meeting of the American Educational Research Association, Chicago.

Lewin, K. (1948). Action research and minority problems. *Journal of Social Issues, 2*(4), 34–46. Reproduced in G. W. Lewin (Ed.). (1948). *Resolving social conflicts: Selected papers on group dynamics* (pp. 144–154). New York: Harper & Row.

Lindahl, R. (2007). Why is leading school improvement such a difficult process? *School Leadership and Management, 27*(4), 319–332.

Little, J. W. (1999). Organizing schools for teacher learning. In L. Darling-Hammond & G. Sykes (Eds.), *Teaching as the learning profession: Handbook of policy and practice* (pp. 233–262). San Francisco: Jossey-Bass.

Lo Bianco, J. (1987). *National policy on languages.* Canberra: Australian Publishing Service.

Luke, A., Freebody, P., Lau, S., & Gopinathan, S. (2005). Towards research-based educational policy: Singapore education in transition. *Asia Pacific Journal of Education, 14*(1), 1–22.

Marzano, R. (2003). *What works in schools: Translating research into action.* Alexandria, VA: Association for Supervision and Curriculum Development.

Marzano, R. J., Waters, T., & McNulty, B. A. (2005). *School leadership that works: From research to results.* Alexandria, VA: Association for Supervision and Curriculum Development.

McDonald, J., Hatch, T., Kirby, E., Ames, N., Norris Haynes, M., & Joyner, E. (1999). *School reform behind the scenes.* New York: Teachers College Press.

McDougal, D., Saunders, W., & Goldenberg, C. (2007). Inside the black box of school reform: Explaining the how and why of change at getting results schools. *International Journal of Disability, Development and Education, 54*(1), 51–89.

McLaren, P. (2003). *Life in schools: An introduction to critical pedagogy in the foundations of education* (4th ed.). Boston, MA: Pearson Education.

McLaughlin, M., & Mitra, D. (2001). Theory-based change and change-based theory: Going deeper, going broader. *Journal of Educational Change, 1,* 2–24.

McNamara, J., & Thompson, D. (n.d.). *Teaching statistics in principal preparation programs: Part 1: Commerce.* College Station, TX: Research Department, Texas A&M University.

McNaughton, S., & Glynn, T. (1998, October). *Effective collaboration: What teachers need to know about communities.* Paper presented at the annual conference of the New Zealand Council for Teacher Education, Hamilton.

McNaughton, S., Glynn, T., Robinson, V., & Quinn, M. (1981). *Parents as remedial reading tutors: Issues for home and school.* Studies in Education No. 2. Wellington: New Zealand Council for Educational Research.

Meade, P. (1996, July). Measuring graduate and employer satisfaction in higher education. In *Proceedings of the eighth international conference on Assessing Quality in Education* (pp. 373–382). Melbourne: RMIT.

Metge, J. (1990). *Te kohao o te ngira: Culture and learning.* Wellington: Learning Media.

Miles, K., & Darling-Hammond, L. (1998). Rethinking the allocation of teaching resources: Some lessons from high-performing schools. *Educational Evaluation and Policy Analysis, 20*(1), 9–29.

Miles, K. H. (1995). Freeing resources for improving schools: A case study of teacher allocation in Boston public schools. *Educational Evaluation and Policy Analysis, 17,* 476–493.

Mills, G. E. (2000). *Action research: A guide for the teacher researcher.* Upper Saddle River, NJ: Merrill / Prentice Hall.

Ministry of Education. (1993). *The New Zealand curriculum framework.* Wellington: Learning Media.

Ministry of Education. (1995). *Ngā haeata mātauranga: Annual report on Māori education.* Wellington: Author.

Ministry of Education. (2004). *Educate: Ministry of Education statement of intent 2004–2009.* Wellington: Author.

Ministry of Education. (2005a). *Better relationships for better learning: Guidelines for boards of trustees and schools on engaging with Māori parents, whānau, and communities.* Accessed 13 May 2005, from http://www.minedu.govt.nz/index.cfm?layout=document&documentid=4231&CFID=4375397&CFTOKEN=47131613&goto=00/

Ministry of Education. (2005b). *Educate: Ministry of Education statement of intent 2005–2010.* Wellington: Author.

Ministry of Education. (2006). *Educate: Ministry of Education statement of intent 2006–2011.* Wellington: Author.

Ministry of Education. (2008). *Ka Hikitia: Managing for success: Māori Education Strategy 2008–2012.* Wellington: Author.

Moll, L. C. (1992). Funds of knowledge for teaching: Using a qualitative approach to connect homes and classrooms. *Theory into Practice, 31*(2), 132–141.

Mortimore, P., & Whitty, G. (1997). *Can school improvement overcome the effects of disadvantage?* Institute of Education occasional paper. London: Institute of Education.

Murphy, S. (2002). Literacy assessment and the politics of identities. In J. Soler, J. Wearmouth, & G. Reid (Eds.), *Contextualising difficulties in literacy development: Exploring politics, culture, ethnicity and ethics* (pp. 87–101). London: Routledge Falmer.

Murrell, P. (1993). Afrocentric immersion: Academic and personal development of African American males in public schools. In T. Perry & J. Fraser (Eds.), *Freedom's plow: Teaching in the multicultural classrooms* (pp. 231–254). New York: Routledge.

Nash, R. (1993). *Succeeding generations: Family resources and access to education in New Zealand.* Auckland: Oxford University Press.

Nieto, S. (2000). *Affirming diversity: The sociopolitical context of multicultural education* (3rd ed.). New York: Longman.

Nuthall, G. (2004). Relating classroom teaching to student learning: A critical analysis of why research has failed to bridge the theory–practice gap. *Harvard Educational Review, 74*(3), 273–306.

Nuthall, G. (2007). *The hidden lives of learners.* Wellington: NZCER Press.

Organisation for Economic Co-operation and Development. (2002). *Education at a glance: OECD indicators.* Paris: Author.

Organisation for Economic Co-operation and Development. (2007). *Evidence in education: Linking research to policy.* Paris: Author. Retrieved 22 January 2009, from http://www.oecd.org/document/56/0,3343,en_2649_35845581_38796344_1_1_1_37455,00.html/

Phillips, G. E., McNaughton, S., & MacDonald, S. (2001). *Picking up the pace: Effective literacy interventions for accelerated progress over the transition into decile one schools.* Final report. Wellington: Ministry of Education. Retrieved from http://www.minedu.govt.nz/web/document/document_page.cfm?id = 6444/

Ratteray-Davies, J. (1994). The search for access and content in the education of African-Americans. In M. Shujaa (Ed.), *Too much schooling, too little education: A paradox of Black life in white societies* (pp. 123–142). Trenton, NJ: Africa World Press.

Reid, A. (2004). *Towards a culture of inquiry in DECS.* Occasional paper no. 1. Adelaide: Department of Education and Children's Services, Government of South Australia. Accessed 29 June 2006, from http://www.decs.sa.gov.au/corporate/files/ links/OP_ 01.pdf/

Reyes, P., Scribner, J., & Scribner, A. (1999). *Lessons from high-performing Hispanic schools: Creating learning communities.* New York: Teachers College Press.

Robinson, V. (2007). *School leadership and student outcomes: What works and why.* Monograph 41. ACEL Monograph Series. Wimmalee, SA: ACEL.

Robinson, V. (2008). Forging the links between distributed leadership and educational outcomes. *Journal of Educational Administration, 46*(2), 241–256.

Robinson, V., Hohepa, M., & Lloyd, C. (2009). *School leadership and student outcome: Identifying what works and why: A best evidence synthesis iteration.* Wellington: Ministry of Education.

Robinson, V., Lloyd C., & Rowe, K. (2007). The impact of leadership on student outcomes: An analysis of the differential effects of leadership types. *Educational Administration Quarterly, 44*(5), 635–674.

Robinson, V., & Timperley, H. (2007). The leadership of the improvement of teaching and learning: Lessons from initiatives with positive outcomes for students. *Australian Journal of Education, 51*(3), 247–262.

Rosenholtz, S. (1989). *Teachers' workplace: The social organization of schools.* White Plains, NY: Longman.

Rubie-Davies, C., Hattie, J., & Hamilton, R. (2006). Expecting the best for students: Teacher expectations and academic outcomes. *British Journal of Educational Psychology, 76,* 429–444.

Ryan, W. (1976). *Blaming the victim.* New York: Vantage Books.

Sarason, S. (1990). *The predictable failure of educational reform: Can we change course before it is too late?* San Francisco: Jossey-Bass.

Sarason, S. (1996). *Revisiting the culture of the school and the problem of change.* New York: Teachers College Press.

Scheurich, J., & Young, M. (1997). Coloring epistemologies: Are our research epistemologies racially biased? *Educational Researcher, 26*(4), 4–16.

Schmoker, M. J. (1999). *"Results": The key to continuous school improvement.* Alexandria, VA: Association for Supervision and Curriculum Development.

Schmuck, R. (1997). *Practical action research for change.* Arlington Heights, IL: IRI / Sky Light Training and Publishing.

Scribner, J., Young, M., & Pedroza, A. (1999). Building collaborative relationships with parents. In P. Reyes, J. Scribner, & A. Paredes Scribner (Eds.), *Lessons from high-performing Hispanic schools: Creating learning communities* (pp. 36–60). New York: Teachers College Press.

Senge, P. (2000). *Schools that learn: A fifth discipline fieldbook for educators, parents, and everyone who cares about education.* New York: Doubleday Currency.

Senge, P., Kleiner, A., Roberts, C., Roth, G., Ross, R., & Smith, B. (1999). *The dance of change: The challenges to sustaining momentum in learning organizations.* New York: Doubleday.

Shields, C. (2003). *Good intentions are not enough: Transformative leadership for communities of difference.* Lanham, MD: Scarecrow.

Shields, C. M., Bishop, R., & Mazawi, A. E. (2005). *Pathologizing practices: The impact of deficit thinking on education.* New York: Peter Lang.

Sidorkin, A. M. (2002). *Learning relations: Impure education, deschooled schools, and dialogue with evil.* New York: Peter Lang.

Slavin, R. E. (1986). Best-evidence synthesis: An alternative to meta-analytic and traditional reviews. *Educational Researcher, 15*(9), 5–11.

Sleeter, C. (2005). *Un-standardizing curriculum: Multicultural teaching in the standards-based classroom.* New York: Teachers College Press.

Smith, G. H. (1997). *Kaupapa Maori as transformative praxis.* Unpublished PhD thesis, University of Auckland, Auckland.

Smith, G. H. (2002, January). *Kaupapa Māori theory: Transformative praxis and new formations of colonisation.* Paper presented at the second international conference on Cultural Policy Research, Te Papa National Museum, Wellington.

Smith, L. (1999). *Decolonising methodologies: Research and indigenous peoples.* London and New York: Zed Books; and Dunedin: University of Otago Press.

Smylie, M. (1995). Teacher learning in the workplace: Implications for school reform. In T. Guskey & M. Huberman (Eds.), *Professional development in education: New paradigms and practices* (pp. 92–113). New York: Teachers College Press.

Smylie, M., Wenzel, S., & Fendt, C. (2003). The Chicago Annenberg Challenge: Lessons on leadership for school development. In J. Murphy & A. Datnow (Eds.), *Leadership lessons from comprehensive school reforms* (pp. 135–158). Thousand Oaks, CA: Corwin Press.

Sparks, D. (2005). *Leading for results: Transforming teaching, learning, and relationships in schools.* Thousand Oaks, CA: Corwin Press.

St George, A. (1983). Teacher expectations and perceptions of Polynesian and Pakeha pupils and the relationship to classroom behaviour and school achievement. *British Journal of Educational Psychology, 53*, 48–59.

St John, M. (2002). *The improvement infrastructure: The missing link or why are we always worried about "sustainability"*. Paper presented at the second annual conference on Sustainability of Systemic Reform, Center for School Reform at TERC, Cambridge, MA.

Stoll, L., & Fink, D. (1996). *Changing our schools*. Buckingham, PA: Open University Press.

Stoll, L., & Seashore Louis, K. (2007). *Professional learning communities' divergence, depth and dilemmas*. Berkshire: McGraw-Hill, Open University Press.

Street, B. (Ed.). (1993). *Cross-cultural approaches to literacy*. New York: Cambridge University Press.

Stringer, E. (1999). *Action research*. London: Sage.

Thrupp, M. (2001). Sociological and political concerns about school effectiveness research: Time for a new research agenda. *School Effectiveness and School Improvement, 12*(1), 7–40.

Thrupp, M. (2008, April). *Secondary teaching, social contexts and the lingering politics of blame*. Keynote address to the New Zealand Post Primary Teachers Association conference, Secondary Teaching on the Move, Waipuna Hotel and Conference Centre, Auckland.

Tillema, H. H., & Imants, J. G. M. (1995). Training for the professional development of teachers. In T. R. Guskey & M. Huberman (Eds.), *Professional development in education: New paradigms & practices* (pp. 135–150). New York: Teachers College, Columbia University.

Timperley, H. (2003a). Addressing teachers' expectations of student achievement in New Zealand schools. *New Zealand Journal of Educational Studies, 38*(1), 73–88.

Timperley, H. (2003b). Shifting *the focus: Achievement information for professional learning*. Wellington: Ministry of Education.

Timperley, H., Phillips, G., & Wiseman, J. (2003). *The sustainability of professional development in literacy—Parts 1 and 2*. Auckland: University of Auckland.

Timperley, H., Wilson, A., Barrar, H., & Fung, I. (2007). *Teacher professional learning and development: Best evidence synthesis iteration (BES)*. Wellington: Ministry of Education.

Timperley, H., & Wiseman, J. (2003). *The sustainability of professional development in literacy part 2: School based factors associated with high student achievement*. Wellington: Ministry of Education.

Tomlinson, S. (1988). Why Johnny can't read: Critical theory and special education. *European Journal of Special Needs Education, 3*(1), 45–58.

Tomlinson, S. (2001). Sociological perspectives on special and inclusive education. *Support for Learning, 16*(4), 191–192.

Tuuta, M., Bradnum, L., Hynds, A., & Higgins, J., with Broughton, R. (2004). *Evaluation of the Te Kauhua Māori mainstream pilot project*. Wellington: Ministry of Education.

UCLA Center of Mental Health in Schools. (2006). *Systemic change for school improvement: Designing, implementing, and sustaining prototypes and going to scale*. Los Angeles: Author.

Valencia, R. R. (1997). *The evolution of deficit thinking: Educational thought and practice*. London: Falmer Press.

Villegas, A. M., & Lucas, T. (2002). *Educating culturally responsive teachers: A coherent approach*. Albany, NY: State University of New York Press.

Vincent, C. (1996). *Parents and teachers: Power and participation*. London: Falmer Press.

Waite, J. (1992). *Aotearoa: Speaking for ourselves*. Wellington: Learning Media.

Walker, R. (1990). *Ka whawhai tonu matou: Struggle without end*. Auckland: Penguin Books.

Wearmouth, J., & Berryman, M. (2009). *Inclusion through participation in communities of practice in schools*. Wellington: Dunmore Publishing.

Weinstein, R. S., Gregory, A., & Strambler, M. J. (2004). Intractable self-fulfilling prophecies fifty years after Brown v. Board of Education. *American Psychologist, 59*(6), 511–520.

Wenger, E. (1998). *Communities of practice: Learning, meaning and identity*. Cambridge: Cambridge University Press.

Wenger, E., McDermott, R., & Snyder, W. M. (2002). *Cultivating communities of practice.* Boston, MA: Harvard Business School Press.

Wheatley, M., & Frieze, D. (2006). *Lifecycle of emergence: Using emergence to take social innovations to scale.* Retrieved from http://www.berkana.org/articles/lifecycle.htm/

Witziers, B., Bosker, R. J. & Kruger, M. L. (2003). Educational leadership and student achievement: The elusive search for an association. *Educational Administration Quarterly, 39*(3), 398-425.

Wong-Filmore, L. (1991). When learning a second language means losing a first. *Early Childhood Research Quarterly, 6,* 323–346.

Wylie, C. (2007). *What can New Zealand learn from Edmonton?* Available at:
www.educationalleaders.govt.nz

Wylie, C., Thompson, J., & Lythe, C. (1999). *Competent children at 8: Families, early education, and schools.* Wellington: New Zealand Council for Educational Research.

Wylie, C., Thompson, J., & Lythe, C. (2001). *Competent children at 10: Families, early education, and schools.* Wellington: New Zealand Council for Educational Research.

Young, I. M. (2004). Two concepts of self-determination. In S. May, T. Mahood, & J. Squires (Eds.), *Ethnicity, nationalism, and minority rights* (pp. 176–192). Cambridge: Cambridge University Press.

Young, R. (1991). *Critical theory and classroom talk.* Adelaide: Multilingual Matters.

Index

accountability
  and assessment 146–7, 180–1
  school principals 178
  schools 15, 39, 98, 109, 145–7, 148, 150, 167, 177, 178, 180–1
  teachers 85, 158
action research 139
agentic positioning 18, 25, 29, 37, 63, 67–8, 69, 70, 71–2, 73, 87, 112, 150
ako 19
Alton-Lee, A. 12, 60–1, 64, 107, 134, 135, 166, 167, 176
American Education Research Association (AERA) 50
Aro Matawai Urunga-ā-Kura (AKA) 172
Asian students 52, 62
assessment
  and accountability 146–7, 180–1
  formative 61, 73, 84, 98, 103, 108, 132–4, 183–6
  national policy 183–6
  norm-referenced testing 183–4
  summative 84, 134, 142, 147
  as tool for enhancing learning 132–4, 148, 183, 185
assessment literacy 135

Assessment Tool for Teaching and Learning (asTTle) 30, 52, 58, 61, 108, 141–2, 174
AtoL (Assess to Learn) programme 174
attendance data 154–5
Australia
  educational disparities 53, 54
  goals, and performance 55
  Quality Education movement 64

Becroft, Judge Andrew 12
Belgium 53
Best Evidence Synthesis programme 99, 173, 174
between-group equity 50
biculturalism 13
bilingualism 48–9, 123–5
Black, P. and Wiliam, D. 132, 147
Bolman, L. G. and Deal, T. E. 16, 88–9, 92, 93, 107
Brooks, A. and Kavanaugh, C. 123
Bruner, J. 67, 79, 84
Bryk, A. and Schneider, B. 98–9
Burr, V. 69

This book makes an important addition to New Zealand educational research. Its focus on developing culturally informed approaches has relevance to other international indigenous contexts at a time when most indigenous populations are struggling to overthrow high and disproportionate levels of learning underachievement.
This book has moved away from doing the same things that have traditionally failed to make change, and develops innovative and new strategies.

GRAHAM HINGANGAROA SMITH, Distinguished Professor and CEO at Te Wānanga o Awanuiarangi

Thoughtful, thorough and passionate, this book provides valuable insights on sustaining and extending educational reforms that make a real difference for those least well served by many improvement efforts. Powerfully interweaving stories and findings from the Te Kotahitanga project with a wealth of other sources, the authors make a compelling case for changing the way schools and systems address marginalised and minoritised students' needs, and offer a useful model that can be tested in other settings.

LOUISE STOLL, former President of the International Congress for School Effectiveness and Improvement and Professor, Institute of Education, University of London

Scaling up Educational Reform *is a refreshing and welcome alternative to today's many discussions about improving student achievement or "turning schools around". Drawing on several years experience with Te Kotahitanga, this book presents a very well conceptualised model for school reform that links relationships, pedagogy, culture and achievement with leadership and systemic reform.*
A "must read" for anyone who is concerned with school improvement!

CHRISTINE SLEETER, Professor Emerita, California State University, Monterey Bay

Russell Bishop and colleagues from Te Kotahitanga offer us all profound lessons about the education of minoritised students and communities: these are fundamentally matters of cultural engagement, of political will and good faith, and indeed, damned hard work.

ALLAN LUKE, Research Professor, Faculty of Education, Queensland University of Technology

Bishop, O'Sullivan and Berryman's text on scaling up educational reform is a major scholarly work. In addition to providing a carefully reasoned and evidence based account of the conception, development and implementation of Te Kotahitanga they address a core concern in educational interventions. It is the question of how to scale up a successful intervention, after the initial resourcing, enthusiasm, and expectations have been put in place. Few other academics have added answers to this question and none with the depth and insight that this text provides. The text adds a major new chapter to our understanding of the hardest and most pressing educational interventions, those designed to make a difference for the communities they call "minoritised": an enduring challenge in New Zealand as well as internationally.

STUART MCNAUGHTON, Professor of Education and Director of the Woolf Fisher Research Centre, The University of Auckland

www.ingramcontent.com/pod-product-compliance
Lightning Source LLC
Chambersburg PA
CBHW080554270326
41929CB00019B/3300